E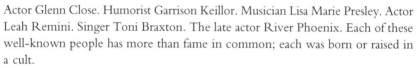

Actor Glenn Close. Humorist Garrison Keillor. Musician Lisa Marie Presley. Actor Leah Remini. Singer Toni Braxton. The late actor River Phoenix. Each of these well-known people has more than fame in common; each was born or raised in a cult.

Many of us think of cults as bizarre groups that only strange people inhabit, but in truth, cults are not unusual at all—and the social pressures and controlling structures that create cults exist (to some degree) in every human relationship and every human group. Cult behavior is *human* behavior—and by studying cults, we can learn remarkably useful things about the world and our place in it.

In *Escaping Utopia*, Janja Lalich and Karla McLaren (both cult survivors) explore the life stories of sixty-five people who were born in or grew up in thirty-nine different cults spanning more than a dozen countries. This original research explores fundamental questions about human nature, human development, group dynamics, abuse and control, and triumphs of the human spirit in the face of extended suffering.

The lessons we can learn from these cult survivors can inform and protect each of us—so that cultic groups cannot gain influence over us or our loved ones.

Janja Lalich is a researcher, author, and educator specializing in self-sealing systems (cults, terrorist groups, extremist groups), with a focus on indoctrination and methods of influence and control. She is Professor Emerita of Sociology at California State University, Chico, and has studied the social psychology of exploitative groups and relationships for over thirty years.

Karla McLaren is an award-winning author and social science researcher who grew up in a New Age healing cult. Her research focuses on emotions, empathy, autism and neurodiversity, social-emotional learning, within-group and inter-group dynamics and conflict, agnotology, and influence techniques.

ESCAPING UTOPIA

Growing Up in a Cult, Getting Out, and Starting Over

Janja Lalich and Karla McLaren

Routledge
Taylor & Francis Group

NEW YORK AND LONDON

First published 2018
by Routledge
711 Third Avenue, New York, NY 10017

and by Routledge
2 Park Square, Milton Park, Abingdon, Oxon, OX14 4RN

Routledge is an imprint of the Taylor & Francis Group, an informa business

© 2018 Taylor & Francis

The right of Janja Lalich and Karla McLaren to be identified as authors of
this work has been asserted by them in accordance with sections 77 and 78
of the Copyright, Designs and Patents Act 1988.

Library of Congress Cataloging-in-Publication Data
A catalog record for this book has been requested

ISBN: 978-1-138-23973-9 (hbk)
ISBN: 978-1-138-23974-6 (pbk)
ISBN: 978-1-315-29509-1 (ebk)

Typeset in Bembo and Stone Sans
by Florence Production Ltd, Stoodleigh, Devon, UK

Important Note

The material in this book is intended to provide an overview of the life experiences and resulting issues of individuals who were born and/or raised in a cult or cult-like environment. The memories and opinions stated herein are those of the individuals who were interviewed during the research project, and are not necessarily the views of the authors. Every effort has been made to provide accurate and dependable information, and this book has been written in consultation with professionals. Readers should be aware that some professionals and academics within this field of study may have differing views, and that change is always happening within groups, across locations, and over time. Therefore, the authors, contributors, publisher, and editors cannot be held responsible for any error or omission.

The material in this book is presented for informational and educational purposes only. It is not a substitute for legal or clinical advice, and should not be used to diagnose or treat any problem. If needed, always consult licensed legal counsel, social workers, or health or mental health providers.

To each of our sixty-five narrators: We thank you for your courage, your openness, your hard-won resilience, and your wisdom. You fought and dreamed to save your own lives; your stories can and will change the world.

Janja Lalich and Karla McLaren

CONTENTS

Acknowledgments   *xi*

Introduction   1

1. We Weren't There by Choice: Meeting Our Narrators   10

2. The Transcendent Belief System: Purity, Perfection,
   and the Eradication of Individuality   29

3. Charismatic Authority: Exhilarating Vision, Electrifying
   Charisma, and Total Domination   41

4. Systems of Control: Official Rules, Formal Structures,
   and Webs of Authority   61

5. Systems of Influence: Social Pressures, Rigid Expectations,
   and Constant Manipulation   83

6. Landing on Mars: Finding Their Way in an Alien World   104

7. Surviving and Thriving: Trauma, Resilience, and Integration   125

   Appendices

   Appendix A: Research Methodology   143
   Appendix B: Print and Multi-Media Resources   147

Appendix C: Cult Information and Resource Websites   153
Appendix D: Influence Methods that Support a
Behavioral-Control System   158

References   *160*
Index   *164*

ACKNOWLEDGMENTS

My inspiration for this book came to me in 2003 while I was attending a cult-education conference in Orange, California, sponsored by the American Family Foundation (now the International Cultic Studies Association). One of the panels focused on growing up in the Children of God/The Family cult, and featured Julia McNeil (sadly now deceased) and Daniel Roselle. Listening to them speak about their lives as children in the cult moved me to tears. Later, we spoke at length, and I so admired their courage, fortitude, and humanity. They gave me a deep understanding of this new generation of cult-leavers and how we as a society have neglected to recognize them or offer them much-needed services or resources to aid them in their integration into the mainstream world. I left that conference knowing that children of cults would be my next research project, and this book is the culmination of that dream.

Grants from the Strategic Performance Fund and the Faculty Travel Funds of the College of Behavioral and Social Sciences at California State University, Chico, enabled me to develop and complete the project. So I thank then-Dean Gayle Hutchinson for seeing the value in this project. I also thank the College's Sabbatical Committee for awarding me a semester-long sabbatical in Fall 2008, which gave me time to complete the interviews. And it goes without saying that the sixty-five individuals who granted me an interview about their lives both in and after the cult are forever in my heart. Often their stories were difficult to listen to because of the neglect and abuse, so I can imagine how difficult it must have been for them to share their experiences with me. Yet, they did so with honesty, grace, wholeheartedness, and the desire to help others who may find themselves in situations similar to theirs. They are the true champions of this book.

There are so many others who contributed in one way or another along the way. First, I am so grateful to my undergraduate Sociology students who became my research assistants who transcribed the recorded interviews and entered data from the surveys: Allison Cross, Maggie Dean, Catherine Foerster, Shannon Simmons, and Jessie Parsons. Also Mandee Kleene worked diligently on searching out relevant literature for me to review. Later in the project, others helped in much-appreciated ways in the final stages of the manuscript process: Alexandra Kokkinakis, a former student and Teaching Assistant of mine, and now Adjunct Faculty in the Sociology Department; Nicole Quinn, a nursing student; and Joni Giraulo, who grew up in the Children of God/The Family and is one of the sixty-five who were interviewed.

I am indebted to my friend Scott McNall for suggesting our book proposal to Dean Birkenkamp at Routledge, who immediately saw the significance of the material and gave Karla and me mounds of encouragement along the way. Thank you, Dean.

I also want to thank those friends and colleagues who were early readers of the manuscript, offering helpful critiques and general enthusiasm for the book: Polly Thomas, Miguel deCruz, Alyson Juers, Shagay Anselment, Emily Gallo, Miriam Boeri, and Alexandra Stein. They, along with other friends, Barbara Besser, Kate Transchel, Marny Hall, and my sweet dog, Ollie, were invaluable in keeping me on track and able to bring the narrators' stories and wisdom to the light of day. And last but certainly not least, I cannot say enough about my dear friend and coauthor, Karla. She's brilliant. She's empathic. She's a terrific writer, and a joy to work with.

Janja Lalich

I thank each of our narrators, whose bravery, pain, griefs, and triumphs have lived inside my heart since the first moment I read their stories. I also thank and admire Janja for discovering a hidden world of pain, despair, and systematic injustice, and walking right in to see what could be done. Her willingness to not only confront the worst of human nature, but to willingly engage with, study, and work to change it is a vital skill for times like these—or indeed, for any times.

I thank Janja for bringing me into this project, and I am indebted to each of the research assistants who organized this voluminous data. I thank our editor, Dean Birkenkamp at Routledge, for his sensitive and enthusiastic encouragement. I also owe a huge debt of gratitude to my husband, Tino Plank, and my colleagues at Empathy Academy, Amanda Ball and Sherry Olander, for keeping the world turning as I made journey after journey into the underworld of cults, and wrote my way back out.

Karla McLaren

INTRODUCTION

Actor Glenn Close. Humorist Garrison Keillor. Actor Winona Ryder. Musician Lisa Marie Presley. Actor Leah Remini. Musician Toni Braxton. Actors Alexis, David, Patricia, Richmond, and Rosanna Arquette. Actor Rose McGowan. The late actor River Phoenix. Each of these well-known people has more than fame in common; each was born or raised in a cult.[1]

Most of us think of cults as bizarre, baffling, or otherworldly groups that only strange people inhabit, but cults and abusive cultic relationships are not unusual at all. In fact, the behaviors, social pressures, and controlling structures that create cults exist (to some degree) in every human relationship and every human group. Cult behavior is *human* behavior—and by studying cults, we can learn remarkably useful things about the social world and our place in it.

In this book, we'll explore the life stories of sixty-five people who were born in or grew up in thirty-nine different cults spanning more than a dozen countries. These stories come from the original research of sociologist and cult expert Janja Lalich, Ph.D., who interviewed these survivors and analyzed their stories to identify the key features they shared. Though each story is unique, these individuals were chosen for the study because of two important similarities: (1) They were all brought into their cults at a very young age or at birth; and (2) They all escaped from their groups on their own, without any help from inside or outside their cults. This focus on the children of cults gives us new information about how cults treat and affect their most vulnerable members, and reveals how we as a society can ease their integration into our world.

As you'll see in their stories, very few of these cult survivors found the support they needed once they got out of their cults. Many social service agencies and counseling professionals do not yet understand the unique needs of people who were raised in closed, controlled, and cultic groups—and a main reason that we wrote this book is to share real-life stories and examples of what cult survivors endure, and what types of support they need. Also, the lessons we can learn from these survivors may prevent more of us from joining these controversial and often harmful groups.

As we delve into these stories, we will explore fundamental questions about human nature, human development, group dynamics, abuse and control, and the triumphs of the human spirit in the face of mistreatment, loss, and suffering. We will also explore the ways that cultic groups are similar to all other groups, and the specific ways in which they differ.

Many of us have encountered controlling or cult-like groups—but for many reasons, we tend to feel unsure about what we see. We may notice something off; yet the people involved will assure us that everything is wonderful, exciting, or life-changing. Or when we encounter a troubling group, we might ask ourselves, "Is this a cult, or is it just a very close-knit group? Am I being too judgmental?" While this confusion is understandable, unfortunately it also helps many controlling groups avoid scrutiny.

Additionally, the way that the media portrays cults obstructs our view and makes us less aware of the true nature of these groups. For instance, in 2011, media outlets focused intense ridicule on the seemingly bizarre cult of the Reverend Harold Camping,[2] whose three failed doomsday prophecies became the butt of endless jokes. Yet almost no one pointed out how utterly commonplace end-times predictions are, since most mainstream religions[3] promote end-of-the-world pro-phecies, as did believers in the Y2K, Supermoon, and Mayan 2012 New Age prophecies.

The media feed us shocking and lurid accounts of failed prophets, polygamist cults, and seemingly strange people wearing strange outfits. Because of the way these groups are portrayed, we miss out on important knowledge that could help us. Instead, we mistakenly believe that cult members are different from us because we are constantly told that all cults are made up of wild-eyed followers, bizarre leaders, and gullible fools.

Subsequently and tragically, when we meet up with *actual* cultic groups, we may miss most of the telling signals and unknowingly walk right into danger. This book will help you learn, in a step-by-step way, how to read those signals correctly so that cultic groups cannot gain influence over you or your loved ones.

By focusing on the often-wrenching true stories of children and teens who grew up in small groups, large international movements, unknown family-based collectives, or infamous cults, we will help you learn how to identify the four dimensions that all cultic groups share.

Who Are We?

We are Janja Lalich, Ph.D. and Karla McLaren, M.Ed., and we have a special knowledge of cults. Both of us were cult members, and both of us got out, started over, and created new lives for ourselves. Coauthor Janja is now a retired Professor of Sociology, a researcher and author, and an internationally recognized cult expert; but in her earlier life, she spent more than ten long years in a Marxist political cult that was going to change the world through a workers' revolution. Coauthor Karla is now an author, educator, and social science researcher, but she spent most of her teens in a New Age cult that was going to change the world through spirituality, nutrition, and right living. In both of our cults, the focus wasn't particularly harsh or alarming at first; both of our cults were filled with idealistic and dedicated people who gathered together to save the world in ways that made perfect sense to them at the time. We weren't building cults, as far as we knew. Rather, we thought of ourselves as groundbreakers who were creating utopias. We were certain that our intense dedication was essential to making our utopias flourish and endure. They didn't, of course, but our groups' downfalls weren't due to a lack of our effort.

Janja's pioneering contribution to the understanding of cults is her renowned *bounded choice* framework and theory.[4] This framework shows that all cults share specific features that help them control their members—and that cult leaders tend to capitalize on their members' idealism, intelligence, utopian dreams, and intense dedication (rather than their ignorance or weakness, as the media would have us believe). The bounded choice framework reveals that cults are not bizarre, outlandish groups filled with zombie-like followers; instead, it helps us see that the social pressures and controlling structures that all cults share (and exploit to the fullest) are also found—to some extent—in every human relationship and every human group.

That's why cults can be so hard to identify. They're not freakish, otherworldly groups that set off all your internal alarms right away—if they were, no cult could ever gather enough followers to grow and survive. Instead, cults often feel like intensely hopeful and promising utopian communities that just might save the world. In fact, that's how many cults begin.

Why Do We Use the Word *Cult*?

A great deal of confusion and controversy surrounds the definition of the word *cult* and the use of it as a label for specific groups. Some people think that the word itself is insulting and should never be used, but as cult survivors, we strongly disagree. The two of us spent many years in cults, and we would have been spared many years of trouble and loss if we and/or our families had only known what a cult was and how cults work.

If we had known what to look for, and if we had been able to identify specific cultic behaviors, we might have avoided a great deal of unnecessary pain and suffering. Janja might not have lost more than a decade of her life in an increasingly controlling and bankrupting environment, and Karla might not have ended up excommunicated and homeless at the age of seventeen. And if the parents and families of the sixty-five cult survivors who were interviewed for this book had known about cults, they might have been able to protect their children and themselves from decades of disruption, isolation, trauma, and despair.

As social scientists, we understand that great care must be taken with the word *cult* because it can be used to belittle any group that people don't like or trust. Nevertheless, the fact remains that a cult is a very specific kind of social group that uses similar methods to entice supporters, transmit its ideology, control its members, and put its worldview into practice. Once you know what to look for, you will see that all cults are very similar to one another, even though their stated goals, actions, and worldviews may be completely different. Identifying cults is not something we should shy away from; we need to understand them so that we can protect ourselves against cult indoctrination and manipulation.[5]

Aren't Cults Just Strange Religious Groups?

No, they're not. Many people mistakenly believe that cults and religions are somehow connected, that all religions are cults (or were cults when they started out), or that all cults promote religious beliefs. That's one of the arguments used to defend the problematic use of the term *new religious movement* (or NRM). Some scholars are offended by the word cult, and fear that religious freedoms are being threatened—and they insist that all cultic groups be identified as NRMs instead. Some of these scholars have spent many decades trying to convince other scholars, the media, the courts, and the general public to banish the word from our vocabulary.[6] Again, we strongly disagree. Not only does this tactic muddy the waters, but also it lets some unethical, harmful, or illegal groups off the hook. When scholars intentionally confuse religions and cults, or suggest that cults are young religions going through growing pains, they may grant First Amendment rights and protections to questionable groups that don't qualify for or deserve the NRM title.

True NRM groups exist all over the world; some are as small as an offshoot church that uses a member's home for its weekly services, and some are as large as the American Buddhist Movement. Merely being new or religious doesn't make a group a cult. For instance, Janja's Marxist cult was atheist, while Karla's cult called itself "spiritual but not religious"—and in this book, you'll meet people from nonreligious cults that focused on such things as Transcendental Meditation, obscure philosophies, and martial arts training. Simply put, religious beliefs are not the key to identifying cults.

When you understand modern-day cults clearly, you'll realize that a cult is not simply a new religion, nor is any religion necessarily an old cult. In fact, the two may have nothing to do with one another. This mistaken connection between religions and cults is one of the reasons that so many cults are able to gather followers even today. Why? Because if people mistakenly believe that cults are always based on religious beliefs, then they'll be on alert for and possibly protected from only one kind of cult—and they'll be dangerously unaware of all the rest.

Some cults may promote religious beliefs, while others may promote political change, racist beliefs, psychotherapeutic approaches, meditation, terrorism, revolution, esoteric philosophies, sexual freedom, celibacy, polygamy, spiritual enlightenment, New Age metaphysical and/or psychic beliefs, nutrition and dietary regimens, improved health or wealth, addiction recovery, self-actualization, yoga, belief in UFOs and extraterrestrial life, martial arts, management and leadership courses, communication techniques, and even multi-marketing schemes. Many cults promote a combination of two or more of these dogmas. And as seen in the infamous case of Enron, a wildly charismatic energy company that failed disastrously and lost billions of dollars, even a corporation can become a cult.[7]

Cults are not defined by *what* the cult leader or its members believe. Rather, cults are defined by *how* those beliefs and goals are transmitted, *who* is transmitting them, and *how much* freedom and autonomy group members have.

What Is a Cult?

Our definition and understanding of cults comes not only from our own life experiences but also from Janja's work and the work of contemporary researchers Robert Jay Lifton, Edgar Schein, Margaret Thaler Singer, Philip Zimbardo, Benjamin Zablocki, Bruce Perry, and Robert Cialdini, as well as scholars like Max Weber, Erving Goffman, Leon Festinger, Solomon Asch, and Stanley Milgram.

Regardless of its beliefs or its size, a cult is simply this:

> A cult is group or a relationship that stifles individuality and critical thinking, requires intense commitment and obedience to a person and/or an ideology, and restricts or eliminates personal autonomy in favor of the cult's worldview and the leader's wants and needs.

Janja's groundbreaking contribution to the understanding of cults is her identification of the four specific features that all cultic groups share. We will explore them in detail in Chapters 2 through 5, and we will simplify her theory here so that you can quickly understand the features that cults of all ideologies and all sizes share (a cult doesn't have to be large; it can be as small as a family unit).[8] The four dimensions of bounded choice are:

1. A Transcendent Belief System
2. Charismatic Authority
3. Systems of Control
4. Systems of Influence

We will focus more deeply on each of these dimensions, and we will contrast the many ways that cults employ them with the ways that healthy groups employ them. For now, the quick sketches that follow will allow you to grasp the basics of the bounded choice framework.

1. The Transcendent Belief System

Though not all groups organize themselves around transcendent beliefs in a higher power or a higher purpose, groups nearly always gather around some kind of ideology about the *right* ideas, the right approaches, and the right kinds of people. Healthy groups tend to support this sense of rightness in non-polarizing and relaxed ways, but in cultic groups, the need for purity and perfection is paramount and intense. In many cults, devotion to the *transcendent belief system* or the utopian ideal becomes the main focus of everyday living as members strive to transform themselves into better and more dedicated believers. This intense focus, which is a cult requirement, often leads to the enforced eradication of any behaviors or ideas that challenge the group's (or its leader's) beliefs. Also, total commitment to these beliefs often leads to fierce distrust and even hatred of outsiders. This us-versus-them polarization increases the feelings of unity and dedication inside the group, and makes it very hard for people to leave, since outsiders are seen at best as lost and in dire need of the group's salvation—or at worst, as evil, or in the extreme, as worthy only of death.[9] In short, the transcendent belief system instills group members with a deep, internalized knowledge that they are right and specially chosen, and that everyone else is wrong and unworthy unless they become believers themselves.

2. Charismatic Authority

We've all experienced hero worship or madly-in-love feelings that erased our good sense. In healthy relationships, these precarious moods tend to fade, and we become able to view our love objects in more calm and rational ways. However, cult leaders and/or leadership teams find ways to keep members exhilarated through electrifying displays of charisma, seductive utopian visions, demands for commitment, demonization of outsiders and less committed group members, and constant emotional manipulation. In many cults, favoritism, nepotism, or jockeying for position will create a leadership group of insiders (the inner circle) who develop and exercise their own kind of charismatic authority, known as "charisma by proxy." This takes some of the stress off the leader while it makes the cult itself stronger. This way, when a cult leader dies, there will be someone to take his or her place and keep the cult going. Of the four bounded choice dimensions, *charismatic authority* is probably the most difficult to escape (as many of us may have experienced in our own dramatic and unhealthy love relationships) because it engages powerful emotional and biochemical reward systems that essentially turn the relationship with the cult into an addiction.[10] When charismatic authority is present in a group, members can become so physically and psychologically addicted to the drama, intensity, and hero worship that leaving the group can feel like leaving all meaning, all purpose, all love, and all hope behind.

3.   Systems of Control

Effective groups create social structures and rules that help them organize internally and distinguish themselves from other groups. In healthy groups, these *systems of control* tend to be non-coercive and tolerant. But in cultic groups, internal systems of control, strict rules and behavioral norms, and constant discipline enclose members inside a tightly controlled universe, or "bounded reality," as Janja has called it. In some cults, every aspect of life is controlled, such that communication, education, diet, exercise, clothing, personal hygiene, sexual habits and partners, health care, family planning, child-rearing, and even friendships are monitored so that group members conform, are obedient, and eventually become isolated from any outside influences. These systems of control dovetail with the overarching belief system of the group and with each member's sense of dedication, such that each member may come to see their behaviors as perfectly logical choices that they made intentionally and willingly. This tends to create in each member a false sense of free will and free choice.

4.   Systems of Influence

In effective groups, social and emotional bonds are developed and nurtured to create a sense of belonging and unity. These *systems of influence* help people learn that they fit in, that they share core beliefs, and that they are in sync with other group members. In healthy groups, this bonding tends to be positive and compassionate, but in cultic groups, this bonding serves to reduce independence and autonomy. Through persistent peer influence, various types of monitoring, rigid expectations, and constant social and emotional manipulation, cultic groups make sure that the needs of the group outweigh the needs, ideas, and dreams of individual members. For instance, highly dedicated cult members may shun or shame anyone who steps out of line, and openly suggest or insinuate that the wayward person's dedication is not what it should be. And when enough people are rooted in and dedicated to the cult's systems of control, the systems of influence tend to arise from within the cult members themselves. Thus, the deep desire to live up to the cult's ideals can create a group where members self-police and other-police and therefore have a very strong influence on each other. It is commonly understood that peer pressure is one of the greatest motivators for us humans, and cults capitalize on this to their benefit.

With the help of the bounded choice framework, you can begin to understand not just what cults are, but how they form, how they grow, and how they affect their members psychologically and physically. These four dimensions of bounded choice are present, to some extent, in most groups—but in cultic groups, they take on a life of their own and are intricately intertwined and interdependent. In this book, we'll help you understand how cults can gain a foothold in our lives, in the lives of the people we love, in our society, and on the international stage.

We will also explore how each of these dimensions plays out in very different groups by sharing the stories of children and teens who were raised in cults. You will be able to observe the everyday life of cults and their members, and see into the thought processes and actions of children inside these cults. Children born or raised in cults have very different experiences and aftereffects than individuals who join as adults, and their stories can help you understand cults in valuable new ways.

Of equal importance, we focus on the fortitude and resilience that helped these children resist, break free, and heal from mistreatment, loss, and trauma. These stories can help you understand how people can survive in and break free from controlling environments, and how you and your loved ones can apply these lessons of survival in your own lives. It is also our hope that this book will alert society and helping professionals to the kinds of resources and social services that are needed to support this growing population of survivors who were born and/or raised in cultic groups—because more and more of them are leaving every day.

Understanding cults is vital to your understanding of human groups, human relationships, and the universal human longing for perfect and transcendent utopias. Cult behavior is *human* behavior. By looking at these very human behaviors with clear eyes and the support of the original, in-depth social science research and interpretation presented here, you can learn how to identify cults. In so doing, you can keep yourself and others safe from coercion, manipulation, and harm—and you can effectively support people who want to escape, or who have already escaped.

In Chapter 1, we will highlight the stories of six of the sixty-five cult survivors Janja interviewed so that you can meet them and learn about their lives. Each of these people grew up in a utopian cult that their parents or grandparents (or even great-great-grandparents) chose to join, and each of them has a unique view of what life was like inside the closed world of their cult.

Notes

1. Glenn Close: Moral Re-Armament. Garrison Keillor: Plymouth Brethren. Winona Ryder: The Rainbow Commune. Lisa Marie Presley: Scientology. Leah Remini: Scientology. Toni Braxton: Pillar of Truth. Alexis, David, Patricia, Richmond, and Rosanna Arquette: Subud. Rose McGowan: Children of God/The Family. River Phoenix: Children of God/The Family.
2. Harold Camping (1921–2013) was a Christian evangelist and president of the California-based Family Radio station, which broadcast in more than 150 markets across the United States. His fire-and-brimstone style and absolute certainty about the return of Jesus on May 21, 2011, garnered a great deal of media attention and millions of dollars in donations. Camping promised that the faithful would be raptured into heaven on May 21, while the damned would be consumed in plagues and fires until October of that same year, at which time the world would actually end. After May 21 came and went, Camping re-prophesied the true end of the world to October 21, 2011, but he had a stroke in June of that year and was fairly quiet on the subject for the rest of his life. Camping died in December 2013. Family Radio suffered huge losses after the failed prophecy, and had to lay off staff and sell many of its stations. However, as of 2016 it is still broadcasting Camping's sermons on eighty-six stations in the United States.
3. End-time beliefs are found in Christianity (Catholic and Protestant), Judaism, Islam, Buddhism, Hinduism, Baha'i, Norse religions, Rastafarianism, and Zoroastrianism. See https://en.wikipedia.org/wiki/End_time.
4. This framework was originally published in Lalich's book *Bounded Choice: True Believers and Charismatic Cults* (Berkeley: University of California Press, 2004), based on the findings from a comparative study of two cults with utterly dissimilar belief systems (her Marxist-Leninist cult and the Heaven's Gate UFO cult, whose members committed mass suicide in 1997).
5. Sociologists have written numerous articles concerning the difficulties of research on cults. See, for example, Marybeth Ayella, "'They Must Be Crazy': Some of the Difficulties in Researching 'Cults,'" *American Behavioral Scientist* 33, no. 5 (1990): 562–77; Janja Lalich, "Pitfalls in the Sociological Study of Cults," in *Misunderstanding Cults: Searching for Objectivity in a Controversial Field*, Eds. Benjamin Zablocki and Thomas Robbins (Toronto: University of Toronto Press, 2001), 123–55; and Rob Balch, "How the Problem of Malfeasance Gets Overlooked in Studies of New Religions: An Examination of the AWARE Study of the Church Universal and Triumphant," in *Wolves within the Fold: Religious Leadership and Abuses of Power*, Ed. A. Shupe (New Brunswick, NJ: Rutgers University Press, 1998), 191–211.
6. For an example of the scholarly debates on this topic, see Benjamin Zablocki and Thomas Robbins, Eds., *Misunderstanding Cults: Searching for Objectivity in a Controversial Field* (Toronto: University of Toronto Press, 2001).
7. See D. Tourish and N. Vatcha, "Charismatic Leadership and Corporate Cultism at Enron: The Elimination of Dissent, The Promotion of Conformity and Organizational Collapse," *Leadership* 1, no. 4 (2005): 455–80.
8. See Lalich and Tobias's *Take Back Your Life: Recovering from Cults and Abusive Relationships* (Berkeley, CA: Bay Tree Publishing, 2006) for more on family cults and one-on-one cults.
9. Current evidence of this "death-to-outsiders" feature can be seen in the violent actions of groups like ISIS, Al-Qaeda, al-Shabab, and other terrorist groups as well as in some white supremacist and ultra-nationalist groups in the United States.
10. See Benjamin Zablocki, "Hyper Compliance in Charismatic Groups," in *Mind, Brain and Society: Toward a Neurosociology of Emotion*, Eds. David. D. Franks and Thomas S. Smith (Stamford, CT: JAI Press, 1999), 287–310, for a discussion of relational addiction and hyper-compliance in charismatic groups.

1

WE WEREN'T THERE BY CHOICE

Meeting Our Narrators

Childhood is usually romanticized as a time of wonder, laughter, and magic—as a time when we're surrounded by nurturing support that helps us form our identities, discover our unique skills, and grow up happily . . . if we're lucky. Sadly, the individuals you'll meet in this chapter weren't lucky.

Instead, our six narrators were born into cults, or brought into cults in early childhood by their parents. When their parents (or their great-grandparents, in some cases) joined these groups, they did so because each group's ideals and promises captivated them, made sense, or felt profoundly meaningful. But our narrators didn't have any say in these decisions; they weren't there by choice. Sadly, because they were children, they often experienced some of the harshest effects of the practices linked to their groups' utopian ideals and world-changing beliefs.

In many cases, the cult survivors you'll read about in this chapter didn't grow up in their family unit and weren't raised by their own parents. Many of the groups you'll learn about placed children in collective homes so that their parents could work for the cult. The childcare duties often fell to people who didn't have any training or the support they needed to nurture the children properly, because the business of these cults wasn't about raising children. The business of these and most other cults is to grow, bring in money, and build their influence.

In some of these cults, children were far down on the list of importance, and many experienced neglect in the face of the cult's main focus of gathering more followers, gathering money, and building power. Some of these groups developed specific rules that separated children from their parents so that bonding could not occur; instead, all members were expected to bond with the cult, its leader(s), or its ideology.

Other cults controlled women's fertility and actively promoted pregnancy and childbearing to increase their numbers. The children born into these groups were often treated as blank slates who could be trained (usually communally) to be ideal and untarnished examples of the perfection of the cult's beliefs. For many of these cult babies, early life was filled with discipline, hard work, endless indoctrination, and a constant demand for perfection. For many of the individuals you'll meet in this book, childhood was not a time of wonder, laughter, or magic; it was more like doing time in a boot camp.

Janja interviewed sixty-five people who were raised in cults and escaped, in all cases on their own without any inside or outside help. In this chapter, you'll meet six individuals, each of whose names have been changed to protect his or her privacy. We are, however, identifying their cults, all of which are still active as of 2017.

The many cults we studied seem very different on the outside. Some were strictly religious; others were focused on martial arts, while still others were focused on meditation or metaphysical philosophies. Nevertheless, the four dimensions of bounded choice that characterize all high-demand groups and relationships were and still are active in all of these groups. *All* of these groups rely on a transcendent belief system, charismatic authority, systems of control, and systems of influence to transmit their ideology, control their members, and put their worldview into practice—even though each group has its own unique organizational structure, philosophy, and utopian vision.

Some of these groups focus on religious ideals that reach back to the fundamental early teachings of their respective religions; some focus on preparing their members for the end of the world or the end of human existence as we know it; some focus on metaphysical ideas about energy and health; and some focus on creating a more perfect world (or perfect health) through complete devotion to the group's rules and dogma. But as you'll see, no matter which ideals these groups promote, the most important ideals are related to transcendent beliefs, systems of control and influence, and the demand for unquestionable dedication to a charismatic and controlling authority figure.

We chose these six stories to help you enter the seemingly strange world of cults through the eyes of real people. As we continue onward into the book, we'll bring in examples from the entire group of people Janja studied. For now, we will focus on the true-life stories of Samantha, Iris, Matthew, Jessica, Joseph, and Lily (all of these names are pseudonyms).

Samantha G.

The Sixth Child of a Tenth Wife in the Third Generation

My mother had six kids. My father tried to keep that as the average for each of his nineteen wives. He didn't feel like they needed to have any more than six. Some of them had fewer and there were two or three that had a few more. Well, one had eleven kids, one had nine kids, but I think the average was six. He would decide for them: four for you; on to the next.

Samantha

Samantha G. is the sixth child of the tenth wife of a Fundamentalist Mormon man who had nineteen wives and seventy-four children. Samantha was born in the 1970s, and is a third-generation Fundamentalist Mormon (also known as Fundamentalist Church of Jesus Christ of Latter-Day Saints, or FLDS[1]). She grew up in a large polygamist community in Arizona, surrounded by hundreds of polygamist families who believe in the religious doctrine of plural marriage for Mormon men (but not for women, who are allowed only one husband at a time).

In the mainstream Mormon faith, plural marriage was abandoned in the late nineteenth century as a response to pressure from the U.S. government. However, many Mormons at that time denounced the change as both politically spineless and spiritually endangering—they were certain that the loss of plural marriage threatened devout Mormons' chances of ascending to the most exalted of the three heavens prophesied by Mormon founder Joseph Smith. Smith believed that the third and highest heaven, the Celestial Kingdom, was where only the most faithful Mormons would be nearest to God. In his original prophesies, Joseph Smith proclaimed that entry into this most exalted kingdom could be attained only by men who had undertaken Celestial Marriage (plural marriage).

The Mormon Church splintered over the issue of Celestial Marriage in the 1880s, and many polygamist Mormons left the new state of Utah (where plural marriage was outlawed) for Mexico,[2] Canada, and then-unincorporated areas of Colorado and Arizona. Samantha's large family consists of direct descendants of the Arizona faction of this rupture, and in her community, it is understood that a man with fewer than three wives has very little chance of ascending to the Celestial Kingdom. Accordingly, most men accumulate numerous wives. Samantha's father had nineteen wives, but some men in the community have more than fifty. The legal and financial situation for these wives and their children, however, is very precarious. Because plural marriage is illegal in all parts of the United States, these plural marriages are not recognized—and typically, many plural wives raise their many children on public assistance and food stamps as if they are single mothers.[3]

Growing up, Samantha lived in a large home with eleven of her nineteen mothers and thirty of her seventy-four brothers and sisters. She was raised primarily among half-siblings who were near her own age, and she didn't really get to know her own full siblings (who were segregated by age into other homes) until she was an adult. Samantha's mother was expected to stay at home and care for all thirty of the children while some of the other mothers worked, but she found the work overwhelming and often retreated into her bedroom or into nervous breakdowns. Though Samantha was the youngest of her mother's six children, she became a caretaker and medications manager for her mother at home and during her many hospitalizations.

Samantha and her many siblings went to a public school funded by the state of Arizona, though the curriculum was controlled and directed by the church. Many of the teachers were plural wives from the community, so there were not a lot of outsiders who could provide support to the children. Consequently, Samantha's (and her siblings' and friends') many complaints about the systematic sexual abuse they endured were not reported to any authorities.

Samantha was raised in a very tightly controlled community where rules of dress, behavior, and worship were strict—but also where, unfortunately, sexual abuse by brothers, uncles, and cousins was not controlled at all; instead, it was commonplace. In fact, Samantha's own father molested her repeatedly, though he was never able to remember her name (or which of his nineteen wives was her mother). As Samantha reached puberty, she avoided making direct eye contact with adult males at parties or gatherings because she was afraid that she would be forced to marry one of them. In Samantha's community, marriages are arranged by male church elders; young girls have little to no choice in the matter, and many girls are married before their sixteenth birthdays.

One consequence of the large number of early enforced marriages in FLDS communities is a high infant and child mortality rate, along with a high number of miscarriages and stillbirths. The youth of the mothers is a factor, as is the sheer number of pregnancies some women experience. It isn't uncommon for FLDS women to become pregnant every year or two from their early teens into their late thirties. Another factor is that inbreeding among members of the same family (such as first cousins, uncles and nieces, and other close relations) isn't monitored; therefore, genetic birth defects are prevalent.[4] Samantha once counted the graves in the baby cemetery in her small community and found over 150 hand-dug graves, including seventy graves for stillborns and babies under one week of age.

Samantha's mother went in and out of mental hospitals throughout Samantha's childhood and adolescence, so no one was available to protect Samantha from incessant sexual and physical abuse. Things changed when her father died suddenly. Samantha was fourteen then, and before an already-arranged marriage could be forced upon her, she escaped from the cult and lived with a non-fundamentalist Mormon family nearby. Samantha struggled for many years to rebuild her life, and is now an advocate with the HOPE Organization, which offers support and a kind of underground railroad to freedom for survivors of abuse in polygamous relationships.

Fundamentalist Mormon groups are still active in Arizona, Colorado, Utah, Mexico, and Canada, with more splinter groups and family compounds forming every year. For instance, Elizabeth Smart wrote the 2013 bestseller, *My Story*, about being kidnapped from her own bedroom when she was fourteen and being held captive for nine months. She was abducted by a fundamentalist Mormon couple who wanted to start their own polygamist cult—with the teenaged Elizabeth as their first, unwilling plural wife.

Iris D.

The Enlightened Child Freed from Karma

> My parents felt an obligation for us to be given the key to enlightenment and the universe so that we would never have to reincarnate again. And so, my brother and I were brought to the home of some TM leaders to go through this initiation process. We did not know what it was going to be other than we were very excited and very hyped up about how mystical and important this was. We had our special little holy flowers and hand-kerchiefs and we went with a group of other children—my brother and me. He was five and I was eight. A young woman performed a ceremony with some incense and candles and she started chanting. And then she kneeled down and bowed down to a picture of somebody. I didn't know who it was. She motioned for me to bow down as well. And I didn't. I didn't know what it was about. And then we sat down and she gave me my special mantra and told me how to use it. And it was supposed to be a huge turning point for our spiritual state in the universe. We were now better than everybody else who had not yet been initiated, and so we were kind of the spiritual elite.
>
> *Iris*

Iris D.[5] was born into the Transcendental Meditation (TM) community in California in the late 1960s. Her parents met at a TM teacher training and dedicated their lives and their home to the growing movement. Iris and her brother grew up meditating and following TM's spiritual teachings, and their home was a training center for adults and teens who were interested in TM. As some of the first children born into the movement, Iris and her brother were considered especially spiritual and enlightened.

TM was founded by an East Indian man called Maharishi Mahesh Yogi. He was born in 1921 (as Mahesh Prasad Varma) and began teaching meditation in India in the late 1950s. Mahesh traveled and lectured throughout the world, and rose to international fame and power after the Beatles (and other celebrities) briefly joined his ashram in Rishikesh, India, in the late 1960s. Though the Beatles stayed for only a few weeks, their presence and apparent devotion[6] made meditation seem exciting and fashionable. Mahesh became the international face of the meditation movement and TM soon became the most famous form.

TM uses deep breathing and silent repetitions of a special mantra (usually a single, meaningless syllable) to supposedly help people transcend their bodies, their emotions, and their thoughts in favor of a depersonalized form of consciousness.

TM is generally suggested as twice-daily twenty-minute practice, but devotees in TM's inner circle meditate in two-hour sessions (or more) every morning and evening. TM devotees claim that their form of meditation brings relaxation, stress relief, lowered blood pressure, creativity, inner peace, protection from disease, and spiritual enlightenment. However, many studies[7] suggest that lengthy meditation may also exacerbate underlying mental illnesses and/or induce anxiety, depression, dissociation, paranoia, grandiosity, and even hallucinations in vulnerable people. Iris remembers many psychotic episodes occurring in TM community members; however, those events were explained in spiritual terms, as awakenings. There were also several suicide clusters among young TM devotees that were also explained in spiritual terms: the victims were portrayed as fully awakened beings who no longer needed to cycle through birth, death, and reincarnation.

Iris's parents were deeply devoted to teaching TM and building the presence of TM in the United States and throughout the world. They often left Iris in the care of other members during their four-hour daily meditation sessions, and during their recruiting trips in the United States and abroad. When Iris was three years old, her family moved to Fairfield, Iowa, where the TM community had developed a large compound with a grammar school, and soon, a university.[8] Iris's mother gave birth to Iris's little brother there, and in the first few months of his life, she left him and Iris in Fairfield so that she could take a six-month training directly from the Maharishi in his compound in Holland (children weren't allowed at Mahesh's compounds). As an adult, Iris asked people in the TM community about her mother's travels, and while there was some concern about her mother leaving a breastfeeding child, Iris also heard praise about the depth of her mother's devotion to TM.

Children in the Fairfield compound knew and lived with their parents, and while being left for months at a time was difficult, it was a normal and expected part of community life. The children also had relative freedom because the adults were so focused on recruitment, teaching, and building TM. This freedom was especially enjoyable during the adults' lengthy daily meditation periods, when the children were free to run around and play (or get into trouble as they got older).

Life in the TM compound in Iowa was fairly pleasant. Everyone believed the same things, ate the same vegetarian diet, and shared the higher purpose of creating world peace through TM. This sameness, however, meant that stepping out of line was very socially dangerous; without any use of overt force, the community was able to keep people in line with threats of expulsions.

Iris and her friends went to the private TM grammar school in Fairfield—the Maharishi School of the Age of Enlightenment. The school taught all subjects through the lens of Mahesh's beliefs; and though it was intended primarily for TM children, the tuition was very expensive. Iris remembers all of her friends feeling very anxious during the summers as their parents struggled to come up with or borrow money for their children's tuition. The community portrayed their only other option—the public grammar school in Fairfield—as rough, mean, and spiritually ignorant.

Iris and her brother went to grammar school in Fairfield, but then moved numerous times as her parents traveled throughout the United States doing recruitment and TM teaching. Iris went to seven different high schools, and because her parents were so busy, she had to enroll herself at each one. As they grew up, her brother got tired of all this upheaval and tried to leave a few times, but he didn't have many job skills or life skills. He also didn't feel comfortable out in the world, where most current events and common knowledge were foreign to him. He ended up, as many of the teens who left TM did, in yet another close-knit religious community.

Iris married a young man from the TM community when she was eighteen and got pregnant by him. She eventually had three children who were raised inside and outside of TM communities as she and her husband tried to build a life for themselves in the outside world. Iris watched many of her friends struggle to leave and then return several times, or join another similarly closed religious group, as her brother had. She also kept an eye on younger TM community members, many of whom were getting into drug use, falling into depressions or psychoses, or attempting suicide. These troubled members struggled without the help of doctors, medications, or support because the TM community focused only on ancient Indian herbal medicines, vegetarianism, and meditation for their health care. Iris also watched older members, her father included, struggle through serious diseases without medical support. Iris began speaking out to leadership about the troubles she saw; as a result, she lost her elite status as a revered and enlightened child. She came to be seen as a troublemaker who was continually threatened with expulsion for speaking out.

Iris finally left with her husband and three children when she was twenty-nine years old. She credits her husband for helping her get out and stay out, as so many of her friends had not been able to do on their own. However, both Iris and her husband had tremendous trouble fitting into the outside world, finding and keeping jobs, connecting with outsiders, or even engaging in small talk (which is built on everyday knowledge that they didn't have). In their first year away from the cult, Iris and her husband mostly played video games all day while they figured out how to live in an alien world. Even today, she has trouble feeling part of everyday life and is often filled with anxiety about not being perfect enough, not fitting in, or possibly being expelled from wherever she happens to be. She and her fellow ex-TM friends also have a hard time connecting to people who don't share a higher purpose or spiritual values. She still feels like an outsider in many social situations.

Iris and her husband divorced a few years after they left TM, but they remain friends. They both visit the Fairfield compound with their children so that they can see their friends and visit with their parents, all of whom are still in the cult. While they enjoy those visits, they are all relieved to pack up and go home.

Iris's parents are not financially prepared for old age, and they have no retirement savings. Her invalid father lives with her brother, while her mother and other impoverished elders live in a kind of makeshift retirement community in Fairfield. All of the money and property they had when they joined—and all of the money they made as TM recruiters and teachers—went to tuition, tithing, and building the Maharishi's empire.

After she left TM, Iris put herself through community college and then university, and is now a licensed medical professional. In addition to her career, she regularly counsels and supports people who are trying to leave TM and other cultic groups. Though she tends to keep her cult upbringing to herself, she was also able to speak up in her new community and stop her children's high school from buying a TM program developed for schools. Today, Iris still meditates, but only when she feels like it.

Matthew O.

The Outsider Who Got Out, Came Out, and Survived

> So I worked in the restaurant there and can you believe that many of these kids worked seventeen hours a day? I worked seventeen hours every day and I never earned any money for that work. We weren't allowed to earn any money for our pockets. We just slaved away, day in and day out. We would wake up at four or five o'clock in the morning and we would go until we would close at midnight. We would go to bed at like two or three in the morning, you know, you only got two or three hours of sleep and that's how the commune worked. Everyone experienced very limited sleep and it was just a real brainwashing experience with the sleep deprivation. You never had a good eight hours of sleep. If you had eight hours of sleep, they felt like you were spoiled and lazy when you should be preparing yourself to be in heaven with Jesus Christ.
>
> *Matthew*

Matthew O.[9] was born in Tennessee in the 1970s in a spiritual commune called the Twelve Tribes. The Twelve Tribes formed in the early 1970s and was a part of the "Jesus Movement" that arose within the American youth counterculture, in part as a response to the Vietnam War. In the Jesus Movement, many disaffected teens and adults wanted to live as they imagined Jesus had lived, so they focused their lives on spirituality, communal living, Bible study, and constant hard work to prepare themselves for a wonderful afterlife with Jesus. Many of the original Twelve Tribes members met each other in 1969 at the famous Woodstock Festival in upstate New York, and some of the early members were "Deadheads" who followed the Grateful Dead from concert to concert. Twelve Tribes communities are now located throughout the world, and several are still active in the Woodstock area.

Twelve Tribes members engage in extensive Bible study and communitarian living, often with forty or fifty people in the same house. They isolate themselves from the evil "worldly" society so that they can focus on their spiritual lives and prepare for the end of the world. Members work constantly from the age of five or seven for no pay in order to support their community, and homeschool their children to protect them from outside influences—including television, toys, computers, music, dancing, politics, and public education. Members use prayer as their primary form of health care, avoiding dental care and vision care as well. Twelve Tribes members also maintain strictly old-fashioned gender roles, with women dressing modestly in long dresses with bloomers (never pants), never cutting their hair, speaking only through a man such as a husband or an elder, and giving birth to as many babies as they can.

Matthew's parents were dissatisfied Christians who were looking for a deeper form of religion. By chance, they met up with Twelve Tribes recruiters at a concert and were immediately drawn to the idea of living as Jesus had and separating themselves from the evils of the modern world. They sold their home and belongings and moved into a communal compound in Chattanooga, Tennessee, and Matthew was the first midwife-birthed baby born in the Chattanooga commune. Sadly, he was born ill with spinal meningitis and a high fever that was not treated, and he lost his hearing. Sadder still, his parents didn't realize that Matthew was deaf until he was three years old. Up until that time, they and other Tribe members spanked and punished Matthew constantly for not paying attention. Unfortunately, his eventual diagnosis of deafness did very little to improve Matthew's early life.

Illness and disability were looked upon by the Twelve Tribes as punishments from God that required diligent and continuous prayer (and little to no medical care). Matthew's grief-stricken parents prayed for him and felt tremendous shame for whatever they had done to cause Matthew's deafness. Matthew was worried about and punished, but he was not given language support or special education until he was seven. Only one person in the commune knew American Sign Language, and he had to work for years to get the elders to understand the value of teaching Matthew a language. Though this man helped Matthew learn and catch up, no one else learned to sign—so Matthew got by through close observation of others and a gestural language of homemade signs that helped him communicate and follow orders.

Even without a dependable way to communicate and understand, Matthew was expected to follow all the rules of the commune, which included waking at four or five each morning to begin work. Matthew reports that he saw children as young as three working in the communal kitchens, and that many of the girls in the cult provided communal childcare when they themselves were just five years old. By the age of eighteen, Matthew and his teenaged friends and siblings were expected to work unpaid seventeen-hour shifts in one of the many Twelve Tribes' farms, shops, bakeries, industries, restaurants, or construction firms.

Life in the commune was filled with hard work, minimal sleep, and scant food, and Matthew remembers having to confess on several occasions after he had eaten toothpaste because he was so hungry. The punishments for this and other transgressions (which could be meted out by any adult) were a form of caning with oiled switches, rods, or paddles. Public nude canings were a regular occurrence for many of the children, who were expected to be perfect children of God. Play and toys were forbidden, and trips to nearby towns were strictly monitored so that evil worldly influences couldn't affect the children. Matthew remembers being forced to close his eyes as the group walked past worldly toy stores or magazine racks, though he always peeked through his eyelashes.

Matthew struggled throughout his life to fit into the commune, yet he was never happily a part of the community—or of his family of eight siblings. He was ostracized and treated as a second-class citizen because of his deafness, which was seen as constant proof of God's displeasure, and he endured endless rounds of forced prayer to atone for the alleged sins that had made him deaf. Matthew endured a great deal of physical and emotional abuse, and his linguistic seclusion added to his struggles. For instance, one of the Twelve Tribes' beliefs was that their true homeland was in Israel, so children were taught Hebrew in preparation for the eventual move to their imagined home. Many of the children then used Hebrew as a secret language among themselves so that they could bond and share their concerns and troubles, but Matthew was never taught to speak or sign in Hebrew, which further isolated him.

Matthew's mother, who had a history of depression and migraines before she joined the cult, found herself falling into regular depressions and excruciating migraine episodes. Medication was not allowed, so her only treatment was forced prayer and confessions. As a result, she became less and less functional as she aged, and so was not able to support or protect Matthew. Matthew's father, burdened by endless hard work and the notion that he had two sinful and imperfect family members, was not able to provide support either. Matthew attempted to leave the commune—and he attempted suicide—numerous times before he finally escaped at the age of twenty-one. The Twelve Tribes elders prohibited contact between Matthew and his family. They told Matthew that he was now evil and worldly, and that God would kill him and send him to Hell. Matthew told them in return that God would judge them for their actions, and for allowing so many children and adults to be abused.

On the outside, Matthew struggled to learn how to live in an alien world where he didn't understand even the basics of how to take care of himself, manage money, rent an apartment, apply for a job, do math, drive, or vote. He struggled to shake off the Tribe's toxic belief that the outside world was evil. In fact, many Twelve Tribes escapees eventually return to the cult because they can't tolerate the supposed evils of the outside world. Luckily, Matthew found a good social service agency that helped him study for his GED, apply for disability support, and learn about Gallaudet University for the Deaf, where he was accepted as a full-time college student. Matthew studied and mastered American Sign Language in his twenties at Gallaudet, and experienced yet another culture shock as he learned about his deafness and Deaf culture—not as a sign of failure or evil, but as a valuable cultural identity with a rich linguistic tradition.

Matthew saw a counselor at Gallaudet who helped him work through many of the issues of abuse and loss that haunted him. He also realized that he was gay (which was also considered evil in the Twelve Tribes) and he was grateful that he had the freedom to learn about gay culture and be himself away from the cult's influence. Matthew is now an out and proud gay man who provides online support and counseling to other cult survivors (including some of his siblings, who have since escaped from the Twelve Tribes), and he works as a social services case manager.

Jessica A.

The Magical Jesus Baby

> We were called The Family because we were supposedly one big, happy family. All husbands were everybody's husbands, all wives were everybody's wives, and all the children were everybody's children. And our Law of Love said that anything done in love was fine. Any form of discipline was fine, as long as it was done in love, you know? That really included some very over-the-top things, like kids getting beaten black and blue, nude public spankings, or putting kids in tiny little closet rooms, and fasting for, like, a month.
>
> *Jessica*

Jessica A. was born in Southeast Asia in the 1970s. She was one of the first "Jesus babies" born into the large, multinational group called The Children of God[10] (now called The Family International, or simply The Family). Jessica and her fellow Jesus babies were the offspring of a practice (which has since been terminated) called "Flirty Fishing," where young women from the group were told to have sex with men in order to bring them into the group and produce a generation of children created especially for and by The Family. As a result, many women in The Family have no idea who the fathers of their children are.

The Family is a fundamentalist Christian group that focuses on Bible studies and prepares for the prophesied end of days with the help of the Sixties-era free-love teachings of their prophet, the late David "Moses" Berg. As part of the Jesus Movement of the 1960s and 1970s, The Family gathered many converts among the disillusioned hippies of the era; in the 1970s, The Family was believed to have over 30,000 members in fifteen countries. Today, The Family International claims to have thousands of members in more than ninety countries. If this is true, they may be one of the largest cults in the world.

In the early days, as The Family was growing by leaps and bounds, the group achieved cohesion and unity through strong devotion to their leader, who followers called "Dad." Berg's teachings were often contradictory and based on his whims, or focused on creating a sexually open, free-love atmosphere that included scheduling required daily sexual contact between group members of all ages, known as the "sharing schedule." Money was very tight in the early days, and all members (including children) worked ten to twelve hours a day and often busked, danced, and sang on the streets for money, sold booklets of Berg's teachings, and begged for donations of clothing and food.

As the group expanded and more children were born into or brought into The Family, schooling was added to the work and busking schedules. However, the only books allowed were the rambling tracts written by Berg, which were studied on no particular schedule, given that the main focus for everyone, young and old, was to build and support the cult. Jessica remembers being taken away from her work and being rushed with other children into a classroom when visitors or local officials would come to check on them. Jessica and the other children would sit at desks and raise their hands as if they were in school, but this classroom was only for show: the central work of Family members was to acquire donations, keep the group going, and bring in more converts.

Jessica's life in The Family was harrowing. She had asthma, which was considered a sign of satanic possession. From her earliest years, her asthma was treated with exorcisms, solitary confinement (often in dark closets), or extended rounds of enforced fasting. At the age of seven, Jessica was included in the enforced sexual sharing schedule, and along with the other children in the group, she was the victim of constant physical, sexual, and emotional abuse at the hands of Family members and their potential recruits. Jessica's parents weren't able to protect her; they worked long hours to support the cult, and family closeness was not encouraged. Childcare was performed communally and at the whim of whichever adult was nearby, and the Law of Love was used to excuse nearly any form of punishment or abuse. Jessica fought against this abuse, but her defiance only brought more stringent punishments upon her, including an enforced nine-month silence fast when she was eleven years old.

In numerous attempts to discipline and retrain Jessica, The Family moved her between the cult's compounds in Holland, France, and Belgium—and away from her parents and her siblings. Jessica tried very hard to be an obedient member of the group, but she failed over and over again—and was disciplined, silenced, hit, punished, isolated, forced to fast, and moved around constantly.

As Jessica neared adolescence, Berg (who had many teen wives) decreed that girls could be married at the age of twelve so that they could start producing babies as soon as they were able to. However, Jessica's defiance and multiple punishments kept her out of the cult's marriage market. Jessica slit her wrists at the age of twelve and was sent to a Family compound for troubled children, at which time the sexual sharing schedule was thankfully stopped because the cult was being scrutinized in many countries for child abuse.

For the next few years, Jessica was bounced from country to country, sometimes living near her mother and sometimes being forcibly separated from her. In one of the retraining compounds, Jessica was violently raped by a peer; yet, instead of punishing him, the compound leaders bizarrely—and cruelly—had her feed and tend to her rapist so that she could learn forgiveness. Jessica escaped from The Family at the age of fifteen, with no skills, education, money, or contacts. Jessica slept on couches, panhandled, sang in bars, and moved from place to place to keep herself going, but before long she returned to The Family out of sheer exhaustion and desperation.

Jessica stayed in the cult for about eighteen months after her first escape, but she left for good at seventeen and spent many years homeless and in chaos until she put herself through school and started building a life for herself from scratch. Today, Jessica has a Bachelor's degree in Political Science and was an advocate with the group Safe Passages, which acts as an underground railroad and provides support, housing, and counseling to people who were raised in and escaped from The Family and other cults.

Joseph L.

The Excluded Member of the Exclusive Brethren

> There was some fairly genuine friendship and a sense of community in the early days before 1960, and the way of life that they encouraged was in some ways admirable. The negatives were mostly after 1960: genuine friendships became strained by internal political conflict; learning and scholarship were discouraged and ridiculed; hypocrisy became almost essential for survival; and the organization became one that seemed to exist purely to deceive, control, and exploit its members. The atmosphere became harsh and demanding. The worst of the negatives was being separated from loved ones, and I was. Many people suffered more than I by being separated even from their spouses. The worst emotional stress was suffered by members who were excommunicated and who were denied any social contact with their friends and family who were still in the sect. Excommunication usually meant losing all of your friends and family. Often it meant losing your home, too, and sometimes your job.
>
> *Joseph*

Joseph L.[11] was born in London in the 1950s as a third-generation member of the Exclusive Brethren. The Exclusive Brethren movement was founded in Dublin in 1825 as a fundamentalist evangelical Christian denomination with no officially appointed clergy. The original Brethren focused instead on the inerrancy of the Bible, on the literal existence of heaven and hell, on close studies of scripture, and on isolating themselves from the outside world. Any male Brethren can contribute to religious services (called assemblies) and biblical discussions; however, women are not permitted to do so. Women and girls are not allowed to pray out loud in Brethren assemblies; and once they are married, women's lives and bodies are under the control of the cult. Married women are not permitted to use birth control, and until recently, they were not permitted to work outside the home. Today, many Brethren women are allowed to work, but only in positions where they do not have any power or influence over men.

The Exclusive Brethren (and their many offshoot branches) promote powerful internal unity with required nightly assemblies, weekly communal meals called The Lord's Supper, two Saturday morning assemblies, and three assemblies on Sundays. The Brethren firmly separate themselves from worldly outside influences (the official doctrine is called "Separation from Evil"), and frequently distance themselves from anyone who disagrees with them. Joseph reports that, as a result, the Brethren have undergone more than a dozen schisms since 1848, such that there are now over twenty different Brethren branches[12] in fourteen countries existing in what Joseph calls "a state of mutual excommunication." Joseph's branch, called the Raven/Taylor/Hales group, is headquartered in London and is considered the most strongly separatist of the Brethren's many competing branches. It is estimated that there are now more than 45,000 members in Exclusive Brethren branches and offshoots worldwide.

Children in Joseph's Exclusive Brethren branch were raised in their own family units and attended public schools, but they were not allowed to take classes in music, art, literature, Bible studies (Brethren have their own interpretations of scripture that don't agree with mainstream Christianity), drama, dance, computer studies, evolution, paleontology, geology, sex education, or physical education where revealing clothing was worn.

Joseph recalls that when he was young, he and his family were able to interact with outsiders and neighborhood children. However, a change of leadership in 1959 led to a series of decrees that required members to donate large sums of money to the Brethren, actively shun any dissenters, and end all contact with outsiders. This new leadership enacted many authoritarian and exclusionary changes, so that by 1960, no one in Joseph's group was allowed to live in a house or apartment that shared walls with non-members, or to share meals or socialize with outsiders. One consequence of these changes was that Joseph lost touch with all of his aunts, uncles, cousins, and grandparents who weren't in the Brethren.

By the age of nine, Joseph was expected to attend assemblies every evening, plus two meetings every Saturday morning, and three daytime services every Sunday. This made finding time for school or homework very difficult for him.

He dreamed of escaping and living wild in the trees of a nearby forest, and he has fond memories of a teacher who would secretly let him read novels at school (novel reading was strictly forbidden in his group). Joseph was fortunate to be in the last generation of Brethren children who were allowed to go to college, because the relative freedom he found there allowed him to quietly set himself up in the outside world with a small rented apartment and a job. As he met people from other churches and discovered that the Brethren's ideas weren't supported by the Bible, he began to question all parts of his cult's ideology—but only to himself, as questioning and debate weren't allowed.

Joseph secretly planned his escape by applying for non-Brethren jobs and connecting with outsiders he met at college. He escaped from the group at the age of nineteen and was excommunicated completely, meaning that no one in any Brethren branch was allowed to communicate openly with him for the rest of his life.

Joseph built a life on his own and reconnected with his non-Brethren family, but he didn't really know them or have much in common with them. When he was twenty, he met a young woman who was also trying to leave the Brethren, and they developed a close and supportive friendship that turned into love, and soon into marriage. Joseph and his fiancée invited both of their families to their wedding, but no one attended. However, a few family members broke their enforced silence and wrote terse notes to let Joseph and his wife-to-be know that their marriage was immoral, worldly, and evil.

After an uncomfortable period of learning to adjust to the outside world, Joseph has lived a good life away from the Brethren. He found an online group of ex-Brethren, and has been able to share his story with people who truly understand what he went through. However, even though he's been out for more than forty years, he reports that his feelings of anger, grief, and loneliness have increased rather than decreased over time. As the only immediate family member to have left the Brethren, Joseph has missed all the important life events of his siblings, parents, and grandparents—and sadly, he wasn't even notified about the deaths of his parents or his grandparents. When he misses them the most, he sometimes imagines talking to them and hearing their voices. Today, Joseph counsels other cult escapees online and in person, and has created a history and genealogy of the Exclusive Brethren and its many combative offshoots.

The Exclusive Brethren and all its competing branches are still active today, but many have finally relaxed their extreme prohibitions against contact with outsiders and non-Brethren family members. The Brethren are considered a New Religious Movement by some religious scholars; however, there is ample evidence of each of the four dimensions of bounded choice in Brethren groups: a strongly transcendent belief system; a severe and demanding authority structure; and powerful systems of influence and control that isolate followers, bind them to the group, and regulate every aspect of their lives.

Lily E.

The Highly Disciplined Martial Artist in the Inner Circle

> I wasn't able to have a normal childhood because I didn't live in a normal
> household with normal parents. After I was ten years old, I was out of my
> parents' picture. My mom lived in house with other women and didn't
> raise me anymore. And my dad lived in a house for the men. And then I
> lived with another family. It wasn't normal. I couldn't do normal things,
> couldn't have normal friends, couldn't go over to anybody's house, couldn't
> even do a normal school project.
>
> *Lily*

Lily E. was born in Vermont in the 1980s. Her parents were earnest seekers who
had converted to Mormonism before Lily was born, but only truly found what
they were looking for when they started martial arts training under the direction
of a Korean-born woman named Tae Yun Kim. Kim had created her own form
of martial arts, called Jung SuWon, which incorporates Korean tae kwon do,
spiritual teachings about marshalling and purifying your *ki* (or *chi*: your life energy,
power, and healing ability), Bible-based studies, and self-help teachings on
discipline and success. Kim claimed to have achieved the status of Grandmaster
of martial arts in her native Korea (which is disputed); thus, she required her
followers to address her as Grandmaster and bow to the many large color portraits
of herself that adorned the walls of her martial arts studio.

Lily's parents became members of Grandmaster Kim's inner circle (of about
forty or fifty people) called the College of Learning when Lily was three years
old. When Kim left Vermont to start a larger martial arts training school in
Fremont, California, Lily's parents left everything behind and moved to California
to study with Kim and help her build her new school. In Fremont, Grandmaster
Kim created very strict living arrangements for her College of Learning followers,
segregating men and women into separate household compounds. Lily was one
of the few children in the inner circle. While she was allowed to live in the same
communal women's home as her mother until she was ten, Lily was urged not
to attach too strongly to either of her parents. For instance, if Lily wanted to go
shopping alone with her mother, Grandmaster Kim had to be asked for permission
first.

Grandmaster Kim felt that parental attachments were weakening, and would
only get in the way of the acquisition of spiritual purity and martial arts excellence.
Lily's parents were not expected to provide for Lily in any way, so she received
care, food, clothing, and even toiletries from other women in the communal
home (most of whom had no dedicated time or energy to spend on Lily). Lily
remembers feeling very nervous and guilty about using shampoo or eating
something from the sparsely stocked refrigerator because nothing truly belonged

to her. Lily's mother soon became Kim's personal assistant and primary caretaker, and Lily was left on her own most of the time.

Lily began intensive martial arts training at the age of six, and she attended lengthy Jung SuWon classes every weeknight. Grandmaster Kim also personally taught Bible study classes where she subtly suggested a connection between herself and Jesus and took personal credit for bringing her followers to Christ. Daily life for Kim's followers was strictly controlled: children slept on the floor; constant dietary restrictions were enforced for members of the inner circle; total obedience to Grandmaster was required; and military-style discipline such as doing push-ups, running laps, and being berated in public for laziness or alleged wrongdoing were ways that Kim kept members of her inner circle in line.

Lily went to public Christian schools, but she lived a double life. While she wasn't strictly forbidden to play with other children, Grandmaster Kim continually warned that outsiders were untrustworthy or might even be Satanists. Lily also didn't know how to explain her home life or training schedule to other kids, or why she had to bow to an enormous portrait of Grandmaster every time Lily came in the door. Her intense nighttime Jung SuWon training also meant that visiting other kids' homes after school wasn't feasible. Lily did well in school, but she didn't form any lasting friendships.

Lily's parents divorced when Lily was nine (most of the marriages in Grandmaster's inner circle ended in divorce), and her father left the group a few years later. As was customary in this group, Lily's father was portrayed very negatively by Grandmaster Kim and other members of the inner circle. (The group habitually portrayed people who left as abusive, evil, or even as child molesters.) Although Lily knew that her father was not an evil man, these attacks made maintaining a relationship with him nearly impossible.

In 1998, when Lily was seventeen, Grandmaster Kim's group was exposed as a cult on a television program called *Inside Edition*. After that scandal, child protection agencies investigated the communal houses, and Kim quickly bought the children beds and stocked the refrigerators. For a little while after this exposé, Kim allowed Lily and the other children more freedom, and even allowed friends to come to their homes—but that freedom didn't last. Grandmaster Kim and members of the College of Learning became even more suspicious of outsiders, and the cult became more isolated, secretive, and paranoid.

Grandmaster Kim encouraged her followers' children to go to college, but no money was made available for any of them to do so. Lily put herself through state college and lived on campus, where she found some freedom from the group. Nevertheless, she wasn't able to make her escape until she was twenty-five years old. After Lily left, Grandmaster Kim denounced her as an embezzler and a person with "dark energy," and even called Lily late one night to tell her that she had a vision of Lily dying in a horrifying automobile accident as a direct result of her disloyalty. Lily knew rationally that this vision was a manipulative tactic meant to punish her, yet she felt frightened and unsettled about driving for years afterward.

Lily's mother is still the primary caretaker for Kim. Lily's mother now allows Lily to contact her, but she remains deeply disappointed that Lily left and is uninterested in maintaining a close relationship with her daughter. Lily's father is now involved in a New Age community, and while he is somewhat more available than her mother is, Lily and her father aren't close.

Lily found post-cult support in an online group of defectors from the College of Learning (and other similar martial arts cults), and she has been able to make some sense of her early life. She paid off her student loans, and put herself through graduate school to become a legal paraprofessional. Lily now lives in the San Francisco Bay Area and no longer practices martial arts.

★ ★ ★

In the next four chapters, you will learn about how these cults attracted and then retained our narrators' families, and how each of the four dimensions of bounded choice combine to create the closed and isolated world of these (and other) cults. We will begin by exploring the dimension that was most alluring for our narrators' parents or grandparents: the transcendent belief system.

Notes

1. For more accounts of children raised in the FLDS, see Andrea Moore-Emmett, *God's Brothel* (San Francisco: Pince-Nez Press, 2004).
2. Miles Park Romney (1843–1904), the great-grandfather of former Massachusetts Governor Mitt Romney, was the son of one of the founding members of the Mormon Church. Miles was also one of the founders of the splinter Mormon Church colonies in Colonia Juárez and Colonia Dublán, Mexico. Miles and other American Mormons founded the Mexican faction in1885 to continue the practice of plural marriage after it had been outlawed in the United States. Miles Romney had five wives; however, his son Gaskell Romney (Mitt's grandfather) and his grandson George Romney (Mitt's father) were not polygamists.
3. This form of welfare fraud pales in comparison to a multimillion-dollar case pending against imprisoned FLDS leader Warren Jeffs and his brother Lyle Jeffs. According to Federal prosecutors, the Jeffs's followers in Utah and Arizona were instructed to use their food stamps to buy specific items that were then turned over to the Jeffs to distribute. Followers also spent their food stamp money at cult-run stores without receiving any merchandise. The prosecutors estimate that over twelve million dollars of Federal benefits were diverted and money-laundered by the Jeffs.
4. See M. Oswaks, "Tiny Tombstones: Inside the FLDS Graveyard for Babies Born from Incest," *Broadly* (March 9, 2006). Accessed December 23, 2016, https://broadly. vice.com/en_us/article/tiny-tombstones-inside-the-flds-graveyard-for-babies-born-from-incest.
5. Iris D.'s story is a combination of the life stories of two people who grew up in the TM movement.
6. Conflicts between the Beatles and Mahesh have been reported over the years, but have not been confirmed.
7. A review of seventy-five published studies on meditation found that prolonged meditation could provoke "relaxation-induced anxiety and panic; paradoxical

increases in tension; less motivation in life; boredom; pain; impaired reality testing; confusion and disorientation; feeling 'spaced out'; depression; increased negativity; being more judgmental; feeling addicted to meditation; uncomfortable kinaesthetic sensations; mild dissociation; feelings of guilt; psychosis-like symptoms; grandiosity; elation; destructive behavior; suicidal feelings; defenselessness; fear; anger; apprehension; and despair." See A. Perez-De-Albeniz and J. Holmes, "Meditation: Concepts, Effects and Uses in Therapy," *International Journal of Psychotherapy* 5, no. 1 (2000): 49–58.

8. Maharishi International University, which is now Maharishi University of Management.

9. Matthew O.'s story is a combination of the life stories of two people who grew up in the Twelve Tribes.

10. Actors Rose McGowan and River Phoenix (and his siblings) grew up in The Children of God/The Family cult.

11. Joseph L.'s story is a combination of the life stories of two people who grew up in the Exclusive Brethren.

12. Garrison Keillor grew up in an American offshoot of the Exclusive Brethren called the Sanctified Brethren. In his autobiography *Lake Wobegon Days* (New York: Penguin Books, 1985), Keillor wrote, "We were Sanctified Brethren, a sect so tiny that nobody but us and God knew about it, so when kids asked what I was, I just said Protestant. It was too much to explain, like having six toes. You would rather keep your shoes on" (101). "We were the 'exclusive' Brethren, a branch that believed in keeping itself pure by avoiding association with the impure. . . . Once having tasted the pleasure of being Correct and defending True Doctrine, they kept right on and broke up at every opportunity, until, by the time I came along, there were dozens of tiny Brethren groups, none of which were speaking to any others" (105–6).

2

THE TRANSCENDENT BELIEF SYSTEM

Purity, Perfection, and the Eradication of Individuality

I was told to believe that I was evil, because the Exclusive Brethren believe in the Calvinistic doctrine of original sin, and in a literal heaven and hell. Throughout my childhood I experienced, and still sometimes experience, a strong sense of shame even in situations where I now logically "know" that I have done nothing wrong.

Joseph

Someone who left TM and became ill—we were told that he was meditating with the wrong mantra and how fortunate we were to know the right mantra, to protect ourselves from spiritual injury. There were also people who died or became extremely sick—including my father—because they believed to the core of their being that the true answer was long-term meditation and to use the Maharishi products. Or to pay thousands of dollars for ritual prayer services to be performed in India while the cancer or arthritis, or whatever it was, ate away their body and their money went to Maharishi's coffers. They were so indoctrinated.

Iris

There was a lot of abuse that we went through. The Twelve Tribes believed that kids are supposed to suffer more than the adults and they think that kids are very evil and that they have to be 100 percent perfect. If they are born into the commune that means that they have to follow the Bible scripture and revelations that say that Jesus Christ will come and save 144,000 perfect children out of this evil world. So the commune expects the children to be perfect and to be involved with that revolution with Jesus

Christ in heaven. The kids just suffered with all kinds of rules and judgment and criticism and it was very oppressive.

Matthew

The FLDS believes in and practices polygamy, and believes that a man must have at least three wives in order to get into heaven. It's a very patriarchal group where women are subjugated and expected to obey their husbands, and everyone has to follow the gospel to the letter. Everyone in the world outside was called "gentiles," or nonbelievers. We were taught that they were bad but that the apostates (people who left the FLDS) were worse because the gentiles, they didn't know they were bad. They had never heard the gospel, so it wasn't their fault they were bad. My dad would study the gentile news before he gave his sermons, and use real-life situations, real-life occurrences, and then make them a blanket statement for the whole world: This is the way the outside world is. If a child had been abused and neglected to the point of death, then that's what the gentile world did to the kid.

Samantha

What Is a Transcendent Belief System?

For centuries, people have asked, "What is the meaning of life? What is my purpose? Why am I here?" Through the ages, these questions have led philosophers, religious scholars, and artists to reflect deeply, and to develop an endless number of transcendent belief systems to answer them. The concept of transcendence relates to God and gods, certainly; yet it also relates to the universe beyond our understanding, to the realm of ideas, and to concepts that we are not yet able to comprehend. In many transcendent belief systems, wonder, free thinking, and doubt are welcomed and supported. But in the controlled and sealed-off world of cults, free thinking and doubt are not allowed.

Religions and philosophies promote many different transcendent belief systems. Each one has different answers about the meaning of life, and most will expect you to become a better person as you grow to understand the belief system. Conversely, in many cults, your purpose is to become a *perfect* person: a perfect, unquestioning martial artist like Lily; a textbook-perfect meditator like Iris; or a perfect, doubt-free child of God, as Matthew and Joseph were supposed to be. In other cults, your purpose may be to support your idealized leader or to spread your group's perfect belief system throughout the world, as Jessica's group, The Family,[1] did and still does today. In most cases, each cult member's needs, ideas, and individuality are irrelevant; rather, the value of members is measured by how flawlessly they live up to their group's vision of absolute, transcendent perfection.[2]

Though not all groups organize themselves around transcendent beliefs in a higher power or higher purpose, groups nearly always unite around their support for the *right* ideas, the *right* approaches, and the *right* kinds of people. For instance, top executives at Enron, an energy company that rose to great power and wealth and then failed disastrously, passionately promoted the belief that they were changing the very face of business. Everything that people at Enron did, they assured themselves, was not simply right; it was better than any other business practice that had ever been developed. Enron promoted itself as the truth and the way and the light of business, and their evangelical belief in the rightness of their model had the effect of silencing almost everyone in the company, even as it became clear that their unorthodox methods were endangering not just their own financial futures, but the stability of the world energy market itself.[3] Even when there are no obvious religious or spiritual beliefs involved, a transcendent belief system filled with certainty and righteousness can take over a group and erase the critical abilities of everyone inside it.

In healthy groups, a sense of rightness tends to be shared and supported in nonpolarizing and easygoing ways. In cultic groups like Enron and the groups Janja studied, however, the push for purity and perfection is intense and incessant. Public displays of unquestioning dedication to the group's beliefs become a main activity that often leads to the enforced extermination of any traits, behaviors, or ideas that challenge those allegedly perfect beliefs. In the private lives of cult members, the internalization of this intense dedication often leads people to willingly suppress or even erase their own individuality. When a transcendent belief system is strong enough, external forms of control may not be necessary; each member's idealism and dedication may kick into overdrive so that they will apply increasingly stricter controls on their own behavior.

In many cults, indoctrination into a transcendent belief system interferes with all aspects of life—and especially with the psychological development of children and teens. In most cases, family ties, socialization, schooling, play, health care, financial security, and preparation for the future are pushed aside, because all cult members—babies, children, teens, and adults—are required to demonstrate complete devotion to the group's ideals and beliefs.[4]

The Unique Features of Cultic Belief Systems

There are four dimensions to Janja's bounded choice model, which describes how people are attracted to and then trapped in cultic groups. As a reminder, the four dimensions are: (1) the transcendent belief system; (2) charismatic authority; (3) systems of control; and (4) systems of influence. It may strike you as unusual that we begin with the transcendent belief system instead of the charismatic cult leader, because without a leader or leaders, there would be no cult in the first place. Yet because we're focusing on the children, we believe it's important to start with the dimension that most likely captured the hearts and minds of the parents, who then brought or birthed their children into the cult environment. Though the cult leader is a crucial feature of bounded choice, it's typically the transcendent belief system that attracts followers to the group and keeps them loyal to its rules and beliefs.

Cultic belief systems contain a seemingly contradictory yet powerful combination: they are *all-encompassing*, yet also *all-exclusive*. These belief systems are all-encompassing because they offer a complete explanation of the past, present, and future—and they promise the one and only path to salvation. They explain everything and tell followers precisely how to behave and how to live, and they require followers to rewrite their own personal histories and future goals in order to be accepted into the group. Of course, many religions, political ideologies, and grand philosophies offer similar all-encompassing ideologies, but cults have a specific feature that makes them different: besides explaining everything about human existence then, now, and ever after, the leader also specifies the exact methods followers must adopt and the personal transformation they must undergo in order to walk the group's sacred and perfect path.

Cultic groups are also *all-exclusive* and sealed off, in that only special individuals can access the cult's information, deep beliefs, and transformative processes. Additionally, the cult's doctrine is all-exclusive because it is not simply true; it is The Truth—it comes down from on high, and it is never to be challenged. It is the only way to salvation. It makes the group exceptional and gives members a powerful sense of privilege and superiority, such that anything or anyone else becomes unworthy of consideration. One consequence of this type of thinking is that the group becomes walled-off and elitist—as Joseph's Exclusive Brethren group was toward outsiders, or as Iris's TM group was toward non-meditators. Other groups and belief systems are ridiculed or seen as evil, and this across-the-board prejudice justifies the attitude (and sometimes the requirement) that followers must exclude or reject any idea, belief, or person that is not approved by their group.

The combined pressures of the all-encompassing ideology that explains everything, the exclusivity and prejudice toward other beliefs, and the constant demand for change interact strongly with the dedication and idealism that motivate cult members. The belief system is urgent, undisputable, and unyielding: once you fully understand the perfect belief system, how can you not follow it to the letter? Once you commit yourself body and soul, how can you not follow through? As we'll explain in Chapter 4, this sense of obligation is even more compelling when you've testified openly to your commitment in front of others. These beliefs are so entrancing and magnetic that you come to believe that your life depends on following them with complete devotion.[5] These beliefs require strict obedience to rigid rules, a secluded lifestyle (even if you are living in the midst of an urban area), and a complete break with the thoughts, attitudes, and behaviors of your pre-cult life. Naturally, for children raised in cultic environments, there is no pre-cult life. This is all they know day after day.

For children who grow up in cults, there can be a harsh contrast between the group's utopian ideals of perfection and the often-grueling process of trying to achieve that perfection in everyday life. Cultic demands for transcendent perfection can be especially harmful for children and teens, who are often subjected to systematic abuse ("for the higher good") as a way to eliminate any traits, behaviors, or ideas that do not fit into the group's belief system. For instance, Matthew spoke of working long hours and being forbidden to play, or being forced to close his eyes as he passed "worldly" toy stores or bookstores—just as Jessica was punished, isolated, and forced to fast repeatedly to cure her of the allegedly satanic condition of asthma.

The outcome of this transformational process is a deep internalization of the belief system. Cult members quite willingly submit themselves to an intensive training and indoctrination process because they come to believe that their group holds the only path to freedom. Although we can easily see from the outside that cult members are not free, the transcendent belief system guarantees freedom through a sense of grand purpose, connection to a higher goal, and the promise of spiritual, political, or personal salvation. A cult member's subservience doesn't feel like subservience; it feels like devotion, zeal, and transcendence.[6]

How the Transcendent Belief System Captures and Retains Followers

The transcendent belief system ensnares people in a number of ways. Each member's constant striving for an impossible ideal makes them feel inadequate about themselves and their accomplishments. All they know is that they must work harder to live up to the group's demands, change themselves, and become more perfect. A large part of this push for perfection is that people are encouraged to constantly scrutinize, criticize, or even berate themselves and other group members. Each follower's dedication and personal commitment impels him or her to become self-recriminating and self-critical—and to be deeply critical of others as well.

This interplay of critical attitudes and self-condemning behaviors means that people don't have the time or clarity to seriously question their leader's actions, rigid ideas, or the workings of the controlling social system that the leader has created. Cult members become so consumed with criticizing themselves for their incessant failures, criticizing others, and working endless hours to achieve the group's goals that they enter into a state of denial. They are assured that once they become perfect and achieve their group's goals—either the short-term ones (such as recruitment and daily duties) or the longer-term ones (such as building a compound or working to reform the cult's public image)—then freedom, self-fulfillment, and transcendence will be bestowed upon them. However, the goalposts are constantly moved out of reach so that even if everyone—children and adults—toils full-time with perfect dedication for no pay, their efforts will never be enough. In this environment, no one has time to question the leader or the belief system; everyone is working too hard for that.

Additionally, there are dire consequences for questioning the leader or the group's beliefs. If a member fails to exhibit appropriate behaviors or voice the appropriate opinions, he or she will be reprimanded according to the standards of the group—which could include physical punishment, enforced silence fasts, shunning, demotion or change of assignment, exile to a different location, or other penalties. These reprimands—or even the threat of them—create an atmosphere of self-denial, exhaustion, and overwhelming feelings of guilt, shame, and fear. For parents, this imprisoning environment may also mean not having the time or energy to properly care for their children, such that child neglect may become an unintended feature of life in many cults. For the children, it means growing up without much parental contact or the chance to develop healthy parent-child bonds.

For instance, Iris's parents were required to be more dedicated to TM than they were to their children:

> My mom would semi-regularly leave town for long periods of time to go be with the Maharishi or to take a course. She felt very dedicated to the movement and the teachings, and being part of that sometimes got in the way of her taking care of the family. My parents believed that TM was very important, and they told us that their sacrifice in doing meditation to enhance their consciousness—which they said would benefit our entire family—was the same sacrifice that Jesus made by dying on the cross to benefit the whole world. This was very, very important to them. But what that meant was that I raised myself. I didn't really have parents.

Jessica's parents were similarly committed to The Family:

> My parents' reasons were that basically they were following God, living like disciples following Jesus, so they forsook everything, gave it all to the group, and just followed God. That was their initial reasoning. But it got pretty sick along the way because the founder was, for lack of a better word, insane, perverted, etc., so, you know, it was a very different childhood growing up.

Because their parents were too busy, too indoctrinated, or often physically absent, many children lived essentially without family connection or protection. In some cults, family ties were intentionally severed. For instance, Lily's mother and father were segregated into all-female and all-male homes, and Lily lived in a yet another home without them so that her mother could care for their College of Learning leader, Grandmaster Kim. In the FLDS, Samantha lived in a home with thirty children her age, but didn't really get to know her own full siblings (who were in other, age-segregated homes) until she was a teenager. In many cases, children in cults are on their own and unprotected from the often-severe beliefs of the group.

For Matthew, the Twelve Tribes' push for transcendent purity meant constant hard work and a lack of basic health care:

> They believe that with each generation, the children are supposed to get purer and purer until they are the perfect generation and then God will come. This meant that we had to work every day to be perfect. Since I was five years old, I started work at 5:00 a.m. every morning in the Tribes' businesses, and when I was a teenager, I had many, many health problems. I wasn't an unhealthy person; it was that I didn't have enough sleep. They didn't believe in letting people have a full night of sleep, or that kids should use medicine or go to the doctor or go to the hospital. They didn't believe in that, so they didn't take us to the dentist or the doctor. I mean, glasses weren't given, or braces; they didn't fix our teeth. They didn't provide any of that; they didn't allow medicine for kids with ADHD, or give older people hearing aids—they didn't provide any of those basic needs. People had to suffer and pray to God to heal them back to normal.

Jessica's group, The Family, believed that illness was a sign of evil, and she would often be subjected to harsh treatments without her parents' knowledge or permission:

> They would exorcize demons every once in a while when I had an asthma attack. They would anoint me with oil—they'd make this cross with kitchen oil on my head. And they'd gather all around me, and lay their hands on me, and pray, and scream prophecies, and speak in tongues, and try to cast the demon out of me while I'm having an asthma attack and can't breathe. I laugh now, but it was terrifying at the time.

Children in these groups also grew up in an environment of continual indoctrination. Many of them did not go to regular schools in the outside world, which typically was seen as evil. This meant that the children did not have access to ideas that could counter the all-encompassing and all-exclusive beliefs of their groups. If they did go to outside schools, their relationships to school friends were often strained because of the cult's odd beliefs and behaviors.

One woman grew up in a philosophical group called Aesthetic Realism, which enforced a rigid sense of mission and purpose:

> There was an expectation that wherever we went over the years, increasingly our main function was to spread to others the knowledge of what our leader had done for our lives. I really felt that my mission in life was to either recruit people or guard against them if they didn't see how

important Aesthetic Realism was. And I had to choose my friends based on that. I had a best friend all through high school whom I completely rejected when I was a senior. Just cut her off because she would not agree with these ideas. And that was a heartbreaking thing for me—and for her, I think.

One of The Family's first-born "Jesus babies" remembers internalizing the group's dogma so completely that she spent her childhood knowing about and planning her own death:

> Of course, Moses Berg was the End-Time prophet, and of course we were the End-Time Army. That's just the way it was. I remember thinking when I was about six or seven that I would die when I was fourteen, when Berg said that Jesus would come back and the End Times would begin. I hoped I wouldn't end up being martyred by being burned alive because that seemed like a pretty painful way to go. I preferred being beheaded, as I figured it would at least be quick. I'd been instructed in religious literature from the time I could first speak; we memorized scripture and we were always told how special and different we were. I don't remember ever doubting it as a child; I didn't know there was an alternative.

In cultic groups, the push for ideological purity and perfection is intense and incessant for adults and children alike. Public displays of unquestioning commitment to the imagined perfection of the belief system (and the leader) become a required activity that often leads to the enforced eradication of any traits, behaviors, or ideas that challenge that imagined perfection. Privately, the internalization of this unquestioning commitment often creates members who become willing to suppress or even erase their own critical thinking and individuality.

A young man raised in a fundamentalist Pentecostal church remembers having to prove his devotion in very public ways:

> The church services were supposed to break down your natural boundaries, or you were supposed to do that willingly. You know, so that visitors would see how powerful being in the church was, I guess. We were supposed to get up there, I mean, all up there and cry. Cry, cry, cry . . . just have these emotional breakdowns in front of everyone for attendance purposes or something. It always made me really uncomfortable. But, I just tried to participate, and I remember constantly feeling these panic sensations, because we were supposed to be in these emotionally really extreme states—every Sunday!

A young woman who was born into the Church of the Living Word cult remembers proudly telling other children of the benefits of being physically abused:

Our leader told my parents to have lots of babies to serve the church. But when I was born, he ascertained psychically that I was rebellious and so they had to break my spirit. They started spanking me at three months old and I remember going to kindergarten in my church school for Show and Tell and saying that when your parents spank you, it's good for you. It was kind of like a proud thing, even in kindergarten: That's why I'm a good person, because they were hitting me. But I also started to dissociate when I was five. I remember the first time it happened. I was sitting in my room and this overwhelming feeling came from out of the blue, and I did a deep internalization thing where everything got really small. But sometimes it would happen when they would just spank me and spank me and spank me so that my spirit would be better. You know, if you have a bad spirit or whatever, then that spirit gets spanked. So I remember having no internal life; I felt like they could see right through me and they could see what I was thinking, and I really didn't feel I was allowed my own thoughts. That was my young life.

These children grew up in the shadow of powerful belief systems that severely restricted their choices, their psychological development, and their lives. Each one of them was destabilized and damaged by their cult upbringing; yet all of them found a way out and were able to build new lives for themselves. How did they cope? How did they endure?

Coping Mechanisms for Surviving in a Closed Belief System

Throughout this book, we'll focus on the resilience and coping mechanisms our narrators relied on; these traits helped them escape and build new lives for themselves. But it's also important to understand the ways they coped when they were children, and the different ways they guarded themselves against their groups' all-encompassing, all-exclusive, and self-denying belief systems.

Imagination was one escape, and many children in abusive or neglectful environments create a private world for themselves. For instance, Joseph escaped into forbidden novels and dreamed of living wild in the forest instead of being trapped inside the Exclusive Brethren's world. Some children, like Iris and Samantha, became hyper-responsible as a way to avoid too much notice. Samantha managed the mental health care of her overburdened mother (who was expected to look after thirty or more of Samantha's siblings), and Iris took care of herself and her brother whenever her parents abandoned them to go on extended TM retreats.

Many children in controlling and abusive environments create alternative social structures or secret codes. Iris's friends in TM had complete freedom twice every day when all of the adults in the compound meditated for hours. The children's close relationships with each other helped them deal with the group's rules and the continual absenteeism of their parents. And though Matthew's deafness prevented him from joining in, the children in the Twelve Tribes used the Hebrew they learned in school as a secret language among themselves.

One unusual (though painful) form of protection came from being an outsider. For instance, Matthew's deafness and Jessica's asthma marked them as unclean or evil in the belief systems of their cults. Though each of them endured enforced isolation, exhaustive prayer and confession sessions, and abusive punishments, both fought persistently to maintain their own dignity and autonomy. The humiliation and abuse they endured took a harsh toll on both of them, but it did not break them; instead, it made them more stubborn and more determined.

Unhealthy transcendent belief systems are very powerful; and though they can entrap and imprison people, our narrators' stories show that people can escape. If you are or have been involved in an unhealthy belief system, it's important to know that you, like our narrators, can get away and rebuild your life. Healthy transcendent belief systems do exist, and the checklists below can help you learn how to clearly identify them.

Evaluating the Transcendent Belief Systems in Your Own Life

The following checklist can help you identify whether a transcendent belief system is healthy, hope-filled, and supportive—or controlling, perfectionistic, and dehumanizing. Healthy groups with a transcendent belief system encourage critical thinking, debate, and individuality. Unhealthy cultic groups use their transcendent belief system as a form of control, and don't allow any questioning.

If you're involved in any group with a transcendent belief system, you can use this checklist to gauge the health of your group. Place a check mark by any of the following statements that are true.

☐ The group's sense of purpose is intense and urgent.

☐ The belief system is rigid, righteous, and exclusive; other beliefs are criticized or ridiculed.

☐ Members are expected to become perfect true believers; there is no room for doubt.

☐ The belief system is elitist; it is the only true path and the ultimate solution.

☐ The belief system promotes specific and demanding tools, practices, and rules, and has a structure that converts members into perfect followers.

☐ Members endure extensive indoctrination sessions—through Bible lessons, political training, recruitment training, self-awareness lessons, meditation, criticism sessions, group rituals, study and lectures, punishments, and so forth.

☐ The belief system is perfectionistic, with all-or-nothing requirements that must be followed to the letter.

☐ Members are rewarded for subordinating themselves utterly and/or shedding their previous identities (family, job, home, finances, name, etc.).

☐ The group is strongly hierarchical, with an inner circle of true believers who have special access, power, and privileges.

☐ Members are expected to contribute their money, their time, their resources, and their labor to the group in order to be seen as serious and loyal followers.

☐ The belief system is transmitted personally by the leader, who cannot be questioned. If the leader is deceased, this may be done through writings, videos, and/or audiotapes, as well as by top leaders' testimonials.

☐ The group creates internal and external enemies who are portrayed as threatening the very survival of the group.

☐ Members who question, break the rules, or leave are shunned or demonized, and may lose all contact with group members, including their own family members.

If you checked yes to one or more of these statements, your group may be under the influence of a controlling and unhealthy belief system. However, this doesn't mean that your group is dangerous, and it doesn't mean that it's a cult. Your group would need to have all four dimensions of bounded choice active (which includes a charismatic leader, systems of control, and systems of influence) before it could be considered a cultic group. However, if your group's transcendent belief system feels unhealthy to you (even if the other dimensions of bounded choice aren't present), you may be able to suggest changes and see if your group is willing to alter its troubling behaviors.

You can share the features of healthy transcendent belief systems below to help your group understand the specific ways in which it is veering toward controlling and abusive behaviors. If the group or its leader(s) can't or won't change, you can use the following list to find a group that provides hope and answers without rigidly enforcing its beliefs, controlling its members, or shutting out the outside world.

Signs of a Healthy Transcendent Belief System

• Members have the right to question, to doubt, and to think their own thoughts.

• The belief system makes room for other beliefs and other ideas.

• Members are treated as equals, and are not expected to be subordinate or perfectionistic.

• The belief system allows for personal autonomy, dignity, and freedom.

• Members retain their identities, finances, relationships, personal time, and private lives.

• The belief system includes rather than excludes people and ideas.

- Members can leave without being shunned or forced to abandon their friends and family.
- The belief system opens members to the world rather than isolating or segregating them from it.

When a transcendent belief system is healthy, people have choices. When it's not, their choices get tangled up with the group's rigid vision of perfection and purity. With the help of Janja's bounded choice model, we can see that unhealthy belief systems can create an entrapping situation for believers. They work hard to be devoted, to live up to the group's beliefs, and to become perfect. These actions are admirable; they require energy, intelligence, and dedication. However, because cultic belief systems are perfectionistic and unhealthy, all of this hard work and devotion only serve to exhaust and ensnare followers (and their children) in a never-ending cycle. Breaking free is very difficult, but it can be done, and people can find healthy groups with healthy systems of belief.

In the next chapter, we'll look at the individuals or groups who create these unhealthy transcendent belief systems in the first place: the *charismatic authority*.

Notes

1. This group is also known as The Children of God.
2. Emile Durkheim's *The Elementary Forms of the Religious Life* (New York: The Free Press, 1915) is the classic sociological study of religion and cults. He wrote: "In reality, a cult is not a simple group of ritual precautions which a man is held to take in certain circumstances; it is a system of diverse rites, festivals, and ceremonies which *all have this characteristic, that they reappear periodically*. They fulfill the need which the believer feels of strengthening and reaffirming, at regular intervals of time, the bond which unites him to the sacred beings upon which he depends" (80).
3. See D. Tourish and N. Vatcha, "Charismatic Leadership and Corporate Cultism at Enron: The Elimination of Dissent, The Promotion of Conformity and Organizational Collapse," *Leadership* 1, no. 4 (2005): 455–80.
4. According to Durkheim, both the physical and mental effects of the cult's rites and practices generate forces that "are . . . necessary for the well working of our moral life . . . and it is through them that the group affirms and maintains itself, and we know the point to which this is indispensable for the individual." Durkheim, *The Elementary Forms of Religious Life*, 427.
5. Durkheim explains that the outcome of these processes in the cult "awakens this sentiment of a refuge, of a shield and of a guardian support which attaches the believer to his cult. It is that which raises him outside himself; it is even that which made him" (Ibid., 465). In that sense, the believer psychologically merges with the cult and the cult leader.
6. This is a complex phenomenon. The higher calling of the cult comes with a moral imperative (i.e., you must do this now) that is intricately linked to renouncing your own needs and desires. Thus, the lure of freedom (salvation) leads to self-criticism, denial, and loss of self. But the strength of this moral imperative makes your self-denial feel, strangely, like a source of pride. See *Bounded Choice: True Believers and Charismatic Cults* by Janja Lalich (Berkeley: University of California Press, 2004) for a comprehensive explanation of this key process of cult membership.

3

CHARISMATIC AUTHORITY

Exhilarating Vision, Electrifying Charisma, and Total Domination

She claims that she is the world's highest-ranking female martial artist. She says she has a doctorate. Doctor Great Grandmaster Tae Yun Kim! And then she compared herself to Jesus. You know, we would sit in a Bible class and read a passage about him and the disciples, and then her students would be like, "wow, ma'am"—we always referred to her as ma'am or Grandmaster—"This is like how Jesus and his disciples were. And we're following you, and you're teaching us all these things, ma'am, and I can see the similarity." And sometimes she flat out would compare herself to Jesus, but most of it was indirect. But you could see what she was trying to imply.

Lily

I know the charismatic leader has always been part of TM. My mother definitely said things to me like, "A reason for doing something or not doing something is because Maharishi said."

Iris

The Exclusive Brethren changed radically when Jim Taylor took the reins. I remember an excommunication that was done in a way that was a radical departure from the due process that had been practiced for more than a hundred years. Instead of discussing the facts and principles at stake and taking a communal decision in accordance with established practice and long-established principles, the Brethren acted purely in response to the instructions of Taylor, who lived thousands of miles away. It was merely a rubber-stamping exercise, and we were not even told why we were to do it.

Joseph

I remembered hearing that all the adults in the Twelve Tribes were really mad because this one elder used to be able to take all of his kids to Kentucky Fried Chicken. I had no idea what Kentucky Fried Chicken was, but I just knew everybody was really mad about it. I remember that those kids were really heavy and so they used to say that while all of us were starving and skinny, they were overweight because they got to go out and eat Kentucky Fried Chicken. They were up in leadership, so that was allowed. They just said, "Well, that's the way it goes. You can't question our authority."

Matthew

What Is Charismatic Authority?

We can all identify charismatic people in our lives, from actors, musicians, and politicians to the best player on our favorite sports teams. Charismatic people are appealing and magnetic, and they draw us in with their skills, appearance, talents, or perhaps a special quality that we can't quite put our finger on. Charismatic people can stimulate hero worship or feelings of being wildly in love, as many of us may have experienced in our adolescent and early adult infatuations. In healthy relationships, these wild and worshipful moments tend to fade, and we become able to view those individuals in more balanced and calm ways. But in unhealthy relationships and groups, charismatic people find ways to continually activate that intense infatuation and devotion. Successful *charismatic authority figures* keep followers captivated and entrapped through exhilarating utopian visions, constant displays of power, demands for commitment, demonization of outsiders (or of less committed group members), and incessant emotional manipulation.

Charismatic authority is the powerful emotional bond between a leader and his or her followers. It makes the leader seem deeply legitimate and visionary, and it grants authority to his or her actions. Anything he or she does is portrayed as vital to the utopian vision and the survival of the group. The ends always justify the means because the charismatic authority figure isn't merely right; he or she is anointed, chosen, or blessed. When followers internalize the sense that their leader is utterly perfect, they may convince themselves that anything they do in service to the leader is righteous and justified. Eventually, the leader's needs justify the behaviors and actions of everyone in the group. At the same time, a shared sense of urgent duty reinforces each member's dedication and binds them tightly to the leader's ideas, goals, and desires. The deep relationship followers have with their leader's charismatic authority is the hook that keeps them engaged, susceptible, and willing to do whatever it takes to satisfy their leader's every whim and desire.

Magicians, Heroes, and Saviors: Max Weber on Charisma

The concept of charisma was introduced by one of the founders of sociology, Max Weber, in his classic work on ancient religions, bureaucracy, and institution building.[1] Weber is regarded as the leading scholar on charismatic authority, and he identified a follower's response to charisma as an ecstatic state, or a "psychological state accessible only in occasional actions . . . as intoxication."[2] Some of the people he identified as being charismatic were magicians, heroes, prophets, saviors, shamans, and even the founder of Mormonism, Joseph Smith.[3] According to Weber, these charismatic leaders are a revolutionary force in society, in the sense that they offer new radical promises and solutions that may lead to great change or upheaval.[4]

In our everyday lives, charisma is often thought of as a trait that is found in special individuals, a "personal gift made manifest in miracle and revelation."[5] But *charismatic authority* is a powerful social relationship that requires followers to respond to the vision and demands of their excitingly charismatic leader. Weber noted, "What is alone important is how the individual is actually regarded by those subject to charismatic authority, by his 'followers' or 'disciples.' "[6] By this he meant that it is the recognition by others that determines the validity of a person's charisma. In other words: no followers, no charisma. Since charismatic authority is a social relationship and not merely an inherent trait of an individual, it exists primarily in the eye of the beholder. This is why some people can see through a seemingly charismatic leader and ask, "How can anyone follow that charlatan?" while others may be completely smitten. Not everyone responds in the same way to charismatic authority figures.[7]

Once followers have identified a person as a charismatic authority, it then becomes their *duty* to "act accordingly . . . with complete personal devotion . . . arising out of enthusiasm, or of despair and hope."[8] This dutiful obedience is established intentionally by the authority figure through internal systems of control and influence (enforced discipline, rules, rituals, intense study, peer monitoring, etc.) that train followers in how to submit. This submission must occur so that the leader can expand his "sphere of domination."[9] To expand his domination, a clever charismatic leader offers something uniquely special that followers can only get from him or her—the hope of new beginnings, peace on earth, an enchanted afterlife, perfect health, a cancer cure, political revolution, social justice, or something as mundane as weight loss or financial gain.[10]

Through initial encounters with the leader or recruiters, a new recruit comes to believe that this leader is the only one who can offer salvation (be it religious, political, philosophical, health, or otherwise). The recruit is then further convinced by the savvy cleverness of the leader that to be part of the group and reach salvation or perfection, he or she must follow the leader's special transformational process, which always includes self-denial and obedience.

Transcendent beliefs and dogmas seem to be the focus of cults; yet in reality, the purpose of many cults is simply to serve the emotional, financial, psychological, and sexual needs of the leader with unquestioning obedience and disregard for self. The authoritarian personality of the cult leader helps ensure that his or her needs and desires are always the top priority.[11] However, this need backfires reliably. Why? Because even if the leader started out with good intentions, it's rare that a person can handle the kind of adulation and blind obedience that is demanded from and granted by cult followers—even if the worship and obedience are granted under duress. It is commonplace for charismatic authority figures to become unbalanced and egocentric.

In Grandmaster Kim's College of Learning, followers were promised spiritual attainment through martial-arts discipline. Lily remembers that part of that discipline involved praising Kim:

> "Praise the Lord." "Praise Jesus." And "I love the Lord" and "Jesus is my answer." If you had that mentality in the group, that wasn't good enough. You had to praise Grandmaster Kim and she had to take credit for you getting to know God. And in her eyes, her introducing you to God was more important than your relationship with God itself, and you had to be thankful to her for that.

A young man whose family was among the first followers of the Word of Life Fellowship remembers the point when his leader's charismatic authority began to spin out of control:

> I think the church originally started out with good intentions, but then pastor started realizing, "Hey, I have power. I love this sense of power." I think that's the point where people were writing songs about her. They would write songs about God and stuff, but they would be writing these praise songs about the pastor and it's like, this is ridiculous. Are we going to church to worship *her*?

It's important to clarify that charisma or charismatic authority on its own is not evil and does not necessarily produce a cult leader. We can think of such charismatic leaders as President John F. Kennedy, the Reverend Martin Luther King Jr., Aung San Suu Kyi, or Nelson Mandela, to name just a few. These and other charismatic authority figures have been a positive force in society. However, the influence over others that comes with authority—and the inherent power imbalance that is created—must always be kept in check.[12] Charismatic leaders have a responsibility to learn how to maintain their humanity in the face of constant adulation, and to apply rigorous checks and balances to their behavior so that they can protect their followers from harm. In cults, those protections don't exist.

How Charisma Becomes Toxic

Cult leaders do not have checks or balances on their behaviors or their claims. They are the final authority. Beyond utilizing their charisma to attract followers, cult leaders must also be authoritative, domineering, and be able to read people well enough to convince and charm them. Often, a leader will claim that he or she is aligned with or is the spokesperson for some greater authority, such as God, Jesus, Buddha, Ascended Masters, Spiritual Oneness, or even Marx, Lenin, or Mao (in the case of some political cults[13]). Some cult leaders, like Grandmaster Kim, may openly claim to be the reincarnation of a religious figure such as Jesus. This is not unusual; one woman Janja interviewed for this study was raised in a New Age cult called the Brotherhood of the Spirit/Renaissance Community, and she said, "The leader believed he was the reincarnation, of course, of several different things: historical figures, some being Christian, some being Civil War heroes, like Robert E. Lee, various things like that." One cult leader, Gabriel of Sedona, claims to be the reincarnation of, among others, King Arthur, a mythical being.

In Karla's New Age cult, her leader claimed to be a medium for an ancient Chinese sage, and said that he had also lived previous lives as the Egyptian pharaoh Akhenaten, the philosopher king Marcus Aurelius, the mythical wizard Merlin, and the musician Henry Purcell, among others. This seems objectively bizarre now, but at the time it was magical. Everyone in the group was encouraged to imagine who they might have been during those historical periods, with the leader assigning identities, such as Henry Purcell's wife for Karla's mother, one of Akhenaten's daughters for Karla, and the mythical King Arthur for the leader's own young son. This exciting, enthralling, and imaginary history helped everyone in the cult feel that they had been together for centuries, and that being together in this life was an exquisite and necessary aspect of destiny. Their leader had created a deep and meaningful ideology that united everyone, such that anything strange or harmful that happened in the cult was easily downplayed in deference to their extraordinary fate. Though these ideas about reincarnation were one part of the group's transcendent belief system, note that the leader was always a powerful charismatic figure in every reincarnation, and that—in this life—he was the ultimate authority who assigned his followers' identities in their own (alleged) past lives.

Toxic charismatic authority can be difficult to escape (as many of us may have experienced in our own dramatic and unhealthy love relationships) because it engages a powerful need for belonging that keeps followers entrapped by the intense and urgent demands of the leader or leadership group. In cults, the leader combines the exciting and seductive quality of charisma with an unhealthy lust for power and influence. This toxic situation binds followers to the cult so strongly that meeting the needs of the cult or the often bizarre, corrupt, and sometimes illegal needs of the leader begins to feel correct and normal, as if it is second nature. At this point, members have become enveloped in what Janja has identified as a "bounded reality."[14]

In The Family cult, leader David "Moses" Berg was widely known for acting out his sexual fantasies and perversions, especially with children. Jessica remembers a specific demand that Berg made when she was seven years old:

We'd get together and have these big meetings and read all the new mailings.[15] Around that time, the big thing was making videos for Berg, the leader. He had decided that he wanted to come around to the homes and have sex with everybody, but because he couldn't, he wanted all the women to dance and make a video for him. Every woman in The Family. He said he'd like everyone to do it, but that you didn't have to. It was like an honor/requirement, you know what I mean? These videos he asked for, they were called "Glorified God in the Dance." He told us what he wanted, what type of music, and that there should be three songs. The first one should be nice and fast, and the second one should be medium, and the third should be a really slow song. And you should start out with some scarf or whatever, or some small amount of clothes on, and he wanted you to wave the scarf around your body as you got undressed. It was really, really detailed. Everything he wanted, like basically, "Here's my fantasy." I was seven. Oh, yeah. Seven was pretty much the age when we were starting to be integrated [into the cult's sexual sharing practices].

Though meeting bizarre requirements like Berg's might come to feel like second nature, meeting the needs of a cult leader has detrimental effects on individuals and an even more detrimental effect on children. In most of the cults Janja has studied, the children's daily lives were entirely focused on what the leader felt was important. Normal and healthy aspects of childhood, family life, bonding, and development were pushed aside if they didn't agree with the leader's needs and beliefs. For instance, if the leader or group distrusted conventional medical care, as Matthew's Twelve Tribes and Iris's TM cult did, then children weren't allowed to see doctors, dentists, or even optometrists. If the leader or group actively distrusted the everyday world, as most of these cults did, then children received extremely limited cult-based education, or had their public school classes scrutinized and stripped of anything the cult didn't agree with, as Joseph experienced in the Exclusive Brethren. If the leader actively distrusted family ties, as Grandmaster Kim and David Berg did, then the children weren't allowed to grow up with their own parents.

In her book on cults and attachment,[16] social psychologist and cult researcher Alexandra Stein, Ph.D., focuses on the damage to normal bonding and attachment that occurs in cults because leaders tend to want all attention, all love, and all adulation focused on them:

John Bowlby's attachment theory[17] has helped researchers and parents to understand that the need for protection is a fundamental, evolved element of the relationship between children and parents. When all works well, children seek the protection of a safe other—usually a parent—when stressed, or under threat. There is a set of behaviors (visual searching, calling and crying, for example) that children engage in with the goal of ensuring proximity to their caregiver. In general, these behaviors cease on uniting with the caregiver and gaining comfort. This is known as the "attachment behavior system." Parents have a reciprocal "caregiving system" that seeks to protect their children so that in a healthy relationship parents will feel distressed if they are unable to comfort and protect their child. When these systems are functional, the result is protection of the child, which increases chances of survival to adulthood.

While this may seem obvious to those in more or less healthy family relationships, what is less obvious is how and why cult leaders consistently and predictably interfere in these evolved systems of care and protection of the young. But interfere they do, in a multitude of ways, as shown in my book.[18]

Stein highlights the impact of the cult experience on the mother-child bond. According to her research, this bond is controlled in multiple ways in a cult. The ones most relevant here are: (a) mothers are often discouraged from having a special bond with their children; (b) mothers may spend little or no time with their children due to the demands of the cult; (c) the child is physically taken from the parents; and (d) each mother's behavior toward her children is carefully monitored.[19]

Doing "the right thing" (for God, the Revolution, one's personal growth, whatever) becomes synonymous with obeying the leader. To go against the leader's directive is to go against God himself. The mother becomes psychologically trapped: she wants to be a good person, but the definition of goodness resides entirely in the cult's domain. And any attempt to define goodness for herself ensures swift condemnation and an attack on her "faith."[20]

Children who are born into or brought into cults are usually taught that the leader's needs are more important than their own needs, family ties, friendships, health, schooling, comfort, stability, or even sleep. It's important to state here that we're not blaming the children's parents for the abuse and neglect their children endured. After all, the parents became enthralled by the cult and believed deeply in the rightness and omnipotence of the leader. We must acknowledge that parents in cults, like all other members, are indoctrinated to believe that their sole loyalty must be to the leader.[21]

As part of this loyalty, parents are expected to teach their children reverence for the leader and the belief system. Their children's devotion and conformity reflect on the parents' own worth as cult members; therefore, indoctrination of the children becomes a regular daily task. Some of this indoctrination occurs through simply being in the environment; at other times, it's transmitted through direct teachings. For example, one young man who grew up in Scientology said:

Maybe when I was three or four, I started to pick up some of the things from the belief system. I know that there was a lot of talk about L. Ron

Hubbard—how he was going to bring peace on earth, and he was going to prevent a third world war from happening. Those are the kinds of things I remember. Like he was someone—you know, it was written in the Buddhist scriptures thousands of years ago that a person would return and that person would bring peace on earth. Those sorts of things I remember just picking up on. I guess I would say I was around three or four at the time.

Iris remembers indoctrination during events on the TM compound:

Twice a day all the adults would go and meditate at the dome, separately. The men would go to one, and the women would go to another. But regularly they would have events at the men's dome where everyone would attend. The kids would go, too, and usually it would be because Maharishi was going to speak. Every now and then he'd be there in person, but usually it was on a telecast. Either he would speak or other people from the higher-up level of the organization would speak. Or they would also have singing and school-kid events, where the kids would sing or do something. They had these funny movement songs that they taught us. The songs taught the principles that we were supposed to remember.

These cults were very social places in most cases, but without their parents' care and protection, the children were basically on their own, with only their leader to rely upon. However, because the charisma of the leader (or the leadership group) was both deeply compelling and deeply toxic, the children were continually drawn toward or forced to attach to someone who could never and would never meet their true needs. Sadly, this damaging situation was true even for the children of cult leaders.

Divine Neglect: Children of Cult Leaders

Some children of cult leaders receive special privileges and acclaim, but many are treated as burdens or obstacles who stand in the way of their parents' grandiose plans. Janja interviewed the daughter of the leader of Morningland, a New Age cult, who remembers that she and her siblings had to grow up very fast because her mother intentionally avoided parenting them:

I was always being pushed onto other members of the church and being disassociated from my mother. It got to the point where she said, "I have no children." Well, people knew that we were her children, but to us in private, she would let it be known: "You don't call me mother. You call me Sri. You have to look to other people for mother figures." That's when I finally shut myself off, because then I knew—oh, God. At that point I was about 14, so I got myself a part-time job because no one was supporting me or giving me money anymore. I wasn't being given money for school. If I needed clothes or something, I had to go to one of the *Gopis*[22] [her mother's special disciples] and they would go to my mother. At one point, she had her attorney assign one of the *Gopis* as my legal guardian. And when I was 15, she had me emancipated. And that was the last time I saw her. I was not allowed to go see her even when I was getting married.

The most negative part of it, I think, are the abandonment issues—feeling abandoned, not really having a nurturing mother—and, I think, the jealousy. I would feel jealousy with girlfriends and stuff because I would see how close their mothers were to them and I didn't have that. I really didn't.

In the 1960s, a visionary cult leader attracted many young people to her home, where she set up a live-in commune. Her daughter shared one of her more harrowing experiences:

And so it was all these hippies that were flocking to her, mostly—all these dope smoking, smelly people, which is how I perceived them. They were weird and they were scary. They all lived in my home. And during that period of time, I don't remember really having any connection with my mother. My grandmother took care of me. She would make sure I got to school; she'd make sure I had a snack when I got home. And that's pretty much it. Then we moved into a big old store building, and from there to this huge house, where I lived with a bunch of young hippie women. I didn't really get to see my mother very much, unless she was preaching. She pretty much stayed in her study most of the time, getting words from God. And having meetings all the time. Round the clock. Any time of the day. Sometimes they'd last for days.

One time, my mother had been in meetings for, like, three days. I don't remember exactly why, but I had this major need to see her. And I kept trying to go up—there was this big grand set of stairs up to the second floor. And so I would go up, and I'd try to get in to see her. But she had people guarding her so that nobody could get in because she didn't want to be disturbed. And so I would say, "I need to see my mom," and they would say, "Go! Get out of here. She's busy." And for three days this went on. I kept trying to get to her. Finally, I went outside and I climbed up the fire escape out back. I got onto the catwalk. I walked all the way along the catwalk to the last room, where a window was open. So I snuck in and got into the hall, just feet from where she was. And I knew as soon as they saw me that they would grab me and take me, so I started screaming at the top of my lungs, "I need to see my mom! I need to see my mom!" So they're starting to drag me away, and one of the elders came out of my

mom's study and said, "Put her down. Put her down. What's going on?"
And I was just hysterical. Just screaming and crying. "I need to see my
mom, I need to see my mom." And he says, "Okay, calm down, calm
down. We'll take care of this." Then my mom hears all the commotion,
so then of course she magnanimously walks out and exclaims, "Everybody
move aside, move aside. My baby needs me." And it's like, you know,
where were you for three days? Did you even know where your daughter
was for three days? No. Or for the last month and months, who knows?

But my mom just said, "Do you want me to give up this whole thing
and move into a house and raise you myself? You know I can't do that.
God has asked me to do this. Would you really want me to not save them?
Would you want to be responsible for them all going back and being drug
addicts? Would you take me away from loving these people who've never
been loved before? Of course not."

Shortly afterward, her mother sent her away to live with her older sister:

That had a major impact on my emotional development. But I would say
that probably the most harmful thing was actually my development as an
individual. That was not allowed. And that started from the time I was very
small. Basically, my mother started assigning rules for who I was supposed
to be—from a very, very young age. I remember when I was really little
she called me her Mary Sunshine. And it was my job to brighten up her
day, to make her happy, and to make her feel good. That continued for a
period of time, and then I was supposed to be an example. From a very,
very young age, I was supposed to be an example to all these drugged-out
teenagers. And I was supposed to help save them. I was supposed to be there,
and I was supposed to show them how to be and how to act and I was always
supposed to be a good example. I was supposed to grow up and take over
and be the next generation, and this was my job, and this is who I was
supposed to be. And every time any little piece of me, who I maybe was
actually supposed to be, would come out, she'd squash it.

Even for the children of cult leaders, there is no safe place to be, because the
only acceptable behavior is to worship and adore the cult leader. This unhealthy
idolization is not something that children should ever be expected to do in their
own families. These harmful expectations interfere with children's psychological
development, their ability to form bonds, and their ability to individuate and
become their own people. Their personhood is erased, because in a cult, the only
types of people allowed are the leader, special disciples, devotees, and members
or allies with money or connections who can help legitimize the cult. Freethinking
and autonomous individuals are not allowed; the cult leader is truly the only person
who matters.

The Narcissism Inherent in Cultic Charisma

In our narrators' stories—even though they grew up in very different groups—we encounter strikingly similar tales of dramatic and self-absorbed behavior in their leaders. Constant crises and tests of loyalty are common in these groups because in many cases, cult leaders are unstable, egocentric, and deeply needy people. However, these crises actually serve the leader in that they destabilize followers, who then become even more susceptible to the leader's needs and demands.

A young man who grew up in the Greater Bethel Temple described the atmosphere created by the leader, Bishop Nelson Turner:

> Authoritarian, yes. He was very controlling. There were people in the church who held different positions of leadership, but they had no power. They couldn't do anything without his approval. He very much ran the church. He would openly rebuke people constantly. That was his way of manipulating and controlling people. It was open rebuke. Constant. Just constant. By name sometimes. Sometimes not by name, but we would often know whom he was talking about. He would discipline people openly. It was definitely a situation in which everybody was very afraid of moving. Afraid to do anything. No one would start a new program or initiative. Even the other ministers or preachers in the church, if they did get a chance to preach, which wasn't very often, they had to watch what they said. And if they said anything contrary to what Turner said, they would hear about it. They would get blasted over the pulpit, as we would say. They'd get chewed out. Strange thing was, even if Turner wasn't there to hear it, other members of the church who were loyal to Turner would go and chew out the preacher who said something he wasn't supposed to.

Our narrators tell hauntingly similar stories of meltdowns, tantrums, and illnesses that their leaders blamed on group members who were supposedly not devoted enough. They also share stories of bizarre double and triple standards that allowed these leaders (and their inner circle) to get away with almost anything—theft, lying, child abuse, medical neglect, molestation, rape, enforced prostitution, imprisonment, and the intentional alienation of family members. And these stories are not unique; they are a main theme in many research studies, scholarly books, and memoirs about cult life.[23]

In cults like the tragic Heaven's Gate[24] or the deadly Jonestown created by Jim Jones,[25] cult members actually lined up to "willingly" commit suicide (or be murdered in the case of Jonestown) in order to support their leader's devastating delusions.

In the extreme behavior of charismatic authority figures, we find a crucial feature that separates cults from normal groups, and that is that cult leaders often exhibit traits of Narcissistic Personality Disorder (NPD).[26] NPD is a condition where people require a great deal of external validation, may display grandiosity and selfishness, and may have little to no empathy for others. Though people with NPD often appear powerful, they have fragile egos and can be deeply unstable and self-absorbed—and they may inflict a great deal of damage on their mates, family, and friends.

When a charismatic person with NPD develops an alluring transcendent belief system and finds a way to build systems of influence and systems of control, then dozens, hundreds, or even thousands of people can become entrapped in his or her web of domination. If you add political and military power to this potent mix, millions of people—or entire countries, such as North Korea, Stalinist Russia, or Nazi Germany—can be controlled by the exhilarating vision, electrifying charisma, and total domination of their toxic and narcissistic leader.

New York-based psychotherapist Daniel Shaw, who has worked with dozens of cult-involved clients, describes many cult leaders as "traumatizing narcissists":

> The guru is infinitely entitled and grateful to no one; he rewrites history to create a biography that leaves out any trace of his significant misdeeds and failures; he never hesitates to lie for the purpose of self-aggrandizement, and to blame others for his own errors and failures; he is erratic, thin-skinned, belligerent, and constantly involved in attacking and belittling perceived enemies; he persuades followers to see their lives before joining his group as wretched, and he claims exclusive possession of the power to transform followers' lives in miraculous ways.[27]

[Erich] Fromm[28] called such people "malignant narcissists," people out of touch with reality, who exhibit more and more extreme behaviors as the pressures of living up to their delusion of perfection mount, and as they inevitably become exposed to scrutiny and criticism. All too often, enraged by challenges to their fantasy of omnipotence, they lead their followers to acts of violence, against others or even against themselves. In cults, we have the examples of this horrific violence in the Manson Family, Heaven's Gate, Jonestown, and many, many others.

Shaw highlights the most common dynamics that occur between leader and followers as:

1. Purification of ego
2. Only perfection is good enough
3. Incessant urgency
4. Violation of boundaries as a norm
5. Inner deviance must be eradicated (that is, only the leader's moral code is to be obeyed)
6. Defend the leader no matter what.[29]

These dynamics are readily seen in the experiences shared by the adult children of cults interviewed for this book, and by others with similar experiences.[30]

The young woman who grew up in the Brotherhood of the Spirit cult (whose leader claimed that he was the reincarnation of Robert E. Lee, among others) shared what it was like growing up with a traumatizing narcissist:

> So it was all the mental games, all the physical and sexual abuse, all the exhaustion, the sleep deprivation, food deprivation . . . all of it was really tied together. It varied for the members; but in our case, it never came with any privileges and definitely came with some drawbacks. By that time, the leader had drug and alcohol problems so he was very unpredictable and just a scary person. So, for example, when my sister was born, when she was a baby, the leader was the kind of person you could always hear before he appeared—loud, commanding. I remember clearly being in the house we called The Lodge, holding my sister. She was an infant, and we hear him coming and she starts shaking, just trembling. She was just terrified of him. He came in, probably drunk or high or something, and he's trying to get her from me and I'm physically fighting with him over the baby. Now, a lot of people were around, we're talking at least thirty people—it's dinnertime. People are around and no one's doing anything; they're all just pretending it's not going on. I'm twelve years old or maybe thirteen and I'm fighting with him, literally fighting over the baby. So he finally gets her away from me and he's throwing her around and she's screaming and crying, and so I finally get her back and run off with her—and the upshot of all of that is that he went to my mother and said basically, "You better get your daughter in line or you're going to be kicked out of here."

In the narcissistic and malignant environment of cults, obeying the leader is essential if you want to stay in good graces or be allowed to stay at all. Individuality or dissimilarity from the leader, then, is unsafe and unwise. Accordingly, it's common for cult members to emulate the leader—talk like him, act like him, or use the same gestures. The young man who was raised in the Greater Bethel Temple worked hard to become like Bishop Turner, even though the young man's family was the only white family in that all-black fundamentalist church:

> He knew that I was trying to emulate him. He tore down my father in my eyes constantly, so I hated my father. I didn't think of him as much of an example of anything. And I didn't want to be like him. So I tried to be like this man, this black man who has an 8th grade education, who is forty years older than me, who has a totally different life experience than I do, and I'm trying to be like him. And everyone knew I was emulating him. Everybody knew. Turner stood me up in the congregation multiple times and complimented me for being such a good follower of his. He made the

comment once about—I mean, he had a huge inferiority complex, and he would always say to the congregation, and he often used the "N" word in referring to his congregation. "Y'all are a bunch of Ns." He would say, "You all don't want to listen to me because I'm black. Y'all would rather listen to the white man." Then he'd stand me up and he'd say, "Well, here's a white man who listens to me." I mean, I tried to dress like him, I tried to talk like him, walk like him, think like him, handle my finances like him. I just tried to do everything to be like him. And that created a huge struggle for me because I wasn't him.

A young woman who was raised in a small New Age group led by a woman named Anne Haas spoke of her mother's extreme devotion to Anne:

My mom constantly had a fake English accent—because Anne Haas is from England, so she has this very English accent—and so my mom constantly sounded like that. She dressed like Anne, her hair was like hers, everything. And anything that I did wrong or that she didn't like, it was like this preaching hour. An hour lecture of how wrong I am and basically trying to lecture me about how un-perfect I am. Just like Anne would do.

People trapped in the sphere of a narcissistic leader learn to minimize their own needs so that they can meet the needs of the leader and try to become like him or her. When this leader gathers a whole group of devotees, the group itself can mutate into a toxic community.

The Toxic Narcissism of Cultic Groups

Once the leader's charismatic authority is accepted and members work hard to emulate him or her, an inner circle will form. The most devoted or high-ranking members of that inner circle will act in the leader's stead. Many leaders don't like to be around their followers all the time or even at all—they tend to live in better quarters, go on expensive trips, or simply isolate themselves with their favorite devotees, as The Family's Berg and TM's Maharishi did. In those cases, the middle management, as the top lieutenants are sometimes called, will take over the discipline and control of the rest of the members. This is an illustration of "charisma by proxy," where anything inner circle members say or do is allowed because they have the blessing of the leader.

A young woman in a philosophical cult called Aesthetic Realism talked about the inner circle that formed around their leader, Eli Siegel:

Around the leader, this other kind of subculture grew, especially as he grew older. There were people who felt that they were ethically chosen and he treated them that way—as though they were ethically superior. So they came to be the really controlling ones, and everyone was vying for their approval. One of them was a woman who was an unusually mean person and who claimed to be ethically superior; but her actions were so power-hungry and so mean to people. And one word from her and a person would be cast from grace and thrown out.

In Karla's cult, a group of devoted adult women formed an inner circle and managed the day-to-day details of the group for the leader. They were known as the senior women and they ran the group in the leader's absence. During a period when the leader was in Europe gathering money to fund cult businesses, the senior women banded together in a communal meeting and expelled Karla (from the group, from communal housing, and from speaking to group members) for wearing unapproved jeans instead of skirts, talking to unapproved outsiders while grocery shopping, and talking back in meetings. Such was the power of the senior women that Karla didn't attempt to make her case with the leader himself, who had been like a father to her for seven years (or seven lifetimes, according to his tales of reincarnation). Karla was seventeen at the time.

Yet even in the midst of all this loss, domination, and abuse, we discover hope in the stories of our narrators. Even as young children, many of our narrators report that they were repeatedly shocked and offended by the extreme displays of superiority, endless double standards, and habitually abusive behaviors of their leaders and the leaders' inner circles. In fact, the everyday injustices they witnessed awakened many of them to how wrong their situations were. Before they escaped from their cults (or were expelled), many of our narrators questioned, challenged, and protested against what was being done to them, to their friends, and to their families.

Something inside each of us rebels against abuse and injustice. Even children who were raised from birth to worship their perfect leader somehow knew that things were wrong. This inner knowledge is a facet of resilience that helped our narrators get out, stay out, and persevere through often-grueling circumstances. Against all odds, they *knew* that a better world—and kinder people—existed.

Coping Mechanisms for Surviving Toxic Charismatic Authority

Our narrators found ways to guard themselves against their leader's unstable, domineering, and abusive behaviors. These young people were able to maintain a sense of themselves, even in the destabilizing presence of the toxic narcissists who controlled their lives.

Many children who are under the control of a toxic narcissist learn how to cleverly play along and appear devoted so that they can avoid notice or punishment. Lily learned to appease Grandmaster Kim and act like a perfect follower, even though Kim constantly angered and hurt Lily by keeping her away from her own mother. Samantha feared her abusive father and did what she could to avoid his notice; part of this avoidance involved caring for her mentally ill mother and taking on some of her mother's childcare duties for the thirty children in the home so that the house would appear to be well managed.

One of the most important defense mechanisms was defiance, either open or secret. Open defiance, however, exposed the children to more punishment, isolation, and abuse, as Matthew experienced in the Twelve Tribes, and as Jessica experienced in The Family. Joseph's defiance against the controlling Exclusive Brethren was more secretive: he read forbidden novels at school and lived a life of freedom in his imagination. Iris and her young friends in TM had hours of defiance time (unintentionally) built into their days; when all of the adults in the compound were meditating, the children were left alone to speak openly and do whatever they liked. Samantha's defiance was very subtle; at FLDS gatherings, she would intentionally avoid eye contact with adult males so that she wouldn't be forced to marry any of them. Though our narrators did what they could to survive in their sealed-off worlds, it is sad to note that each of them had to develop their own thoughts, opinions, self-protective instincts, and desires—their individuality—in secret so that they wouldn't be exposed or punished for the crime of being different from what their leaders expected of them.

Unhealthy charismatic authority figures can create a destructive and entrapping social world that is overwhelmingly focused on their own beliefs, desires, and delusions. Though these toxic leaders can essentially imprison people, the stories of our narrators show that people can escape, even if they were born into a cult and raised by the leader personally. If you are now or have ever been involved with a charismatic and narcissistic authority figure, it's important to know that you can break free, rebuild your life, and heal—though you will likely have to do some rebuilding of your sense of self as you reestablish your own life again. It's also important to know that healthy charismatic leaders and groups do exist; the checklists below can help you learn how to identify them.

Evaluating Charismatic Authorities in Your Own Life

The following checklists can help you identify whether a charismatic leader or group is healthy and uses its authority appropriately—or if the charisma has decayed into toxic narcissism, self-absorption, and the need to utterly control others. These checklists can also help you identify any toxic or narcissistic people in your everyday life.

Healthy charismatic leadership involves being willing to learn from others, instituting checks and balances, maintaining a sense of humor and a sense of humility, being responsive to complaints and corrections, and treating people well and respectfully. Unhealthy charismatic leadership treats others as means to an end and requires unquestioning devotion to the leader's (or group's) beliefs, desires, and demands.

If you're involved with any charismatic leaders or groups, you can use this checklist to gauge the health of the situation. Place a check mark by any of the following statements that are true.

- ☐ The leader or group has an inflated sense of importance and connection to greatness.
- ☐ Members must idealize and revere the leader and the ranking leadership.
- ☐ The leader claims special powers, knowledge, and lineage—or may claim to be divine.
- ☐ Members are often publicly shamed or berated for not living up to the ideals of the leader or group, or for not meeting the needs and/or demands of the leader or group perfectly enough.
- ☐ The leader's needs, ideas, and desires are overriding; they delegitimize and erase the needs, ideas, and desires of group members.
- ☐ Some members are granted access to an inner circle with special privileges and special access, and often, these individuals (or, at least, the chosen ones) can break the group's rules without punishment.
- ☐ The leader can do or say almost anything without repercussions; there are no checks or balances on his or her behavior.
- ☐ Members are expected to dedicate every part of their lives to the leader or the group, and not doing so has grave consequences.
- ☐ The leader has complete control over the group's belief system, rules, and norms—none of which can be questioned.
- ☐ The leader belittles all other belief systems and any other leaders who may be functioning in the leader's realm (e.g., other New Age leaders if the leader has a New Age philosophy).
- ☐ Members must display complete obedience and devotion to the leader or the group.
- ☐ The leader takes credit for anything good that happens, and blames members for anything bad that happens.
- ☐ The leader treats questions and challenges as threats, and he or she may see enemies everywhere—inside and outside the cult.
- ☐ Members who challenge the authority of the leader or leadership group are punished, publicly humiliated, shunned, or kicked out, and may be portrayed as enemy traitors.

If you checked yes to one or more of these statements, you or your group may be under the influence of a toxic charismatic authority figure. However, this doesn't mean that this person is dangerous, and it doesn't mean that his or her group is a cult. Your group would need to have all four dimensions of bounded choice active (this includes a transcendent belief system, systems of control, and systems of influence) before it could be considered a cultic group. However, if this person's behaviors are concerning you (even if the other dimensions of bounded choice aren't present), you may be able to suggest changes and see if your leader or group can—or is even willing to try to—alter these troubling behaviors.

You can also share the features of healthy charismatic authority below to help the leader or the group understand the specific ways in which they are veering toward trouble. If they can't or won't change, you can use these pointers to find a charismatic leader or group that offers hope without idolizing one person (or one idea) at the expense of everyone and everything else.

Signs of a Healthy Charismatic Leader or Group

- The leader or group has behavioral checks and balances in place.
- Members are treated as valuable individuals; they are not disciples, servants, or pawns.
- The leader has a sense of humor and a humane leadership style.
- Members retain their identities, family relationships and responsibilities, and private lives.
- The leader or group values and promotes members' ideas and beliefs.
- Members have the right to question, doubt, and challenge the charismatic authority.
- The leader or group deals responsibly with conflicts and challenges; there is no belittling, punishing, or shunning.
- Members have the freedom to come and go as they please.
- The leader or group considers and promotes other ideas, other beliefs, and other groups.
- The leader encourages critical thinking and intellectual pursuits.
- The group is open to the outside world and to nonbelievers.

When the charisma of a person or group is healthy, people are drawn to it and invigorated by it. When it's not, their choices get tangled up with the leader's need for total devotion and control.

Janja's bounded choice model helps us see that people who are under the sway of a charismatic authority figure are being manipulated, certainly. But in most cases, they are also finding a sense of purpose, meaning, and pride as they work diligently to demonstrate their perfect devotion. Diligence and devotion are worthy attributes; however, when they are directed at the bottomless pit of an unhealthy person's needs, both attributes only serve to ensnare followers in the web of a toxic narcissist. Breaking away from toxic charismatic authority is hard work, but it can be done, and people can learn how to identify—and support—healthy authority and healthy groups.

In the next chapter, we'll look at the ways that a group's *systems of control* work to change the everyday behaviors of group members, turn them into perfectly obedient followers, and bind them tightly to the group and the leader.

Notes

1. Max Weber, "The Sociology of Charismatic Authority," in *From Max Weber: Essays in Sociology*, Eds. H.H. Gerth and C. Wright Mills, (New York: Oxford University Press, 1946), 196–252; *The Sociology of Religion*, trans. E. Bischoff (Boston: Beacon Press, 1947/1968); "The Nature of Charismatic Authority and Its Routinization," in *Max Weber: On Charisma and Institution Building*, Ed. S.N. Eisenstadt, (Chicago: University of Chicago Press, 1968), 48–65.
2. Weber, *The Sociology of Religion*, 3.
3. Weber, "The Nature of Charismatic Authority," 48–49.
4. Ibid., 51.
5. Weber, *The Sociology of Religion*, 29.
6. Weber, "The Nature of Charismatic Authority," 48.
7. In sociology, we would understand this as an example of the *fundamental attribution error*, where individual behavior and personality are treated as more important while the social situation is mistakenly treated as less important. See, for example, Jeffrey Pfeffer and Robert B. Cialdini, "Illusions of Influence," in *Power and Influence in Organizations*, Eds., R. M. Kramer and M. A. Neale, (Thousand Oaks, CA: Sage, 1998), 1–20.
8. Weber, "The Nature of Charismatic Authority," 49.
9. Weber, *The Sociology of Religion*, 29.
10. See also Len Oakes, *Prophetic Charisma: The Psychology of Revolutionary Religious Personalities* (Syracuse, NY: Syracuse University Press, 1997).
11. See, for example, Stanley Milgram, *Obedience to Authority: An Experimental View* (New York: Harper & Row, 1974); and Herbert C. Kelman and V. Lee Hamilton, *Crimes of Obedience: Toward a Social Psychology of Authority and Responsibility* (New Haven: CT: Yale University Press, 1989).
12. See, for example, Dennis Tourish, *The Dark Side of Transformational Leadership: A Critical Perspective* (East Sussex, UK: Routledge, 2013).
13. See Dennis Tourish and Tim Wohlforth, *On the Edge: Political Cults Right and Left* (New York: Sharpe, 2000); and Janja Lalich, "The Cadre Ideal: Origins and Development of a Political Cult," *Cultic Studies Journal* 9, no. 1 (1992): 1–77. This last entry is a lengthy analysis of the cult that coauthor Janja Lalich was a member of for more than ten years. It is also a focus of her book, *Bounded Choice: True Believers and Charismatic Cults* (Berkeley: University of California Press, 2004).
14. Lalich, *Bounded Choice*, 20–21.
15. Berg communicated with his followers around the world by sending written communications, called "Mo Letters." See, for example, Miriam Williams, *Heaven's Harlots: My Fifteen Years in a Sex Cult* (New York: Morrow, 1998).
16. Alexandra Stein, *Terror, Love and Brainwashing: Attachment in Cults and Totalitarian Systems* (East Sussex, UK: Routledge, 2016).
17. John Bowlby, *Attachment and Loss, Vol. I: Attachment*, 2nd ed. (New York: Basic Books, 1982). The first edition was published in 1969.
18. A. Stein, personal communication, October 1, 2016. See also, Alexandra Stein and Mary Russell, "Attachment Theory and Post-Cult Recovery," *Therapy Today* (September 2016): 18–21.
19. Alexandra Stein, "Mothers in Cults: The Influence of Cults on the Relationship of Mothers to Their Children," *Cultic Studies Journal* 14, no. 1 (1997): 40–57.
20. Ibid., 47.
21. Janja's study revealed that more than one-third of the sixty-five cult survivors she interviewed still harbored anger and resentment toward their parents, especially their mothers: 37 percent said they either had hostile relations with their mother, didn't want anything to do with her, or she didn't want anything to do with them; and

34 percent said the same about their fathers. Another 26 percent said their relationship with their mothers was "neutral"; and 28 percent said the same about their fathers.

22. *Gopi* is a Sanskrit word for female cowherds, lovers of Krishna with whom he dances at the time of the autumn moon. It is used here as a term for devotees.

23. See, for example, Marci A. Hamilton, *God vs. The Gavel: Religion and the Rule of Law* (New York: Cambridge University Press, 2005); Janet Heimlich, *Breaking Their Will: Shedding Light on Religious Child Maltreatment* (New York: Prometheus Books, 2011); Innaiah Narisetti, *Forced into Faith: How Religion Abuses Children's Rights* (New York: Prometheus Books, 2009); Kristina, Celeste and Juliana, *Not Without My Sister* (London: Harper Element, 2007); Ashley Allen, "Impact on Children of Being Born into/Raised in a Cultic Group," *ICSA Today* 7, no. 1 (2016): 17–21; Charlene L. Edge, "Why I Had to Escape a Fundamentalist Cult," *ICSA Today* 7, no. 2 (2016): 15–17.

24. For a sociological analysis of Heaven's Gate, see Lalich, *Bounded Choice*.

25. For a sociological analysis, see John R. Hall, *Gone from the Promised Land: Jonestown in American Cultural History* (New Brunswick, NJ: Transaction, 1987). For a personal account, see Deborah Layton, *Seductive Poison: A Jonestown Survivor's Story of Life and Death in the Peoples Temple* (New York: Anchor Books, 1998).

26. For a unique and compassionate approach to the treatment of NPD and other personality disorders, see Nancy McWilliams, *Psychoanalytic Diagnosis: Understanding Personality Structure in the Clinical Process* (New York: Guilford, 2011).

27. Daniel Shaw, "The Insanity of Narcissism," *The Huffington Post* (August 15, 2016). Accessed November 12, 2016, www.huffingtonpost.com/entry/the-insanity-of-narcissism_us_57b25a19e4b0567d4f12b90b.

28. Erich Fromm (1900–1980) was a German social psychologist who escaped Nazi Germany and focused his work on political psychology, freedom, human character, and the eight basic needs of human beings. His most notable work is *Escape from Freedom* (New York: Avon Books, 1941).

29. Daniel Shaw, *Traumatic Narcissism: Relational Systems of Subjugation* (New York: Routledge, 2014), 49–50.

30. In "Cults: A Natural Disaster—Looking at Cult Involvement Through a Trauma Lens," relational psychotherapist Shelly Rosen wrote: "People who are born and raised in these groups [controlled by narcissistic leaders] are likely also to experience lags in the development of or dissociation from their own agency, identity, and core self-attributes, characteristics of complex post-traumatic stress disorder (C-PTSD)," *International Cultic Studies Journal*, no. 5 (2014): 12.

4

SYSTEMS OF CONTROL

Official Rules, Formal Structures, and Webs of Authority

Never a public school, absolutely not. We might actually learn something that contradicted the beliefs of The Family, so that was absolutely not allowed. There was absolutely no talking to anyone who was not in the group. There was no reading anything at all that had not come from the group. There was especially never, ever listening to any music or radio or talk shows or watching any television. Utterly forbidden. I mean you could get in so-o-o-o much trouble for doing anything like that.

Jessica

There was a dress code, but it's not like what you see in the current FLDS. What we're seeing now is a little bit better. We all had to wear dresses and we could mix up the colors a little bit, but we couldn't wear anything like bright red or strong colors. It was just lighter colors, but we could wear brown or black. The dresses had to be below the knees—it didn't have to be ankle length, but it had to be below the knees for the girls and the sleeves were supposed to be down to the wrist, but we inched them up to the elbows. So half-length sleeves were not acceptable, but were tolerated. The neckline had to be up to the collarbone. Nothing too tight. Hair had to be braided. My dad actually threatened to cut my hair off with a pocket knife once because I didn't have it braided in the early morning.

Samantha

It is worth noting that all Exclusive Brethren children were forbidden to attend certain classes and activities at school—religious education (including comparative religion), sex education and evolution in Biology, and computer studies. Texts in English literature were studied by parents and elders in the Brethren to ensure that the texts contained nothing that the Brethren considered unsuitable. And some subjects were not considered suitable for study beyond a certain age, for example, Dance, Drama, or Art. Reading novels was generally forbidden except where necessary for school. Swimming lessons were also forbidden in senior school because of the clothing (or lack of it) that we were expected to wear. So it could be said that the indoctrination program was a negative program, rather than a positive one, in that it was largely a case of ensuring that certain information did not reach us.

Joseph

In Chapters 2 and 3, we described the first two aspects of the bounded choice framework: a *charismatic leader* who promotes a *transcendent belief system* with a program of required personal transformation. The remaining two aspects—*systems of control* and *systems of influence*—are essential to bringing about that personal transformation in cult members.

What Are Systems of Control?

Successful groups create systems and rules that help them organize themselves, build a sense of group identity, and distinguish themselves from other groups. In healthy groups, these *systems of control* tend to be flexible, and they often provide a consistent and reliable structure for group members. For instance, a singing group might have specific times to meet, assigned parts for each person, and an expectation that people will learn their parts, warm up their voices, and show up on time. This is a simple example, but without these rules, a singing group would not be able to create music worth listening to. Healthy and successful groups create reasonable rules, attainable expectations, and systems of control that help them function as a team and develop a unified sense of group identity.

High-demand groups and cults, on the other hand, create harsh and unbending systems of control that are carried out by rigid authority figures who enclose members inside a tightly constricted universe. These stern systems consist of the recognizable rules, regulations, and procedures (including discipline and punishment) that guide the smooth functioning of the group and control each member's behavior and thinking. The desired outcome is compliance and, better yet, total obedience.

In some cultic groups, every aspect of life is controlled, such that communication, education, diet, exercise, dress, personal hygiene, sexual habits, health care, family planning, child-rearing, social life, and interpersonal relationships are intricately managed. As a result, the group becomes completely self-sealed and closed off from any outside influences. In many cultic groups, hierarchical authority, endless rules, and strict discipline and punishments create a sealed and bounded world that is nearly impossible to break away from. Absolutely every area of life—personal, financial, and social—is regulated by or connected to the group's systems of control. This powerful control system becomes even more effective when it is intertwined with cultic *systems of influence*, which is the focus of Chapter 5.

The Unique Features of Cultic Systems of Control

The social structures in cults can be compared to the concept of "total institutions," introduced by sociologist Erving Goffman in his classic work, *Asylums*.[1] Goffman outlines the essential features of total institutions (such as asylums, prisons, and concentration camps), which include removal of personal boundaries, stripping of a person's identity, interrogations, constraint, forced relations with others, and control of time.[2] We would also add control of information to these features.

While the asylums studied by Goffman were locked facilities, cultic groups can create the same kind of total obedience through systems of control that are focused on each member's submission to the perfectionistic belief system and utter worship of the charismatic leader. No locked cells, debilitating drugs, or pointed guns are necessary to get a cult member to comply (although there are some extreme cults where such measures have been used[3]).

For instance, the energy company Enron created cultic systems and enforced compliance in many ways. One particularly harsh system was a performance review process called "Rank & Yank," in which employees were evaluated on a scale from 1 (best) to 5 (worst). Employees who received a 5 had their photos published on a shaming internal website, and they were given two weeks to find another position within the company or be fired. Up to 20 percent of Enron employees were fired in this way each year. The harshness of the Rank & Yank system turned the Enron workplace into a cutthroat environment where employees—in order to survive and live up to the company's expectations—lied, cheated, and exploited each other, other businesses, and the world energy market before the company ultimately destroyed itself in 2001.[4]

This type of enforced, group-wide compliance doesn't arise overnight; instead, it occurs over a period of time and in a variety of ways. Cult researchers Louis West and Margaret Singer list some of the most common ways that cults control their members, including isolation of the person and manipulation of his or her immediate environment; control over communication and information; debilitation through fatigue and inadequate diet to disable the capacity for critical thinking; alternating harshness and leniency in a context of discipline; and assignment of monotonous tasks or repetitive activities, such as chanting, meditating, praying, speaking in tongues, or copying written materials by hand.[5]

In her interviews, Janja identified four areas where cults exerted these and other types of control upon their members (including children):

1. Indoctrination (education and resocialization)
2. Family Life (child-rearing, parenting, health care, and the atmosphere in the home)
3. Social and Cultural Life (friends, school life, and relationships)
4. Daily Rules (dress codes, behavioral codes, work rules, and discipline)

As you read about each of these control tactics (especially if you were never in a cult), you may ask yourself, "Why would anyone put up with any of this?" It's a valid question, because sometimes a cult's demands and behaviors are outrageous and inexcusable, especially when they involve children. So it's important to remember what you learned in Chapters 2 and 3: cult members become psychologically entrapped in the leader's charismatic belief system and by his or her promise of salvation. Devoted members can become so deeply entangled and indoctrinated that they will truly come to believe that the ends justify the means.

1. The Mind-Numbing Effects of Indoctrination

The ultimate goal of cultic systems of control is to make members submit to the demands of the cult and obey without question. Members are expected to undergo a rigorous self-transformation process in which they learn to believe in and embody the group's rules and norms—and this resocialization process is partially achieved through rigorous education and training sessions (i.e., indoctrination). Indoctrination occurs regularly in cultic groups, and is reinforced constantly so that members will internalize all of the rules, ideas, and beliefs the group wants them to have. For those who are born into a cult or brought in at a young age, this indoctrination starts early.

Two young men who grew up in Scientology recall the beginning of their indoctrination sessions:

> When I was little they had me doing little drills that they do for the communication course—but slanted for kids. You'd stare at clocks, and that's actually all I remember. I remember staring at a clock (laughs).

★ ★ ★

> I ended up taking Scientology courses. I don't remember if it was during the summer or if it was during the school semester. I remember that I was going full-time for the duration of a few months at least. Scientology fulltime doesn't mean, you know, 9:00 a.m. to 4:00 p.m.; no, it means 9:00 a.m. to 11:00 p.m. Except Sundays, I believe, when it's only a half-day. And this lasted for a few months. I guess I was around nine . . . eight or nine.

For Lily, intense martial arts training started when she was still in kindergarten:

> I started training when I was about six. I introduced myself in front of the class for the first time when I was five—I remember that. And then I started training. I was a curious kid, you know. Everybody else was training and I had to sit out. My mom wouldn't let me. And then, I think, Grandmaster Kim pressured her to have me start. You know, she wants everybody to train. So I started and then after that, I was told I had to. It wasn't a choice for me anymore—I had to. They had kids' class and adult class. And they would make us kids go to both sometimes. Sometimes they would make me teach the kids' class. I wasn't qualified. I would always go hide in the back room and try and get out of it. We all did.

Many cults create their own schools because they don't want children to learn anything that would contradict or question the cult's beliefs and practices. The legalization of home-schooling in many areas of the United States has made cult schools easier to start and run, which not only denies cult children a good education, but also keeps them isolated from the outside world. An added problem is that in most states, formal supervision of home-schooling is limited at best. For example, Janja asked Matthew if the home-school or curriculum in the Twelve Tribes was ever evaluated by the state. He replied, "Oh, no," which was a common answer among our narrators, many of whom felt strongly that they did not receive a worthwhile education. Many of them realized this only after they left the cult and found that they didn't even know the basics.

A young woman raised in The Family talked about rambling "Mo Letters" that cult leader David "Moses" Berg would send out to all of his cult compounds around the world. These letters and parts of the Bible were the sole curriculum for children in The Family:

> Of course, we were not given a formal education. We were all home-schooled, so our school basically just consisted of Mo Letters because there wasn't really that much schooling going on. We learned to read by reading the Mo Letters. We learned how to write by writing a reaction to the Mo Letters. And then arithmetic was something that was just kind of taught on the side.

Matthew's education in the Twelve Tribes was similarly poor:

> We didn't really have formal education. It was just whatever they could scrounge together (laughs). I have a very unique view of the commune because I'm deaf and all the other kids, they could hear. I was the only deaf person in the whole commune and we probably had 120 hearing children

there. So growing up there, I had no language exposure until I was seven years old. I had no social skills because I couldn't speak; I couldn't understand language. I couldn't communicate at all until I was seven years old, and people would struggle to understand how to educate a special-ed deaf person. They were really struggling with this in the commune, so I went to classes with many kids in school and we would sit around in a circle and they were all talking and the teachers didn't know how to sign or teach me so they would just give me paperwork and pretty much leave me out. Communication around the commune was very difficult for me as well because people didn't know how to communicate with me. They didn't know how to sign, of course, and that became more and more frustrating for me. I had a lot of anger as I was growing up because I had no method of communication. My parents struggled to understand how to communicate with me and understand my feelings and my needs. The commune really did not have anybody else to support us to provide education for me or for any deaf children. So, the people in the commune were very ignorant about providing special ed for me.

Whether the children were sent to cult-run schools or were home-schooled, the education they received was closely tied to their cult's beliefs and their leader's ideas. And even if they went to public schools, the children were re-educated and re-indoctrinated once they got home. One woman raised in the Fellowship Tabernacle church remembers the re-education she and other Fellowship kids received at home:

The Fellowship didn't have its own school. There was talk about that, but there were just never enough kids to justify it. I went to public school and they would ask me what they taught me in school. They would ask what the school taught me, and they would correct the teachers, of course, specifically the science teachers. They actually had a special Sunday School class for high school kids where they could get help with their homework and be taught the correct way instead of what their high school teachers taught. "It wasn't the teachers' fault that they were confusing you," they would say. "They were probably good people, but those evil liberals in the school systems, they're forcing them to teach you this, even though it's not true."

From birth to childhood and into the teen years, cult children's lives are taken up with indoctrination, work in cult businesses, childcare for other kids (in many instances), and not much else. The children are trained in how to think, feel, behave, and act—and as Joseph recalled in his Exclusive Brethren childhood, this constant training erased his freedoms:

As far as the Brethren were concerned, you had no freedom of choice and were always being watched. Loyalty, yes, but no feelings of love. Those feelings were no longer alive.

A young woman who grew up in The Living Word church experienced a similar loss of her freedoms:

> As far as my intellect: I think when you are controlling what people are thinking and how they think about it, you're putting a cap on creativity and imagination so that people can't really guide themselves. But it's all part of the tactics that keep us all under control, such as literally starting out sentences saying, "Let me tell you how to think about this."

This restriction of freedoms becomes even more severe when a child misbehaves. Jessica, for example, was sent to one of The Family's teen-training programs[6] for adolescents who were starting to rebel or needed correction:

> There were some teen-training camps in Hungary, where they brought all the teens in the area together. Maybe fifteen or twenty of us were there. We got together and lived in an apartment for a couple of weeks for what was supposed to be intense training. We would spend half the day having classes and then go out witnessing during the other half of the day. We liked being together, but we didn't like the control. There were people constantly keeping an eye on us, telling us what we did wrong, laying into us if we did something wrong, and calling us in to be rebuked by the leaders. I was given a long talk because I wasn't smiling enough or strange things like that. I was told if I didn't start smiling more, I would have to wear a sign saying, "Please remind me to smile." So they were definitely doing anything they could to pick on you.
>
> There were also teens wearing "Silence Restriction" signs. I know one boy who spent his first few months there wearing a Silence Restriction sign and being isolated. He had confessed to thoughts of wanting to be an air force pilot or just disagreeing with the leaders. He was always speaking his mind—he was very intellectual, very smart, compared to anybody else around, including most of the adults. His sign would say something like, "I'm on silence restriction. Please don't talk to me." Or "I am on STRICT silence restriction," and that was underlined. And if he so much as did even nonverbal communications, he would get in trouble. Even motioning to try to get you to pass the salt was considered trying to communicate with you. They always had an adult buddy with us, making sure that we weren't doing anything wrong or breaking their rules. And we constantly had to confess everything. For example, a boy who had lied about something got spanked for it, and he had to confess to the whole group about it. Any

time that people did anything wrong they had to get up in front of everybody and share their lesson and share what they had learned.

Living in such an environment of constant correction, often to the point of abuse, can have harmful effects, especially for children and adolescents. Paddy Kutz, Executive Director of Mental Health America in New Jersey, notes that it doesn't matter if child abuse is verbal or physical, frequent or occasional: "It is painful, and the pain can last a lifetime."[7] This pain is a constant companion for many children in cults who are regularly told that they aren't living up to the group's standards. Many come to feel as though they are incompetent at every-thing, and in order to gain approval, they submit utterly and accept whatever role is thrust upon them.[8] The endless indoctrination, expectation of perfection, and harsh punishment create a harmful environment that is very difficult to navigate.

These harmful effects have been studied in depth by Dr. Bruce Perry, Senior Fellow at Houston's ChildTrauma Academy, who examines "how children's brains are molded by the people around them,"[9] especially in response to physical, emotional, or psychological trauma. For example, Perry found extremely elevated heart rates in the children who survived the 1993 raid on the Branch Davidian cult compound. Typically, the normal heart rate for a child at rest is 70–90 beats per minute. Yet, one child, while asleep, had a heart rate of 160![10] Overwhelming and prolonged stressors, such as restrictions, isolation, and abuse, put children and young people at risk for lasting traumatic damage. Along with that, Perry states that prolonged fear may cause "chronic or near-permanent changes in the brain."[11]

When children are traumatized, their family's response can help them heal and develop resilience—or it can worsen their symptoms. Tragically, many cult families are not allowed to provide the nurturing, love, or healing that traumatized children require.

2. Restrictions on Family Life

Families in cults have an unusual mission, which is to devote their loyalty to the leader (instead of to each other) and constantly display that loyalty—often by ignoring their family responsibilities in deference to the leader's needs. In many cults, parent-child relationships are interfered with, and more often than not, the cult will intentionally disrupt family relationships. Matthew watched this happen throughout his time in the Twelve Tribes:

> They were trying to destroy the family because when one child in a family had a problem and the parents didn't discipline them well enough, the leaders would take the kid and put him or her in another family with other adults, and that's another form of abuse. I would say that 80 percent of the kids lived with different adults, and not their actual parents. They

made kids live in other communes away from their parents. Some even lived in other states.

Lily noted that families in the College of Learning were separated intentionally into single-gender homes, and that most marriages, including her parents', were torn apart:

> I think my parents' divorce was caused by the group. In my opinion, I think it was because my mom and another student would come and dig up stuff on my dad while he wasn't home and they would snoop around the house and things—my mom and my dad were pitted against each other. Yes, couples got split up if they joined COL full-time. If you're full-time, you can't live as husband and wife, so the man and the woman get split up and then they're kind of pitted against each other.

In most cases, child-rearing and discipline were also controlled by the cult, and the discipline was often harsh. These harsh disciplinary measures that children were subjected to were essentially loyalty tests: would the members follow the rules even if their own children were placed in harm's way? A young woman who was raised in The Living Word church remembers a community dedicated to regular spankings and public humiliations of children:

> The founder started telling people that they should be spanking their children starting at six months old. And so my parents were really big on spankings. And I think it was just because my parents were so, I don't know, led by dangling carrots in certain ways because they were so tight with the inner circle, but not enough to have any power. They were just sort of led and persuaded by everyone around them to do these things. For instance, with my younger brother, it was obvious that there was something not quite right. Either he had ADD or just some type of deficit with his attention. But many times instead of directly just having a conversation with us, we were humiliated in front of the group, our small group that we went to church with. They would put my little brother up there and say that he did such-and-such and everyone needs to pray for him. And it was never effective and even I, as a very young child, felt shameful and horrible for him because I knew at that young age that that wasn't right. He didn't need to be put up there and shamed in front of all these people.

A young man who grew up in a Turkish compound of The Family had a particularly difficult experience:

> My parents were based in the same country. They were in Istanbul, but they were based out of a different home. I'd see my dad once every two

or three weeks, and my mom probably a little less frequently than that. I knew I was part of a larger unit, but not being with my parents was very difficult for me. And I developed . . . I was told anyway . . . that I developed serious spiritual issues, stemming from my dependency on my parents. I was about five or six then. The "cure" for that was corporal punishment: regular beatings, isolation, deprivation. Doing chores during regularly scheduled activities instead of joining with the rest of my group. Doing extra reading and memorization assignments. Those were the normal forms of punishment. Silence restriction occasionally. I would not ever speak out against my punishment or try to justify what I considered to be unfair treatment of myself. The people we lived with—the men and women of the organization whom I was instructed to call "uncle" and "auntie"— they all adopted Bible names. They were Uncle John, Uncle James, Auntie Rebecca, whatever. If you refused to include the "uncle" and "auntie", you were punished. They rotated. We would have one for several months or a year, and then they would move on or go to a different home or a different group. Also they would change as we grew older. When I turned eight, I went into a different group and then had a new set of uncles and aunts taking care of us regularly for several months, and then they'd change and rotate.

In the home I lived in for the majority of my years in Turkey, there were about sixty-five children living in there and about thirty-five adults. That would be the average home size; and those thirty-five adults were all uncles and aunts to me. I knew my parents were still in the country. I knew they were still in the city—because I would see them. We'd have what we called a "Family Day," where we'd actually see our siblings and our parents and that happened about once a month; but in general I didn't know how to get in touch with them or have an address or a telephone to reach them at.

In some cases, this family separation had its advantages and was a sort of coping mechanism for the children. For instance, Iris and her friends in TM had freedom twice every day when all of the adults joined together for lengthy meditation sessions. But this freedom had drawbacks, as a young woman raised in the Hare Krishnas explained:

First we moved to the Detroit temple. They had a small ashram that was, well, it was sort of a house that had the girls separated from the boys, and so I went and lived with a few other young girls and I didn't even know where my mother lived. I don't remember how long we were there, but I think I was maybe ten when we moved to New Vrindaban [a Hare Krishna compound in Marshall County, West Virginia]. I didn't like it completely, but there were some fun parts about it because we got to live with our friends. It was kind of weird not being around our parents and not having the thought of them constantly looking after us and loving us and nurturing us. There was this freedom to it, that we weren't looked after a lot, and we had a lot of free time to go and do things. As a kid, it seemed kind of fun. You're like, "Oh, we're on our own," and you're doing your own thing. But I think ultimately I really missed out on a lot of development and self-awareness and self-esteem and those sorts of things. But I didn't realize it at the time.

In most cults, family relationships are restricted or wiped away because they interfere with cult members' time and energy—which is supposed to be focused solely on the cult's beliefs, its purported goals, and the leader's needs and whims. If cults *do* allow relatively normal family relationships within the cult, they almost always restrict or forbid relationships with family members who are not in the cult. These family-damaging systems of control ensure that cult members will not have full access to the love, support, and protection that a strong and healthy family can provide. These restrictive systems also reduce children's opportunity to develop healthy social lives.

3. Restrictions on Social Life

Contact with the outside world and friends or family who weren't in the cult was rare for our narrators, and these losses had lasting effects. In a healthy childhood, varied social relationships are positive and nurturing. Through their relationships, children learn how to communicate, love, develop empathy, negotiate, resolve disagreements, learn new things, and grow as individuals. Unfortunately, cultic restrictions on social life hinder individuation and intellectual growth, and interfere with healthy self-development. These restrictions also teach children how to keep secrets and hide their connection to the cult because, in most cases, outsiders are seen as untrustworthy or even evil. In some cults, this secrecy made the children feel too ashamed or confused to be able to explain their situation to any outsider who might have been able to help—including other children.

Many of our narrators weren't allowed to play with children who were not in their cult. All children in the Twelve Tribes were isolated from outsiders, and Matthew remembers being forbidden to play with outsider children, or to play at all:

No. Not at all. No. Playing with other kids—even looking at them—was really strictly forbidden. We weren't even allowed to go into retail stores except once when we were in Vermont, my mom did runs to this place that used to give us really cheap food or something in bulk. It was leftovers or something. So we used to get to go there, but if we went by a store that had anything that they would call "worldly," like toys or anything like that, we would have to close our eyes. But once again, it depended on whose child you were. Because the elders' kids, they got to go to Walmart or Kmart.

Naturally, enforced isolation breeds loneliness and a sense of remoteness. For instance, Joseph's social life outside the Exclusive Brethren was basically nonexistent:

> I grew up feeling different and alone all the time, and I still feel that way much of the time. I didn't learn to bond with other children either in or out of the Brethren in the way that children normally learn to—for example, learning to compromise to find a way to continue a relationship when differences of opinion arise. Brethren children were strongly discouraged from making "special friendships" with one or more other persons. And my parents frequently forced me to abandon friends even within the group if they felt that I was developing too much of an attachment to one person. The Brethren also discouraged members from having any family loyalties, as these were considered "worldly."

Iris had a few friends outside of the TM compound, but when Janja asked if those friends knew that she and her parents were in TM, she replied, "No, no, no, no. We kept it all secret." And one young woman who grew up in The Family replied:

> You're talking socially, then, I guess. Because we would go out and we would interact with the world in the sense of witnessing to them. And passing out literature. But as far as having peers outside in the world? No. No, no, no, no, no, no, no. No. Any sort of friends that I ever made, um, were all for the purposes of witnessing to them.

A young woman who spent ten years of her childhood in the Jehovah's Witnesses recalled her complete lack of social time with children her age:

> I was monopolized by the church as a child. I really did not have any choices. My choices were taken away from me, almost immediately. My mother sat me down when I was about six weeks into studying with them [the JWs] and told me I could never associate with our relatives again. Not even my own grandma—because Satan might be using them to keep us from learning the Truth. That was how she explained it to me. And so, the family reunions we had every year, those were completely tossed out the window. We never went to another family reunion. Also, my social life was obliterated. I was forbidden to associate with anybody who was not a Jehovah's

Witness in good standing with the organization. And in the small, rural town where I grew up, there were no children who were Jehovah's Witnesses close to my age. The closest person in my congregation, she was nineteen when I was ten. And so I had nobody to hang out with or socialize with for the next nine years.

Cultic restrictions against any kind of social life outside the group are often enforced through surveillance and disciplinary actions. A young woman raised in The Living Word church recalled the intense scrutiny that she and her fellow Living Word teens endured when they attended a public high school:

> We were definitely pretty ostracized as a group, but not very tightknit. We were all zombies. Just kind of zombies. We weren't allowed to do any kind of extracurricular activities, and everybody treated us really strangely. There was definitely a big sports element . . . anytime you're in a Midwest high school scene, that's the only exciting thing. It seems to be all that anyone's ever stoked about. So the whole school is all super into sports, and we're not interested at all or allowed to participate. So that was really strange. We were also definitely not allowed to date. I was allowed to talk with others riding on the bus, but I knew they were watching pretty closely, especially any time they ever decided that there was any inappropriate type of situation going on. We were completely separated and really browbeaten for even being friendly to each other. All living in a state of fear. You don't know what is going to be crossing the line. And at any time you can be pulled into the dreaded conference room to have someone talk to you and kind of tear you apart. For something you don't even understand. I remember there was a boy who had asked me to go to prom with him, and I was told that he was a disgusting Mormon. So I was just having all these horrible teenage, regular things happening, but then you add being totally confused and separated, torn away from my family—and you've got a pretty shattered, helpless, depressed girl. No, there was no joy.

These everyday restrictions on social life created an enclosed and entrapping world—and also kept the children away from any outside person who might have helped them. Inside the cult, the restrictions were not any less severe, since the daily rules and regulations were reinforced through shaming, punishments, isolation, and even banishment from the group.

4.   Daily Rules, Discipline, and Punishments

Daily rules and regulations, along with disciplinary measures, are critical aspects of cultic systems of control. This discipline is used to ensure that the indoctrination takes hold and that members become and remain entirely loyal and obedient.

Both adults and children alike are expected to conform. Lily remembers that the consequences of rule breaking were severe and relentless:

> Grandmaster Kim humiliated all of us. No one in the College of Learning was excluded. Kids included. We were all humiliated. And if she couldn't find something on you, she made something up. Yes, there were physical punishments, but she never physically punished me; she had other people do that. She was a little bit smart, so she had other people handle that. So if it came back to her, she would be like, "I never did that and I never wanted that. That was them; but look, they're gone." We would get disciplined physically to wear us down and also sometimes she would slap people, pull their hair, throw things around the kitchen, beat them with a stick. She's a crazy bitch.

Discipline within cults is often harsh and abusive. Matthew shared details about the types of physical discipline that children in the Twelve Tribes endured:

> The most minimal discipline you could get was that they would use oil dabbles, like rods. And it depended on whom you got, because some of them would oil them really good so they would hurt really bad, while some people would feel bad so they wouldn't oil them as much (laughs). Then you would hold out your hands and they would hit your hands however long they wanted and then it went up from there. They had a bunch of utensils. Bamboo hurt the worst probably and there were wooden paddles and then whatever they had laying around the house if that stuff wasn't available. And they would use that on the bottom, and some people would go all the way up the back and down the legs. It all just depended on whom you got. Then sometimes they did it naked or sometimes just with your underwear. At one point, there was a raid on the community; after that, they said not to do it naked because they didn't want to leave really bad marks that wouldn't heal in a day or two. But a lot of the old timers still really liked to do it naked and some of the men seemed to get some enjoyment out of spanking the girls naked.

One young woman from the Word of Life Fellowship described the "Deliverance Ministry," which was used to keep church members in line:

> If you rebelled, they would say you had an unclean spirit or a rebellious spirit and you needed to get a demon cast out. So you would have to go to the Deliverance Ministers and go through this whole, like, exorcism. And there was a lot of shame attached to that because, you know, clearly you hadn't spiritually taken care of yourself or you wouldn't be in that position to begin with. I had grown up hearing my father giving these

Deliverance Ministries in the other room, and so much screaming would go on. And writhing. You would see it sometimes in church services: the writhing and the screaming and weird voices. Total exorcist sort of stuff, which was really, really frightening.

I had a period of rebellion, and that needed to be taken care of. I had wanted to leave the church since I was eighteen, and now I was in my early twenties. Two Deliverance Ministers were brought in. They prayed with me first and they laid me out on the floor so I'm on my back. They draped me in a cloth and then these two ministers were praying and praying. They got more fervent, more frantic, and they pushed on my stomach. And they got me all worked up emotionally so I'm crying all over the place. I was just crying and crying and crying. And they pushed on my stomach, and pushed and casted, yelling in my ears to cast out the foul demon. Or my unclean spirit, whatever it was. It's just—it was so freaky. This went on for hours. Especially when they saw that there were multiple demons that they had to cast out. Some people would throw up, because it's a lot of stress to put your body under. Plus the emotional stress, and then the whole pushing on your stomach and the yelling in your ears. That's what the Deliverance Ministry was. And then you come out of there. You're emotionally drained. Totally exhausted. You feel like, yeah, I guess something happened because, uh, I don't know how to explain it, except there's this kind of relief. And you feel like oh, yeah, okay, they did cast out the demon because I feel a little bit lighter.

Jessica recalled the punishments in The Family, where the cult's Law of Love was used to excuse nearly any form of child abuse:

The Law of Love doesn't only cover the sex stuff. It covers, for example, discipline. Any form of discipline is fine as long as it was done "in love." That really included some very over-the-top things. Kids were getting beaten black and blue, public spankings, nude public spankings. Putting kids in tiny little closet rooms, and fasting them for like a month. There were the child discipline rules, and those were very, very harsh. But just add it to the fact that little kids were working ten- to thirteen-hour days, schlepping on the streets, selling tracts, in freezing cold weather! And we were like five years old, or if you were lucky, you got to go singing, which was street busking basically, which was fun. We did that so-o-o-o-o much. I mean every one of us when we were really little kids.

I was on silence restriction for a total of two years of my life. I was on silence. I added it up. One time I was on silence for nine months! I could not say a word! And some of the other kids were really little, too. One of my friends who was younger than I, a boy of seven or eight, was put on a year of silence restriction. How the hell can a little boy possibly not talk?

How do they expect you to? He did it. He got in trouble a lot, which is normal. But if you think about these little kids on silence restriction—I'm amazed! We were really, really little kids. They were really, really harsh on a lot of the boys who rebelled. They got a lot of the public humiliation and the public beatings.

The daily rules in cults nearly always involve work requirements and, in many groups, strict gender separations. Joseph witnessed both in the Exclusive Brethren:

Married women were forbidden to have careers. They were expected to produce children, care for them (and/or any elderly persons who were members), and run the home. Brethren were expected to give hospitality to large numbers of people almost every Sunday (usually at least ten to twenty people to a sit-down meal of two courses). The burden of the catering and the cleaning was managed by the women. As I grew older, my mother expected me to help with the daily household chores, and also with preparations for catering on Sundays. I disliked this intensely, and did everything I could to get out of it. Men were required to work to support their families, and the salaries paid by Brethren firms to the men reflected the fact that they were expected to support a large family, as birth control was not practiced.

Children in most cults are required to study, attend lengthy indoctrination sessions or church services, and work. For instance, the many businesses of the Twelve Tribes involved extensive child labor. Matthew described his early childhood, in which he and the other Tribes children worked up to fifteen hours each day:

The group had a cafe and we did a lot of work in the cafe. My sister was working in the bakery, usually during the day, making the desserts, and I worked doing salad dressings or doing prep work in the mornings. But we all worked in the back because the authorities would come around to see if we were there because of child labor laws. So we would have to stay in the back so they couldn't see us. Or the leaders would have us come in late to do clean-up work: closing up, cleaning, stuff like that. Our day was just work, work, work. That was their whole thing.

Besides work, the Twelve Tribes devised many other ways to keep children controlled. Matthew shared his experiences:

We weren't allowed to have things like favorites in the community. No favorite colors, no favorite people, no favorite foods, you know, which to kids in the world is like a staple, right? They had too many rules for kids.

There was no peer involvement allowed at all. No peer involvement allowed with your same-aged kids. You weren't allowed to play sports. The kids weren't allowed to be independent, you know, to do what they wanted. They forced the kids to all work all the time and do service for the commune. We had to clean the house. We had chores we had to do. We had to get up at four or five o'clock in the morning, and you had to be involved with the commune. Things needed to be done to help the parents, the other adults, and you were required to do everything with the adults, who would supervise the kids.

The kids were not allowed to have a childhood. There was no freedom; there was no kid time. We were forced to always act as adults even though we were still children, and they kept imposing these restrictions all the time. There was no fun. There was no inspiration; there were no activities. Everything was forbidden, and you had to work. The kids had to work. They had to help earn their money and they had to help support the commune, so the commune really took advantage of the children. It was using child labor to help support the commune and the household and all of that for food and what have you.

Plus one really negative thing about the commune was that some of the kids were starving. We didn't have enough food available for all of the children that we had. There were no snacks or anything like that. There was a very limited amount of food and you could just barely get by on the amount of food that you were given to eat. And sweets and pop and things like that were forbidden. Juice was forbidden. There were many, many rules, and a lot of the children were very frustrated and felt stressed about this because they couldn't get anything they wanted. You had to go to work, you had to clean the house, and we lived with other people in the house, like thirty or forty other people, and you had to help wash the dishes every single day for three meals: breakfast, lunch, and dinner for everyone. You had to do all of that housework and everything every single day for that large number of people living under the one roof.

When cult members break the daily rules, don't work hard enough, or have the wrong attitude, they may be threatened with banishment. This is a terrifying threat, because most cults isolate their members from the outside world. Banishment can mean leaving behind everything and everyone a person knows, and being cast out into an alien or evil world. Iris told Janja that threats to expel her from TM stayed with her long after she left the cult:

There were several times when I was threatened with being kicked out of the organization when I was younger, which was really frightening at the time. This was my community, and to have been kicked out would have been devastating. And so I learned to be quiet. And even after I had left, there was this fear when I would be called to discuss something at work or at school. I always assumed I would be kicked out . . . I could feel my blood pressure rising, anxieties.

A young woman who was raised in the Worldwide Church of God explained the effect of expulsions on her as a child:

> They had a process of disfellowshipping people, so if you didn't do what the minister said or you didn't do whatever, then you were gone. It was often. I mean this would happen frequently. I would ask, "Where is so and so?" We would go to church and somebody wouldn't be there. I'm asking, "Where are they?" And the reply was always, "Well, we're not to talk about them anymore." So it's just like they were gone. There was one example that was the most painful, but it happened all the time. The most painful one to me was a lady that was just incredible and she just loved me a lot. I was probably seven, and one day she was gone and there was no explanation and we were at the grocery store and I said, "Mom, there's Mrs. S." Mom just grabbed me by the hand, put my brother in the cart, and went the other way. It was like we're not to talk to her, ever, which was really confusing. I remember being really confused by that and no explanation was really given to me. So we just didn't talk to her anymore.

In response to these strict rules and regulations, the children became frustrated and often rebellious—both of which are normal responses to harsh systems of control. Sometimes, the children managed to get away with rebellion; but in most cases, they were punished even more severely. In cults, normal and healthy coping mechanisms such as resistance are usually turned against people. Shelly Rosen, a relational psychotherapist who has worked with former cult members for over thirty years, notes that the trauma of life in a cult, particularly for children, elicits a type of stress response that can be overwhelming.[12] Often, this stress response "gets stuck as a result of social and emotional captivity."[13] According to Rosen, "cult involvement has the potential to be one of the most traumatizing of human experiences."[14]

Coping Mechanisms for Surviving Abusive Systems of Control

The main ways that our narrators coped with the controlling systems in their cults was to rebel against them—either openly or subtly. Some rebelled outright, while others resisted internally, through daydreams that took them to different lives, or through subtle rule breaking that helped them feel some sense of autonomy in their extremely controlled worlds.

Lily was one of those who rebelled openly, and she experienced immediate negative consequences:

> I did rebel a little, and I got disciplined hard for it. You know, they would make me run around the block, do pushups, have my arms out straight like this, you know. Military-style training. I would be kept in a room and yelled at, called manipulative, called provocative. And I think in a way they broke me down so I did want to, um, I wanted to conform. And I did. And when I conformed, Grandmaster gave me more attention and people started recognizing me more and life was easier. And I started to like being a full member of the College of Learning more than being just a kid who everyone dismissed as, "Oh, she's a kid."

Jessica's form of rebellion in The Family was often subtler, yet necessary to her survival because her asthma marked her as a possibly satanic person. Her very existence was seen as a cause for punishment. However, rather than breaking her spirit, this outrageously unfair punishment (like Matthew's punishment for his deafness) provoked Jessica into testing out multiple acts of subtle and overt resistance:

> Yeah. Umm (laughs). Well, I started asking a lot of questions. I started refusing to close my eyes during prayer because I just didn't see the difference, you know. I did stuff that was just silly and childish at first. And then, I started writing stories, my own little stories. I started keeping them when I was eleven, but that was absolutely ended [when adults in the cult found out], and they burned my books. But I kept doing little things like that.

We all develop coping mechanisms to help us deal with abusive systems of control, and these mechanisms always involve resistance and rebellion in some form. Cults and other total institutions answer resistance and rebellion with punishment or abuse, both of which tend to make people fall into line and silence themselves. As you observe the systems of control in your own life, note whether they are healthy or toxic, and also note how you respond to them. If you feel your resistance and rebellion arising in response to them, this may be a sign that you are in the presence of a toxic system of control.

Evaluating the Systems of Control in Your Own Life

The following checklist can help you identify systems of control that are healthy, useful, and appropriate—and it will also help you identify systems that are rigid, unyielding, toxic, or abusive. Remember, as you look through these lists, that systems of control aren't limited to groups; people can be controlled by single individuals as well (think of abusive marriages or unhealthy teacher/student relationships, and so forth).

Healthy systems of control involve rules that make sense, clear checks and balances on power, responsive and respectful leadership, and goals that are attainable and beneficial for everyone. Unhealthy systems of control treat people like cogs in a machine, and they require total submission and unquestioning obedience, regardless of the personal cost.

You can use this checklist to gauge the health of the systems of control you deal with at home, at work, at school, or in any other relationship or social situation. Place a check mark by any of the following statements that are true.

☐ The rules and regulations come from above: members have no say in the system.

☐ The system of control is undemocratic and does not allow for independent thought or action.

☐ Members must be perfect in their obedience or face dire consequences.

☐ Rule breaking is treated as a direct attack on the group or its leader.

☐ Rule breaking has extreme consequences, such as public shaming, beatings, starvation, isolation, shunning, or excommunication.

☐ Publicly shaming or abuse of rule breakers is used as a scare tactic to keep other members in line.

☐ Members are encouraged to report rule breakers—including their own family members.

☐ Leaders or members in the inner circle can break rules without consequences.

☐ The system of control is connected to the working lives of cult members; hard work and even abject slavery are intrinsic parts of the rules and regulations.

☐ The leader can change the rules, regulations, and system at will or on a whim.

If you checked yes to one or more of these statements, you may be dealing with a toxic system of control. However, this does not mean that the person or group that developed the system is dangerous, and it does not mean that you're involved in a cult. This troubling system of control would have to be combined with the other three aspects of bounded choice (a transcendent belief system, a charismatic and narcissistic leader, and a toxic system of influence) before the group or relationship could be considered cultic. However, if this system of control disturbs you (even if the other aspects of bounded choice aren't present), you may be able to suggest changes and see if the people inside the system can address the problems.

You can also share the features of healthy systems below to help the person or group understand the specific ways in which their system has gotten out of hand. If they can't or won't change, you can use these features to find a new person or group with systems of control that are healthy, supportive, nurturing, and fair.

Signs of Healthy Systems of Control

- The system is democratic; all members have a say in how the rules and regulations are developed and implemented.
- Members have the right to question, doubt, and challenge the system.
- Checks and balances are in place so that the system remains fluid, responsive, and fair.
- The system supports equality, and no person is above the rules.
- The system incorporates fairness, justice, and leniency; no one is humiliated, abused, or shunned.
- Members appreciate the sense of structure and discipline that the system provides.
- The system provides a healthy sense of belonging and camaraderie.
- The system helps members develop a unified group identity that does not erase their own identities.
- The group encourages critical thinking and welcomes ideas from outside the system.

When a system of control is healthy, its structure supports and nurtures the people inside it. When a system is toxic, its structure crushes, demeans, and dehumanizes the people trapped within it.

With the help of the bounded choice model, we can see that toxic systems of control use cult members' hard work, obedience, and need for community against them. Though cult members may gain a sense of pride through fitting in and following the rules perfectly, this form of pride has a tragic outcome because it depends on the good opinion of people who actually mean harm to the members. Hard work, community values, and obedience are excellent qualities; however, when they are required by an inhumane and toxic system of control, they lead to enslavement. Breaking free from toxic systems of control can be painful and difficult, but it can be done. And people can learn how to identify—and support—positive groups and relationships that create healthy systems of control.

In the next chapter, we'll look at the ways in which a group's *systems of influence* can combine with each of the three other aspects of bounded choice to create a fanatically devoted believer who would eagerly do anything for a cult or its leader.

Notes

1. Erving Goffman, *Asylums* (Garden City, NY: Anchor Books, 1961).
2. For a study of this phenomenon on a national scale, see Hannah Arendt, *Totalitarianism* (New York: Harcourt Brace, 1951).
3. For example, Jonestown, Aum Shinrikyo, the Manson Family, and the cult coauthor Janja was in, the Democratic Workers Party, to name a few.

4. Frans De Waal, *The Age of Empathy: Nature's Lessons for a Kinder Society* (New York: Harmony Books, 2009), 38–9.
5. Louis J. West and Margaret T. Singer, "Cults, Quacks, and Nonprofessional Therapies," in *Comprehensive Textbook of Psychiatry/III*, Eds., Harold I. Kaplan, Alfred M. Freedman, and Benjamin J. Sadock (Baltimore: Williams & Wilkins, 1980), 3248.
6. For an in-depth article on The Family's teen-training program, see Stephen A. Kent and Deanna Hall, "Brainwashing and Re-Indoctrination Programs in the Children of God/The Family," *Cultic Studies Journal* 17 (2000): 56–78. See also, Stephen A. Kent, "Generational Revolt by the Adult Children of First-Generation Members of the Children of God/The Family," *Cultic Studies Journal* 3, no. 1 (2004): 56–72.
7. Paddy Kutz, "What Are the Effects of Child Abuse on the Brain?" Accessed April 13, 2012, http://www.newarkadvocate.com/fdcp/?unique=1334335352843.
8. Ibid.
9. Bruce D. Perry, M.D., Ph.D. and Maia Szalavitz, *The Boy Who Was Raised as a Dog and Other Stories from a Child Psychiatrist's Notebook* (New York: Basic Books, 2006), 5. Also Chapter 3, "Stairway to Heaven" (57–80), describes Perry's work with the children who were released from the Branch Davidian compound before the final conflagration, and is particularly relevant here.
10. Ibid., 62–3.
11. Ibid., 65.
12. Shelly Rosen, "Cults: A Natural Disaster: Looking at Cults Through a Trauma Lens," *International Cultic Studies Journal*, no. 5 (2014): 12–29.
13. Ibid., 15.
14. Ibid.

5

SYSTEMS OF INFLUENCE

Social Pressures, Rigid Expectations, and Constant Manipulation

Well, I was able to have friends, but I couldn't do anything with them. I could talk to them, but I couldn't go to their house or anything. If you ask them, they will tell you that it was never forbidden, but the reality is that I wasn't allowed. It was kind of weird. If you were to question Grandmaster, she would bring up my high school days when she told me to bring friends over that one time. She never said, "You're not allowed to have friends over," but it wasn't allowed at the same time either. There was always an undercurrent of "You don't know if they worship the devil or not. We can't let you go over there."

Lily

We did TM twice a day. We had advanced meetings at our home a couple times a week. We had to be very quiet around the house all the time, and we were encouraged to attend the meetings. We got a lot of ego strokes if we did, but we were not forced to. Weekends were initiations at our home, where the whole house was taken over by recruitment activities, plus there were always several other meetings and all of them took place at our home, too. So either we could help out, which was a whole day full of quiet whispering with incense burning or people chanting in other rooms, or we sort of wandered the streets on our own. My brother used to get out of the house and he would sleep in the back booth of a Carl's Jr hamburger place rather than come home because it was so uncomfortable at home.

Iris

During my early childhood, I had very little contact with other children as I had no siblings, my cousins were much older, and I wasn't encouraged to join any organizations outside school or bring children from school to my home. Actually, I didn't want to anyway because although we had radio, which Exclusive Brethren didn't normally have, we didn't have television and didn't go to any form of public entertainment. And I didn't want other children to know I was different in that way.

Joseph

What Are Systems of Influence?

Successful groups help their members learn how to create a cohesive group identity that supports individuals—who can in turn strengthen the group. Through social and emotional encouragement and guidance, groups can teach us how to belong, how to share core principles, and how to get into sync with other group members. In healthy groups, these *systems of influence* support individuality and personal freedom while simultaneously helping group members feel as if they belong. For example, a respectful soccer coach helps her team do their best and supports an atmosphere of respect and excellence that permeates throughout the team. Soon, team members will support each other and strive toward personal excellence as a way to demonstrate their dedication to the coach, to the team, and to each other as individuals. Healthy and successful groups develop an internal identity that is respectful of each individual's strengths and challenges. These groups are open to change and growth, and they're mindful of the well-being of the group as a whole.

In contrast, abusive and high-demand groups strip away individuality, are rigid and perfectionistic, and place the needs of the group leader (and/or the transcendent belief system) above all other things. These unhealthy groups use constant peer pressure to enforce intense and self-sacrificing commitment until unquestioning obedience to the group's beliefs, rules, and expectations becomes a daily or even hourly task. An essential aspect of unhealthy influence is that the leader and all members of the group can criticize or report those who stray from the perfect path—and in this toxic environment of self-sacrifice and constant criticism (external and internal), people can become sealed into what Janja calls a "bounded reality," from which it is extremely difficult to escape.

On one hand, people sealed into these systems of influence are striving toward perfection in a group of absolutely dedicated people who are their friends, family, and community—such that leaving would feel like losing everyone and everything they care about. On the other hand, the group's constant manipulation and perfectionistic expectations keep members so hyper-focused on performance—and so unsure of themselves—that they don't have the time, space, or energy they need to even think about leaving. The group is everything and everyone they know. Their leader is like a god (or may actually claim to be the reincarnation of God). Their group's perfect path is the only answer. Therefore, their only real choice is a *bounded choice*: to obey fully, eliminate all

of their doubts and their individual needs, and commit themselves completely—
or risk losing everything.

The Unique Features of Cultic Systems of Influence

Though we are taught to think of our sense of self as our own creation, social
scientists have come to understand that our self is actually a social construction
that is created through our social experiences. We are influenced by the people
around us, and we learn from and embody their values, ideas, beliefs, and
opinions. While each of us establishes and confirms our unique sense of self as we
make our way through life (hopefully without too much undue influence from
others), we are in the end social creations. Our social relationships help make us
who we are, and finding the right balance between external influence and our
own internal moral structure is what individuation is about. But for cult members,
individuation isn't an option, because cultic systems of influence are built to strip
away each member's internal moral structure and replace it with the group's ideals,
beliefs, rules, and perfectionistic expectations.

For children born or raised in cultic groups, their sense of self is shaped in an
environment of extreme influence. For many of them, there is little sense of a
"true self"; instead, any of their thoughts or behaviors that might instinctively
emerge and stray from the norm are ignored, pushed aside, punished, or removed.
A young man who grew up in The Family described the many difficult emotions
he felt as he tried to fit into the destabilizing environment of his childhood:

> Retrospectively, I was a miserable child. I was angry a lot. I was bitter a
> lot. I don't know if stress is the right word, but certainly I was filled with
> confusion. I didn't understand what standards were expected of me. Some
> "uncles" or "aunts" would expect something. Then someone else who
> would be with us one or two days a week would expect something else.
> You never knew what you would do to deserve a punishment or what the
> punishment would entail. The degree of punishment varied as well—from
> mild to severe for the same offense committed by a different individual.
> And so for me, it was a constant state of trying to behave somehow. I tried
> as much as I could to be good and to, you know, go along with the flow
> and try to fit in.
>
> I don't remember being a truly happy child. I don't remember being
> well fed or well educated or anything like that. I don't remember being a
> kid who was very happy or even very popular. I always felt very small. I
> was put down verbally and physically. Honestly, if I was forced to, I could
> probably find something positive about the experience. I guess maybe it
> made me grow up quicker. They suppressed free thought, free spirit. That
> was all suppressed. The fact that I was able to find my voice and get out—
> I don't attribute that to them. I attribute it to myself.

A young woman who was born and raised as a Seventh Day Adventist remembers that her own ideas, feelings, and concerns weren't important:

> I was taught to be very pleasing. And that has been kind of a lifelong struggle trying to put that into perspective. I was very naïve and, in a sense, really immature—because I didn't have any encouragement to develop a sense of self. And that was so apparent when I finally left. It was very frightening.
>
> I also think that I spent much of my childhood kind of depressed. I felt really powerless, without any voice. For instance, I was vaguely aware of pedophiles who were in our church, but it just simply didn't occur to me to talk to my mother—because it wasn't acceptable. I saw things and heard things that felt wrong to me, but I didn't feel like I had a right to say anything. The Adventists always knew best.

A young woman who was born and raised in The Family remembered being astonished that teenagers outside the cult could think their own original thoughts:

> My mom encouraged me to get a job and kind of assimilate to the world. Not to pick up any skills for living in the world, but rather for the purpose of recruiting other people into the group. She was always finding new ways to recruit people, which seemed very normal and wholesome to me at the time. So that's how I got myself into this situation: I'm standing in a group of kids about my age. I'd gotten a little job at the grocery store and a bunch of kids my age worked there. We were all standing around and everybody was joking, being sarcastic, and I was just floored. I was just (sighs) . . . it was the hardest thing for me to grasp. I turned around and looked at one of them and asked him—and it was the most sincere question—"Did you think of that by yourself?" And they thought, of course, that I was being sarcastic with them and they all laughed, and I was like, "Okay, what's so funny?"
>
> I realized that I couldn't even think of these things—because they were funny things, they were sarcastic things, they were things that nobody had told them, they didn't read them in a book, they were just being facetious with each other. And I didn't understand how they could do that without having learned it. Because, of course, nothing came out of my mouth or my brain that I thought of on my own. Everything I thought was there because somebody had taught me or somebody placed it there.

Each of these young people experienced powerful levels of influence, but it's important to understand that systems of influence are everywhere. They're in our relationships, in the media, at work, and in crowds—and they're an essential part of the process of persuasion. As social psychologist Robert Cialdini explains in his landmark book, *Influence: How and Why People Agree to Things*,[1] each of us both persuades and is persuaded countless times each day. We talk our friends into coming out for a movie; we see a pizza commercial and suddenly feel hungry; we give the cold shoulder to a misbehaving colleague at work; or we donate more money than we meant to because everyone else did. We are surrounded by persuasion and influence. Some of it is benevolent; for instance, we learn to take care of our health through the influence of parents, teachers, doctors, and public health campaigns. But some of it is damaging; for instance, we can be manipulated into buying things we don't need, influenced to distrust or hate others, or persuaded out of our own good judgment by someone we respect or fear.

People who want to persuade others and make them comply use many different influence tactics, and Cialdini found that the majority of these tactics "fall within six basic categories . . . [each] governed by a fundamental psychological principle that directs human behavior."[2] These psychological principles are what make these tactics so effective, and in cultic systems of influence, Cialdini's six principles of influence work in these ways:

1. *Reciprocity*: Reciprocity engages your desire to give back by offering you something valuable. They offered me perfection and salvation, so I felt obliged to follow them with absolute dedication.
2. *Social Proof*: Social proof tells you that something is safe and acceptable. Everybody else is going along, and nobody is complaining, so it must be okay. There must be something wrong with me if I feel wary and things don't make sense.
3. *Authority*: Authority engages automatic respect. Early in life I was taught to respect authority figures (parents, teachers, crossing guards, policemen, doctors), so why would I question this superior being with great wisdom who is telling me what to do?
4. *Consistency*: People want to be seen as consistent; they don't want to appear mistaken or foolish. Cialdini notes that "Automatic consistency functions as a shield against thought, [so] it should not be surprising that such consistency can be exploited by those who would prefer that we not think too much in response to their requests for compliance."[3] If I make a public commitment, I'll try to see it through even if I have reservations and concerns.
5. *Liking*: Liking engages powerful social longings. Someone I know and like is asking me to attend a special study session. Why shouldn't I go? When I do go, I'm surrounded by friendly, hopeful people who invite me back. Why shouldn't I go back to the next session? Besides, the leader gave me the most glorious compliment, so why shouldn't I trust him? He seems so likable.
6. *Scarcity*: Scarcity breeds desire. The group is telling me that their way is the *only* way. How can I pass up this incredible opportunity?

In many instances, systems of influence (such as public health campaigns) can have positive effects on individuals. But in cults, these systems aren't focused on the well-being of individuals; instead, they're focused entirely on the needs of the cult and its leader—and on turning idealistic people into fully committed and obedient cult members. In exchange for a sense of meaning, purpose, and deep belonging, each cult member is required to give up her sense of self, her individuality, and her identity.

Matthew remembers watching new people come into the Twelve Tribes, and he describes how the group would attract and then entrap them:

> A high percentage of people who lived in the commune were from the Grateful Dead show at Woodstock. Those people felt like they had a very empty soul and they wanted to feel satisfied, so that's how they came to live in the commune. It was a really easy group to attract at that time, you know, and the commune used two different faces. What I mean by the two different faces is that to the outside world, the commune would look very caring, very compassionate and loving—and everyone would look very happy and blah, blah, blah. But once people would join the commune, they would have to deal with a lot of rules, demands, criticisms, and oppression. There was a lot of peer pressure and a lot of preaching, and a lot of abuse would occur. But it was like an inside thing that they would never show to the outside world. The outside people would look at us, and everybody would try to put on a happy face so that the outsiders would think that everybody loved each other. Inside was very ugly though, and abusive, and that's how people became brainwashed.

Many cults rely on the power of closeness and belonging, and use them as a form of influence and control. Many cult members truly enjoy their close comradeship with each other; it's one of the things that can make it so hard to leave these groups. Yet there is a serious downside to this closeness, because cults exploit the communal intimacy they encourage when they apply their intense systems of influence onto the community.

Criticism, Perfectionism, and Constant Monitoring

In most cults, members are expected not only to bond with each other and strive heroically toward perfection, but are to criticize and report on anyone (including themselves) who veers from the cult's perfect path. Cultic systems of influence enforce and require constant self-criticism, peer monitoring and surveillance, and reporting any wrongdoing to leadership. These requirements help turn members into deployable agents of the cult and its leaders.

A young woman who was raised in Scientology recalls the way her fifth-grade classmates were deployed to bring her back into the fold:

> I went to the Delphian school, which was a boarding school for Scientology kids; but I never fit in. I asked my mom if I could go to public school, and

she said yes. I was about eleven at the time. So I left Delphi one day and didn't tell anyone I was leaving. A few days later, I was walking into a store in town and a van pulled up and it was people from Delphi. They had me get in the van with them, and they took me back up to the school. I remember sitting at a table with other kids, and all of them were talking to me and trying to convince me not to leave. They told me that I was making a mistake: you go to public school, you're gonna get into drugs, you're gonna get pregnant, you're never gonna get out, you know, you're going to have a horrible life. Scientology is *the* way. This is the path, and if you leave, you're sentencing yourself to a whole other life.

Most cultic groups employ peer pressure to keep their followers in line, yet many groups also create public self-reporting rituals that make self-criticism a communal event. A young woman who was born and raised in the International Churches of Christ describes the public confessionals that occurred during church services:

At church, they would ask me to pour out my heart, which was confessing and crying. Sometimes peers would be there with me. They broke you down and got you to say what a horrible person you were. They talked about sexual temptations and worldly thoughts, but never about the true differences between right or wrong, because only the leader was qualified to teach that. It was always intense, always crying, sometimes just from peer-initiated rebukes, where we acted like the grown-ups and criticized each other.

This intense pressure that cults apply to their members causes a great deal of internal tension. While a dedicated cult member may feel relieved to have a sense of commitment and purpose, the triple requirements of total obedience, self-criticism, and surveillance of others become a constant source of tension, anxiety, and dread. Members experience joy and renewal when they commit to the leader and the group (they are born again, literally or figuratively); yet, this joy strangely depends on self-exposure, self-criticism, and the willingness to criticize and accuse their comrades. The strict authority that cult members submit to certainly bonds them to the group in powerful ways, but this submission also creates a power imbalance that invites exploitation and abuse.

As a little girl in the FLDS, Samantha received a great deal of criticism from other mothers who wanted to shame her into compliance with the group's approach to mother-child bonds:

I was considered a brat because I was very clingy with my mom. The other mothers would chastise me and call me names for being clingy with her. My mom had a nervous breakdown when I was six months old and would continue to have them until she was out of the house. So when she would go to the hospital, she would be gone for a couple of weeks; and when she would get home, I would be very, very clingy with her. So the other mothers would berate me, call me names, and tell me that I was going to give her another nervous breakdown if I didn't give her a break. So I would only sit on her lap if I was told to sit on her lap. They said that having me was what caused her to break down, so I was in charge of making sure she took her medication when I was a child. They put that responsibility on me because I shared a room with her. What I remember very clearly one time is that she stopped taking her medication; she told me not to tell anyone and I didn't. She had a nervous breakdown and they blamed me for that. I would have been about nine or ten.

In Samantha's life, there were no outside influences to counter the influence of the other mothers. In the world outside cults, we typically become accustomed to and skilled at responding to the everyday influences around us; yet what is troublesome about cults is that the influences are all pointed in the same direction—toward compliance and conformity with the cult's needs and beliefs. In our lives outside a cult, we have countless influences—parents, relatives, friends of different stripes, the media, various religious creeds, educational institutions, and so forth. Samantha didn't have any of these. Her school was run by the FLDS, all forms of media were banned, and all of her family members were in the cult along with her. She didn't have any other influences to temper the damaging social influence of the group. Samantha was isolated, and this isolation was shared in some form by most of the sixty-five survivors Janja interviewed.

A woman who was born and raised in the Church of the Living Word recalls how literature and art helped her both tolerate and maintain her isolation:

> Socially I felt that if I had any interaction with people outside, I would be tainted. So I spent a lot of time reading literature during school when we had down time or just keeping to myself. I didn't have any friends or people who would try to be friends with me. I didn't know how or what you could talk about with people outside the church. That was also when I really got into art because I was so miserable. It was a good outlet.

In the world outside cults, we encounter different ideas and varying points of view on everything from politics to relationships to the death penalty to art to college majors to flavors of ice cream. And it's up to us to be challenged by these ideas and opinions and make our own choices. Conversely, in cultic groups, individual opinions and choices are frowned upon or forbidden—as is education. Many cultic groups refuse to allow their young people to go to college, and a young woman born and raised in the Assemblies of God recalled her cult's reasons for distrusting higher education:

I was just profoundly naïve because I had not had any experiences with people who weren't involved in the church. And the people who are involved in that church are usually profoundly naïve and anti-intellectual. "Don't send your kids to college because you'll lose them"—was the constant refrain. Colleges will ask your kids, "Could God lift a rock so high?" or something like that. They think that's what happens in college. Someone asks a common paradoxical question and it ruins people's faith, just like that. That's what they assume. Or that people just want to party and have fun and get drunk, and that's the only reason anyone would go to college or leave the church.

For cultic groups, outside sources of information are unnecessary—and they're either denigrated or outright forbidden. Everything is focused on the cult's ideas: there is only one point of view; it comes from the almighty leader; and it is never to be challenged. A cult member is not expected to consider other ideas, but only to obey the leader, embody the transcendent belief system, and follow along with her peers. Her resulting compliance may become an example to others; and soon, compliance and obedience will become the norm. When group compliance reaches a tipping point, leadership tends to become emboldened into exerting greater and greater pressure upon group members. Not only do the group's demands and expectations become more extreme (beyond the typical influence of peer pressure, for instance), but once compliance is a group norm, no one will be left to object or appeal for fairness and justice. If members somehow manage to object—which goes against every rule and norm of cultic groups—they will be reported, shunned, punished, demoted, or threatened with expulsion.

The threat of expulsion or excommunication is a very potent one, due to the way that the outside world is framed by cultic groups. A young man raised in the Holiness Movement recalled constant warnings about the outside world; his group was persuaded to believe that the world was a deeply treacherous place:

> They filled us with fear about leaving. A lot of it was suggestions or examples about people who departed from the movement. They would lose their marriage, or they might end up losing their sanity, and a bunch of other things. I don't remember all the things, but it was all very fearful. Basically, you couldn't survive on the outside.

Cultic systems of influence function as all-pervasive webs of interactions and social norms that serve the goals of the cult and its leadership. In these powerful webs of influence, members learn to adapt their thoughts, attitudes, and behaviors in deference to the group's rules, needs, and threats. For instance, a young woman who was born and raised in the Worldwide Church of God recalled the decisions she made in response to the apocalyptic prophecies of her group:

I grew up in a culture of fear. There were constant images, pictures of nuclear holocausts, of bombs, of people starving to death, of the holocaust itself. Those were the images that were played to me as a kid. There was an idea that our leader had: that we were all going before Jesus came back. We were all going to be whisked off to a place of safety. So there were constant warnings about how we were just going to lose everything. We would have to leave it all behind—and were you willing to leave everything you had? So as a kid, I never really had stuff because, in my mind, we were going to leave it behind anyway.

Each group's systems of influence create a restricted social network and a confining culture that are regularly reinforced by each member's conformity and obedience. This obedience is often imposed—not through obvious punishments, but through an atmosphere of impossible expectations and constant criticisms. A young woman who was born and raised in a small fundamentalist Southern Baptist church remembers feeling as if nothing she ever did was right:

We got in trouble a lot, you know, for whatever kids do. Basically I was told that I should be ashamed and that God was disappointed with me, and mom was disappointed with me. The way I felt was that the universe doesn't love me anymore, and I'm a terrible person because I broke a glass or whatever. We got in trouble for a lot of intangible things, like expressing emotion, strong emotion. You can't be angry. If you're sad, nobody knows what to do. We didn't get punished for being sad, but it was just like, "Oh, my God, she's crying! What do we do!" You can't get angry with your parents. You can't get angry about anything. If we kids were fighting with each other, we would both be told to be ashamed of ourselves, etc., etc. I think that what affected me the most was with my mother; I was just not able to really express myself. Anything that was negative that came out of me was a shameful thing. And both she and God disapproved. When I talk about it, it doesn't sound that serious. But when I was little, it had a big impact. I was a very sensitive kid and very shy and very dependent on my mom. Yeah, it made a big impact.

This confined and confining culture is justified by the promise that each member's obedience and self-denial will lead directly to salvation (however that's defined in each group). In the political cult Janja was in, for example, members were made to believe that the extremely harsh discipline they endured and perpetrated on each other was necessary to reach the alleged freedom of the ultimate social revolution. This glaring contradiction between harsh punishments and so-called freedom was acclaimed as the "dialectic of freedom and necessity" and, as you might imagine, the abuses were rampant.[4]

How Systems of Influence Entrap People

Social scientists have understood for decades that influence can be manipulative, and that group systems can and do affect behavior in powerful ways.[5] One early and classic study by renowned psychiatrist Robert Jay Lifton offers a clear model for understanding the social and psychological manipulation that takes place in cultic groups.[6]

Lifton interviewed American prisoners of war captured during the Korean War, and he also observed and studied the behavioral modification processes that were occurring in Chinese Communist schools under the leadership of Chairman Mao Zedong. Through his studies of people confined in these settings, Lifton identified eight social-psychological techniques commonly used to create what he calls "ideological totalism," or the assimilation of an individual into an all-or-nothing belief system that shuts off his or her ability to even consider other ways of thinking or being. Lifton found that this type of intense and unthinking dedication can be developed in almost anyone—it's a normal human tendency—which unfortunately makes all of us susceptible to systems of influence. In some cases, this susceptibility is exploited by apocalyptic groups to create fanatically devoted cult members who become willing and deadly agents of extremism.[7]

To some degree, all cultic systems of influence and control include a combination of the eight social-psychological influence techniques identified by Lifton.[8] As we describe each technique, we explore its connection to our bounded choice model:

1. *Milieu Control*: The group controls all communication and information, which includes each individual's communication with herself. This sets up what Lifton calls "personal closure," where the person no longer struggles with thoughts of what is true or real. Milieu control works to isolate members and silence internal doubts; it is a part of cultic systems of influence and systems of control.

2. *Mystical Manipulation*: The group asserts that they or their leader have divine, supreme, or political power. The group or the leader may orchestrate events that support their supposed power or verify their central beliefs—and then pretend that these events occurred spontaneously. The leader may also manipulate or reframe information to his or her advantage, and to assert his or her supreme authority. Mystical manipulation is connected to a group's transcendent belief system, charismatic authority figure, and systems of influence.

3. *Demand for Purity*: The group demands absolute dedication, and the leader is the ultimate moral authority who decides whether the dedication is sufficient (it almost never is). This creates an atmosphere of everyday punishment and humiliation. It also sets up an environment of competition, where members will spy on and report each other. This demand fills people with crippling amounts of guilt and shame, such that they may lose touch

with their own sense of morality. The demand for purity is connected to a group's systems of control, systems of influence, and the charismatic authority figure.

4. *Cult of Confession*: The group requires public confession and self-exposure. In many cults, increasingly extreme acts of self-exposure are celebrated as signs of true dedication. Members may lose their sense of balance between self-worth and humility, between what is private and what should be shared, and between their personal self and their idealized group self. This loss of balance and boundaries may entrap members, such that they may feel almost owned by the group. The cult of confession is connected to a group's systems of influence.

5. *Sacred Science*: The group asserts that it has the Ultimate Truth. Challenges are not allowed, and questions are dismissed, treated superficially, or thrown back at questioners. This shuts down members' critical-thinking capacities and inhibits their creative self-expression and personal development. Life is perceived only through the filter of the group's transcendent belief system; no other beliefs or ideas are allowed.

6. *Loading the Language*: The group creates specialized jargon (or communication techniques) that is understood only by insiders, which makes members feel special. However, it also isolates members from the rest of society and reduces their capacity for imagination and original thought. Loading the language is a subtle yet potent way to enforce conformity, and it is connected to a group's systems of influence.

7. *Doctrine over Person*: The group's doctrines, beliefs, and needs take precedence over anyone and everyone. Members must deny their own needs, private thoughts, and personal experiences if any of these contradict the group's doctrine. The past—of society and each member—is altered to fit the group's beliefs, and individuality is erased. The doctrine over person serves to create the cult persona, and it is connected to a group's systems of influence and transcendent belief system.

8. *Dispensing of Existence*: The group makes ultimate decisions about who is an enlightened insider and who is an inferior outsider. Inferior people must be converted, and if they don't join or are critical of the group, they must be rejected and shunned as non-people—or as evil. In extremist cults, these non-people may be punished, harmed, or killed. People outside the group are stripped of credibility and humanity, which teaches cult members that there is no world and no life outside the group. The dispensing of existence strongly suggests that group membership requires fanatical obedience, and it is connected to a group's systems of control, systems of influence, and transcendent belief system.

These eight influence techniques serve to erase individuality and deconstruct members' core selves so that they can become perfect and unquestioning followers. A young woman who was born and raised in The Family describes the point at which she lost her sense of individuality, stopped questioning, and surrendered herself to the group:

> We would have lesson sharing, where we would have to share with the group something we did wrong that week and what we learned from it. Occasionally there would be prayers for deliverance where we'd have to kneel down and everyone would pray over us, casting out demons and so forth. We also had to write periodic "Open Heart Reports." This OHR practice started when I was about eight years old, and we had to write down our feelings and battles as well as our reactions to the religious literature we read, and our shepherds would comment on our OHRs. At first I struggled and thought things were not fair; I was really trying to be good, yet I still got into trouble. My spiritual problem was diagnosed as self-righteousness and daydreaming, which pretty much meant having self-confidence and thinking about anything that wasn't based on the teachings. After a couple of months, I remember things clicking in my mind one day that everything was all my fault, that I was bad and worthless, evil even, and that was why I was always getting into trouble. During this time I also remember making a conscious decision to surrender my family to God, whatever that meant.

Influence techniques like the OHR deliberately attack people's self-image and self-concept (or their core self) and make them feel inherently defective. The core self encompasses all of the ways that people approach, react to, and cope with thoughts, emotions, relationships, and life events. We all develop psychological defense mechanisms to protect our core selves and to perceive, interpret, and deal with reality in our own unique ways. Sadly, systematic attacks on these defense mechanisms (such as the OHR, oral or written confessions, self-criticisms, peer rebukes, and reporting) destabilize our inner equilibrium, our perception of reality, and our core selves.

"Alter the self or perish" is the unstated motto of many groups that require this type of extreme self-transformation. The purpose of these continual intimate assaults on the core self is to tear members down to the point that they begin to identify and merge with the group (or the narcissistic leader). In this environment, members may become extremely anxious about their self-worth—or even about their very existence. Along with this may arise intense feelings of personal disintegration, of falling apart, of feeling that you don't know or understand anything anymore. But the cult is there to pick up the pieces and puts you back together in its desired mold.

Children are especially vulnerable to systems of influence because their selves are not fully formed and are therefore uniquely susceptible to influence and persuasion. Parents in cults do not provide much protection, given that they're often entrapped themselves. In many cases, cult parents are not really parents in the classic sense; instead, they're pawns or instruments of the leader and the transcendent belief system (as we saw in Chapters 2 and 3). In these environments, children are often left to raise themselves or are raised by unrelated group members who have no real interest in them. Consequently, cult children are often at the mercy of whatever rules and influence and control techniques the group has adopted.

A young woman born and raised in the Worldwide Church of God remembers the pressure she felt to control herself and follow the rules:

> I was never allowed to be angry. We weren't allowed to be angry or fearful or show any kind of fear. I think it gave me some compulsions, you know, and some paranoia. I think it affected my eating in terms of just not knowing: Was I hungry? Am I full? So that is a concern. I did struggle right when I left the group. I had some bulimia and anorexia, and I have been diagnosed with an eating disorder that's nonspecific at this point, which was their parting gift to me, I guess. You know, emotionally, not being able to feel, just kind of feeling numb. Not really knowing how to be. I mean, everything was very conditional. Acceptance was very conditional, and so if you were to be loved, you had to be a performer—and not just a performer for your immediate family, but a performer for God's family. So, you know, I wanted to be loved, so I performed well.

The goal of cultic systems of influence is to change and/or shape human beings at their very core so that they will fully accept the group's ideology, adulate the leader, and strive for perfection. Once those goals are achieved, compliance and obedience are almost guaranteed.

How Followers Learn to Entrap Themselves

When powerful systems of influence are active, people may lose their sense of self, their critical thinking, and their autonomy—and when they do, they can be converted into obedient followers. One of the strange side effects of this process is that converts may begin to believe that they have free will, and that they have intentionally chosen to de-self and obey. They become true believers and lose any real awareness of the influence methods that reshaped and resocialized them—and they come to believe that they willingly accepted this personal transformation to be one of the chosen few. This seems bizarre, but it's an intrinsic feature of toxic systems of influence and persuasion. And it's possibly the most difficult feature for someone who hasn't experienced it to fully understand.

Sociologist Benjamin Zablocki focuses on the social-psychological pressures that lead to this willing self-delusion in his work on *hyper-credulity* and *hyper-compliance* in cultic groups.[9] Zablocki explains that cult members learn to erase their critical judgment and wholly accept the beliefs, ideas, and doctrines of the group; members enter into a state of hyper-credulity. Simultaneously, they become strongly attached to and emotionally dependent on the leader and other group members, and cannot bear to be separated from them. This brings about a combined external and internal state in which the idea of leaving the group feels unbearable, and the cult member enters into a state of hyper-compliance. The group becomes everything, and so it becomes rational to comply with whatever the leader or group demands. If these demands are harsh or abusive, the hyper-credulity aspect will arise to erase critical thinking and justify whatever rationalizations or excuses the leader offers, however farfetched they may seem to us on the outside.

Social psychological research has consistently upheld the idea that once a person makes a commitment, especially if he or she takes a strong position in front of others, it is likely that he or she will cling to that position (this relates to Cialdini's concept of *consistency*, discussed earlier in this chapter). This consistency is more likely to lead to hyper-compliance when people spend money, when their family and friends go along with them, or when they have already invested their time and energy. For children, who have no say about joining these groups, adopting hyper-credulity and hyper-compliance may be ways to please their parents or the leader, or may simply become survival responses.

Additionally, social psychological research has shown that a similar form of self-deception occurs in situations of internal conflict.[10] When people are confronted by the possibility that their cherished thoughts, beliefs, or behaviors are wrong, they may be overtaken by a painful internal state known as *cognitive dissonance*. The conflict between their ideas or behaviors and stark reality can evoke many difficult feelings, such as stress, anxiety, anger, nausea, shame, fear, or all of these.[11] In response to this distressing conflict, people tend to alter and distort their perception of reality in order to relieve their cognitive dissonance—and cultic systems of influence help members achieve this relief. When an adult finds a group that becomes a vital source of hope, or when a child or adolescent has little to no experience of any other kind of environment, they will tend toward rationalizations that cause the least amount of psychological turmoil—and they will often choose the group over their own doubts. Having chosen, their sense of consistency will intensify their commitment to the group. This commitment is in turn intensified by the need to belong, or in some cases, to survive.

Many people who have been subjected to harsh systems of influence may deny aspects of their experience. Some become angry at or resistant to the idea that they were changed or directed by psychological manipulation, persuasion, or influence tactics. Some may even develop cognitive dissonance about the knowledge that they willingly supported beliefs, relationships, and obedience to a leader that they now find repugnant. It is very threatening to think that you might have been controlled or changed by another person or group of people; nevertheless, it happens every day. Luckily, so does the resistance that can help people escape these systems.

Coping Mechanisms for Surviving Abusive Systems of Influence

It is no easy task to resist abusive systems of influence, because their purpose is to influence (and thus control) your thoughts, your emotions, your behaviors, and your sense of self. It can be hard to marshal your internal resources when they are being used against you. In this regard, systems of influence can be more difficult to resist than the other three aspects of bounded choice. Many of our narrators were able to rebel against narcissistic leaders, all-encompassing belief systems, or harsh systems of control. But cultic systems of influence engulf and invade the lives of members—who are surrounded in every moment of every day by invisible yet forceful persuasion tactics that impose and reinforce internal and external compliance. Coping with and resisting these powerful forces requires ingenuity.

A young man who was a third-generation Jehovah's Witness appealed directly to God:

> There was no way you could socialize with anybody or have real friends. It was impossible. You couldn't go to a birthday party. You couldn't. I used to pray to God to make me normal. To be like an average kid. To be able to just do fun stuff. To not have to dress up in a monkey suit three times a week, go to all these meetings, and knock on other people's doors. But I felt guilty for praying for something like that, too. You know, God didn't want that. He wanted me out there doing this stuff. Because I know I would feel guilty for saying it afterwards. But I knew also that I didn't enjoy the nervous tension all the time, the ridicule, and everything else I had to go through.

This appeal didn't work because this young man's God was intricately involved with the Witnesses' systems of influence. A young man who was born and raised in the Bible-based cult found another way. He used his analytical skills to assess people, and then shifted his behavior to meet their needs so that he could maintain some level of internal freedom and autonomy:

> Well, I was not emotionally connected to anyone. I never had that. I had strategic connection. The way I operated in the world was to analyze the situation and see what was needed: who was in charge; what were their prejudices, biases, and needs; and how to activate their prejudices and biases to make the situation workable. And also how to meet their needs so that I could possibly get mine met. That was really what I did. From place after place, situation after situation: I would come in, analyze the situation, and figure out how to operate to allow me the freedom to continue to live my life, which was 100 percent in my head, in my books. That's what I did.

We all find ways to protect or assert our individuality in response to abusive systems of influence; however, these maneuvers require subtlety. Such restraint is necessary because cultic systems of influence interfere with us at the ground level of our emotions, thoughts, and self-concept. Resistance against these abusive social systems takes skill, because cults focus most of their energy on influencing and persuading their members, potential members, outsiders, neighbors, the media, law enforcement, the legal system, and even local governments. Even so, the sixty-five people in Janja's study successfully resisted and escaped from their groups' powerful systems of influence. Some of our narrators were teens when they left—with no destination, no money, and not even a change of clothes—yet they were able to create new lives and new selves in the outside world. Cultic systems of influence are indeed very powerful, but they are not all-powerful; they can be resisted.

As you observe the systems of influence in your own life, note whether they are healthy or toxic, and also note how you feel inside them. If you lose your bearings, your boundaries, or your sense of self in response to them, you may be in the presence of toxic systems of influence.

Evaluating the Systems of Influence in Your Own Life

Influence and persuasion are present in all social relationships, so it's important to explore the systems of influence in your life and identify any current problems or any past situations in which you were influenced negatively. Understanding and identifying these situations is the first step toward overcoming their effects.

The following checklists can help you identify systems of influence that are worthwhile and appropriate—and they will also help you identify systems that are controlling, abusive, or likely to undermine your individuality. As you look through these lists, remember that systems of influence are used by individuals, groups, and the media; they are a part of most forms of communication. Influence and persuasion are regular features of everyday life. They can be healthy or toxic, but they're nearly always present.

Healthy systems of influence focus on creating group cohesion that is supportive for the group and for the individuals within it. Healthy influence creates a sense of belonging, dedication, friendliness, and teamwork; and it can help people reach goals that they couldn't achieve on their own. On the other hand, unhealthy systems of influence focus on the group above all other things, including individual rights, dignity, and even safety. These unhealthy systems routinely manipulate their members, pit them against each other, create enemies in and fear of the outside world, and enforce obedience at all costs.

You can use this checklist to gauge the health of the systems of influence in your relationships, in any groups you belong to, in the media, in politics, or in any other place where people attempt to create behavioral change, communal agreements, or group unity. Place a check mark by any of the following statements that are true.

- [ ] There is constant pressure for people to change and conform.
- [ ] The push for change comes from above; the needs or ideas of group members are not important.
- [ ] There are frequent group dedication and commitment ceremonies and activities; oneness is a central goal.
- [ ] The system of influence is built into the powerful sense of community; this deep closeness is both supportive to members and also a way for the group to pry into and control members' private lives.
- [ ] Loyalty to family or friends is discouraged; all loyalty must be focused on the group and the leader.
- [ ] Gossip, informal communication, and off-topic conversations may be forbidden.
- [ ] Members have no privacy; their actions, behaviors, emotions, and even thoughts are monitored.
- [ ] Members soon internalize the pressure to conform, and will obediently monitor and report their own behavior.
- [ ] Members must report on themselves and also each other—as a result, a culture of confession will arise.
- [ ] Confessions are public; and punishment and humiliation are public as well.
- [ ] The leader's behavior is off limits; no one can report on the transgressions of the leader, for he or she is exalted and can do no wrong.
- [ ] Special people around the leader or the leadership group are also protected from any criticism; often there are no consequences for their behavior or actions.
- [ ] Members may be given or asked to choose new names or nicknames, and will be encouraged to let go of previous interests, relationships, loyalties, and goals.
- [ ] The group may develop its own special language that outsiders cannot understand.
- [ ] Any successes or hard work performed by individuals will be attributed to the group or leader, while any difficulty or failure will be blamed on individuals.
- [ ] People in the outside world are treated as non-people: unenlightened, deluded, or evil—and they have value only if they can be converted.
- [ ] The group or the leader may reinterpret events to verify the group's beliefs, fears, or visions of the future; everything will be fitted into their all-inclusive and transcendent belief system.

If you checked yes to one or more of these statements, you may be dealing with a toxic system of influence. However, this does not mean that the person or group that uses the system is dangerous, and it does not mean that you're involved in a cult. This troubling system of influence would have to be combined with the other three aspects of bounded choice (a transcendent belief system, a charismatic and narcissistic leader, and a toxic system of control) before the group or relationship could be considered cultic. However, if this system of influence disturbs you (even if the other aspects of bounded choice aren't present), you may be able to suggest changes and explore whether the people inside the system will address the problems of undue influence and persuasion.

You can also share the features of healthy influence and persuasion below to help the person or group understand the specific ways in which their systems of influence have become unhealthy. If they can't or won't change, you can use these features below to find a new person or group that employs systems of influence that are respectful, compassionate, and healthy.

Signs of Healthy Systems of Influence

- The system helps people feel welcome and important to the group as they are.
- The system encourages healthy community, teamwork, and camaraderie, as well as open discussion and debate about group projects, goals, and decisions.
- Members are role models for each other, but internal competition is a choice rather than a requirement.
- Individual hard work and excellence are celebrated, and are attributed to the individual.
- The group encourages self-awareness and personal responsibility, but does not require public self-exposure.
- The system supports privacy, self-respect, independence, and kindness.
- Communication is direct and open, and secret-keeping is discouraged.
- Members are not required to spy on or report others.
- Members have the right to challenge the ways that group unity is achieved.
- Striving for excellence may be a group value, but the demands are not harsh, and people are not penalized for failure.
- Dedication may be a group value, but the group makes room for casual members.
- The system incorporates fairness, concern for individuals, and acceptance of outsiders.
- The group provides a healthy sense of belonging and realistic levels of commitment.
- The group does not require people to transform themselves or dedicate their lives to the cause.
- Leaders and special insiders are not above the rules, and they can be challenged if they disrupt or ignore group norms.

- The system helps members develop a unified group identity that does not erase their own identities.

When a system of influence is healthy, it supports group identity and individual identity equally. When a system is toxic, it demands change, obedience, and a stripping away of individual identity. With the help of the bounded choice model, we can see that toxic systems of influence exploit close community ties to control and change members into obedient followers. Many cult members feel a deep sense of belonging and comradeship, certainly; but that may come at a terrible price—because even small differences or minor mistakes invite shaming, punishment, shunning, and perhaps even excommunication.

The close relationships people build inside cultic groups are always at risk because their relationships belong to the cult and can be severed at any time. Close community ties, teamwork, and deep dedication are wonderful things; but when they're part of a toxic system of influence, they can turn people into unwitting cogs in the group's machine. Breaking free from toxic systems of influence can be very difficult because these systems hook into our powerful need to belong. However, people can and do break free every day—and we can all learn how to identify and avoid these unhealthy and harmful systems. We can also learn how to recognize and contribute to healthy and worthwhile systems of influence and persuasion.

Systems of influence are the final aspect of Janja's four-part bounded choice model. We placed it last because it is truly the glue that binds groups together; yet, it can be very hard to identify if you don't know about influence techniques and persuasion tactics. Inside toxic groups, systems of influence can be so all-consuming that people might not be able to identify all of the facets until they leave. Plus, the influence may be so powerful that members might not have the time or energy they need to even consider leaving. When you understand influence and persuasion, you can see them in action more clearly; but when you're surrounded by them, or when you're born into or raised inside powerful systems of influence, you may not have any other frame of reference.

Systems of influence can be the subtlest of the four aspects of bounded choice; yet they also tend to exert the most powerful hold on members—even more so than the more obvious aspects of the charismatic leader, the transcendent belief system, or the systems of control. The choice to stay in a system like this—and the choice to self-monitor and report on yourself, your friends, and your family—is truly a bounded choice. In a toxic system of influence, you have no other option than to silence your thoughts, your emotions, and your needs—and obey. Thankfully, our narrators had the courage, strength, and hope they needed to listen to themselves, smash their chains, and break free.

In the next chapter, we'll focus on what it was like for our narrators to escape from their confining groups and land in a world they had been taught to view as evil and unsalvageable. As you may imagine, the rules these children of cults learned in their groups, the transcendent beliefs systems they were taught to embody, the leaders they were taught to worship, and the ways in which they were molded into perfectly obedient followers made their transitions very rocky. Even so, they managed to find their way in the alien world the rest of us know as regular life.

Notes

1. Robert B. Cialdini, *Influence: How and Why People Agree to Things* (New York: Quill, 1984).
2. Ibid., 13.
3. Ibid., 72.
4. See Janja Lalich, "Part Two: The Democratic Workers Party," *Bounded Choice: True Believers and Charismatic Cults* (Berkeley: University of California Press, 2004), 113–218.
5. Any good social psychology textbook explains these phenomena chapter by chapter. See, for example, Elliot Aronson, *The Social Animal* (New York: Worth, 2011); Elliot Aronson, Timothy D. Wilson, and Samuel R. Sommers, *Social Psychology* (Upper Saddle River, NJ: Pearson, 2015); John D. DeLamater and Daniel J. Myers, *Social Psychology*, 7th ed. (Belmont, CA: Wadsworth, 2011); Philip G. Zimbardo and Michael R. Leippe, *The Psychology of Attitude Change and Social Influence* (New York: McGraw Hill, 1991).
6. Robert Jay Lifton, *Thought Reform and the Psychology of Totalism: A Study of "Brainwashing" in China* (New York: Norton, 1961).
7. Ibid., 419. When a group's belief system is especially apocalyptic, members may be convinced to hasten the arrival of Armageddon by carrying out gruesome attacks against the outside world. That was the case on March 20, 1995, when members of the Japanese cult, Aum Shinrikyo, released lethal sarin nerve gas in the Tokyo subway system during rush hour. On an even larger scale, we can look to China under Chairman Mao Zedong in his attempt at a renewal of communist life through his coercive and cruel Cultural Revolution. The outcome was disastrous for the Chinese people. And even today, we witness countless examples of the violence inherent in apocalyptic extremism, orchestrated or inspired by single-minded groups (such as ISIS, Al Qaeda, the KKK, etc.) and/or their beliefs.
8. For a description of these themes, see Ibid., "Chapter 22," 419–37; or Janja Lalich and Madeleine Tobias, *Take Back Your Life: Recovering from Cults and Abusive Relationships* (Berkeley, CA: Hunter House, 2006), 38–9.
9. Benjamin D. Zablocki, "Hyper-Compliance in Charismatic Groups," in *Mind, Brain and Society: Toward a Neurosociology of Emotion,* Eds., David D. Franks and Thomas S. Smith (Stamford, CT: JAI Press, 1999), 287–310.
10. Leon Festinger, Henry W. Riecken, and Stanley Schachter, *When Prophecy Fails: A Social and Psychological Study of a Modern Group that Predicted the Destruction of the World* (New York: Harper Torchbook, 1964).
11. See Carol Tavris and Elliot Aronson, *Mistakes Were Made (but Not by Me): Why We Justify Foolish Beliefs, Bad Decisions, and Hurtful Acts* (New York: Mariner Books, 2015).

6

LANDING ON MARS

Finding Their Way in an Alien World

I didn't know how to talk to people. When I left the FLDS, I moved in with a foster family and I used them as my rock. They taught me how to talk, how to dress, how to be. At school I was very socially awkward. I made friends with the kids who had no friends because that is the only place I knew where to start, and I was very afraid of the kids that were more popular. I remember, just after I left, walking down the halls in junior high school and feeling like someone put a sign on my head that said, "Freak!" Everyone could see where I was from—regular clothes didn't change anything at all. You could look at me and think that maybe I was normal, but I just felt like I was broadcasting that I was from Colorado City.[1]

Samantha

Everything was different from The Family. Just the fact that I didn't have to have sex with everybody I saw, that was different. It's stupid, but it's a concept I had to learn. It really wasn't necessary to have sex with absolutely every male or female you saw.

Jessica

Some days it felt like everything surprised me, and I find it hard to make a list of things that were different, as there were so many things. I think largely I was aware of physical things like, say, being able to eat in restaurants or watch television. But what was a surprise after I left was how people related to one another. Parents loved their children to the extent that they would always put their children's needs first, and they expressed horror at the actions of my parents when I explained that my parents were not allowed to have much to do with me because I had left the Brethren. Friends expected loyalty above issues of right or wrong, which I found completely at odds with what I had grown up with.

Joseph

I grew up with people in the TM compound committing suicide and going psychotic around me. That was normalized. It wasn't until years after I'd left when I was in a graduate school study group that I learned it wasn't normal. Some people were talking about some weird things that happened to them, and I casually mentioned one kid who'd died and his skeleton was found in a cornfield. And someone got really upset and said, "Have you ever noticed that no matter what we say happened to us dramatically, Iris can always outdo us?" And literally, years and years later was the first time I realized that most people don't grow up with that high percentage of psychosis and suicides happening around them.

Iris

Landing on an Alien World

When Janja's radical political cult imploded, she was alone, penniless, and filled with a distrust of outsiders that had been hammered into her for a decade; as a result, she wasn't fully able to access the social support she needed to recover. She struggled for years, as did Karla. When Karla was seventeen, her New Age healing cult kicked her out for breaking rules and speaking her mind. She had nowhere to turn because the group had isolated itself as a way to increase group cohesion and protect themselves from outsiders; as a result, she spent many rootless years without money, a plan, or a sense of her future. All of our narrators have similar tales to tell—of losing everything and everyone they knew and landing unsteadily on the alien planet that most people know as the regular world.

For many of our narrators, leaving their groups meant leaving behind everyone (including family) and everything (including clothing and money, if they had any). After their escape, their groups excommunicated and condemned them—and, tragically, their own families followed suit and abandoned and condemned them as well. Without friends, family, money, or support, these young people struggled to make their way in a world they had been taught to view as flawed, deceitful, or even outright evil. Most of the cult survivors Janja interviewed were utterly unprepared for the outside world—many had no education, no job history, no computer skills, no understanding of finances, and no idea about how to apply for jobs, apartments, social services, or even a driver's license.[2] Many became homeless, turned to drugs, or engaged in risky behaviors and abusive relationships. Many of them contemplated suicide, and some attempted suicide. All of them felt lost, confused, and hopeless. So how did they survive? What and who supported them? And what would have helped them?

Some of our narrators managed to find church-based or social-service programs, and many slowly built a network of support. Others were lucky to find groups of ex-members of their own cult, and were able to give and receive support from people who truly understood the extent of their needs, their reactions, and their deep sense of loss, anger, fear, anxiety, grief, and confusion. Nevertheless, because most people—even people in helping professions—don't understand the unique needs of cult survivors, many of our narrators did not receive the help and support they needed. There is a serious problem here of mutual stigma and ignorance; cults often stigmatize the outside world as evil, and many try to keep their members as ignorant as possible. Yet in the supposedly tolerant outside world, cults and their members are equally stigmatized, such that most people—including counselors and social service professionals—are often deeply ignorant about cults, their members, and the true needs of survivors. In Chapter 7, we'll focus on ways that helping professionals can better understand and meet the needs of people who have escaped from abusive groups, because more and more children of cults are escaping every day.

Learning that outsiders weren't evil and that commonplace things like television and forbidden foods would not harm them was a gradual process—as was learning how to trust people. Our narrators also struggled mightily with larger issues of identity, the meaning of life, and their place in the world—and they wrestled with the damaging ways that their groups had perversely twisted purpose into unthinking commitment, love into fear, community into enslavement, and duty into toxic shame. The struggles of people who leave cultic groups are complex and lasting, even though their relief at being free is powerful.

In this chapter, we'll return to the stories of the six main narrators you met in Chapter 1: Samantha, Iris, Joseph, Jessica, Lily, and Matthew. You may recall that many of them tried to escape at least once before they finally got out. Leaving a cult is probably one of the most difficult things a person can do; leaving is almost always traumatic and painful, and it often takes people a few tries before they finally escape. Most cults threaten defectors with the loss of everything they care about, and warn them that leaving will expose them to danger, misery, or even satanic possession and death. These messages are powerful features of cultic systems of control, and they can make leaving feel like stepping off a cliff into the terrifying unknown. Leaving these controlling groups takes tremendous courage and a willingness to face an uncertain future looming with possible danger, despair, loneliness, or lifelong shame and guilt.

Along with these six main narrators, we are now introducing Rachel, who grew up in the Twelve Tribes along with Matthew, and whose story was combined with his in Chapter 1. Rachel's experience of struggling to integrate—in the outside world and within herself—provides important depth that can give helping professionals a view into the ambivalence many cult children feel about their upbringing. Her story, and the stories of all our narrators, brings awareness to a growing population of second- and third-generation cult members who are leaving their groups. Their experiences and examples provide specific information about the support they found—and the support they needed—as they struggled to adapt to a strange new world.[3]

Alienation and Loss

When someone leaves a cult, especially a very restrictive one (which was the case for most of the sixty-five individuals interviewed for this book), the sense of alienation and loss can be overwhelming. When someone leaves a cult, no matter the circumstances, it is rare for them to be allowed to maintain contact with anyone in the group—yet relationships on the outside can be alienating as well. Even if new acquaintances or coworkers know nothing about a survivor's cult past, the survivor knows, and it sets her apart. Ex-cult members experience a dual separation— both from their former friends and family and from people in the outside world —and this can create intense loneliness. There is also a powerful sense of loss— lost time, lost life experiences, lost emotional growth, and, of course, lost friends and family.

Eighty percent of the people interviewed in this study had no relationship with their group, and they used terms such as "hostile," "have been declared an enemy by the group," or "don't want one" to describe their own or the group's current attitude. Yet many missed their family members or the deep friendships they formed in the cult, especially with other children. More than half still had siblings in the group, with whom they could have no contact.

> *Joseph* **(Exclusive Brethren, EB):** I missed my family enormously, and would make up for the fact that I couldn't actually talk to them by having imaginary conversations with them in my head. I still have them now, but mostly they turn into arguments about whether I was right or wrong to leave. So I have to remind myself that it's not real, and put them out of my head again.

> *Iris* **(Transcendental Meditation, TM):** The way people on the outside treated me wasn't abusive. It was just stigma. It was stigma and being ostracized. So it was more subtle than obvious abuse. Discipline or outward abuse would be easier to identify. Plus, I didn't know how to make friends. I didn't know how to do small talk. And I'm still not very good at it. I just didn't know how to interact with people at all. There was this inner separation. I mean it clearly was inside of me. And it's still awkward for me socially. And it took me a long time, a *really* long time to make friends. Over time I think I started making friends who became a support, and made me feel that I could pick apart my life in TM. But even now, I feel that every year I become more and more socially capable and comfortable. I think it took me a long time to really feel completely comfortable in normal social group settings.

Matthew (**Twelve Tribes, 12T**): Well, I missed my parents. I missed my brothers and my sisters, and the commune wouldn't allow me to see them at all. It was forbidden for me to see them. They didn't want me to have any contact by phone or by writing to my brothers or sisters at all. They cut me off from my family completely, and that was really hard for me because I was really close with my brothers and sisters. To totally disconnect from them was a struggle. That part was difficult.

Rachel (**12T**): I felt really isolated all the time. Just very alone. I wanted to reach out, but every time I reached out, I felt like my hand was slapped away. Then, of course, I had to deal with the kids in the world who totally rejected the person I was in the community because I was different. I used these big words because the community used words differently than the world did, so even if it was the same word, it had a different meaning. So I used words kind of wrong, or the world would think I used the words wrong. So kids didn't really understand me. And of course, they were all talking about Michael Jordan, and I had no idea who Michael Jordan was. I had never even seen TV or a newspaper or heard the radio. I didn't know what country music was. So I was totally ostracized—and I was being told that everything I was was not acceptable.

Now I realize that trauma really binds people like nothing else, and I realize that's why my friendships were so deep and so committed in the community. That's still something I've never found in the world. That kind of bond, that connection; I really miss that and I miss being with people who understand me, who grew up in the same sort of environment, and so they understand all these little things that are still a little bit weird about me.

Lily (**College of Learning, COL**): If we had had a friendlier environment, an environment where my parents helped me, I could have had a chance at going to an Ivy League school. I really believe that. But they just kind of left me in COL and expected me to get good grades and do everything myself. Had my parents paved the way and said, "We'll help you," and had I had a little more direction, I would have at least had a shot. I wanted to do a lot of things. I wanted to figure skate competitively starting as a teenager. I had interests, but I wasn't allowed to have my own interests. I was only allowed to really think about Tae Yun Kim and martial arts. I think I could have had a shot, and it's affecting me now. And I'm trying to start all over, but I'm twenty-seven. You know, it's different than when you're a child and when you're a teenager and you have more of your life ahead of you. But now I'm out and my parents and the whole group, they're against me. My mom was like, "You can't call. Don't call ex-members anymore. Don't come around. You know, they're uncomfortable with you."

Samantha (**Fundamentalist Latter-Day Saints, FLDS**): It wasn't until probably my junior year in high school that I started hanging out with the more popular kids, but I still didn't feel like I could relate to them, like I could talk to them. Because they would be worrying about their clothes, their hair, and here I'm still worrying about my salvation and having troubles with my foster family. I remember one friend telling me that she wanted to kill herself because her parents had grounded her and her boyfriend had broken up with her, or something like that, and I was, like, "Oh, my God, I can't even relate." I was just in a completely different place from the people around me.

Jessica (**The Family, FAM**): I bummed around for a little bit, and I went to Belgium. And I was singing in bars in the countryside and stuff. I was going around with a couple of these musicians, and sleeping in their vans, and singing in bars for a little bit. I finally made my way to be with some others who had left The Family, and stayed with them for a while. But I was really quite lost, you know. I didn't really know what to do or anything. So I just started doing little jobs, and I panhandled a lot because it was pretty much what I knew how to do. What I didn't really want was to be a stripper. Most of the girls I knew from the group ended up being strippers. And I also did not want to work in McDonald's. Because when I left, they said I would be a failure and end up flipping burgers my whole life. So I refused to work at McDonald's. Absolutely not. I think that one reason I never told people about my childhood is . . . it's really weird, but I kind of had the sense that I'm actually an alien and my insides are blue and I landed on this planet a few years ago. And people will probably look at you with the same look when you say, "I was in a sex cult."

Beyond this shared sense of loss and alienation, our narrators dealt with multiple internal and external challenges. The indoctrination and abuse they experienced in their groups destabilized them—and the fact that they were so unprepared for the outside world strongly affected their ability to heal, move forward, and build new lives for themselves.

The Roller-Coaster Ride of the World Outside

Children of cults, for the most part, are not allowed to experience the outside world. When they leave, they often struggle to figure out how to survive, or even how to function on a daily or hourly basis. Leaving their restrictive or abusive groups is necessary; yet landing in the outside world brings countless challenges, both good and bad. Many experience a melding of their fear of the unknown and their joy at being free—and this can make their transition an emotionally intense experience. For instance, the overwhelming majority of people Janja interviewed were astonished by how nice everyone was in the outside world.

Their groups promised them that everyone outside was threatening, corrupt, and evil—yet our narrators found the opposite to be true, and many were shaken by the experience. Leaving their groups was a big push that took courage, but then they found that their courage was still needed as they encountered surprises and shocks in response to seemingly mundane aspects of the outside world.

> *Rachel* (12T): You know, we weren't allowed to have things like favorites in the community. No favorite colors, no favorite people, no favorite foods, which to kids in the world is like a staple, right? You have to pick out your favorites. So, my parents would do that with us: okay now, you have to pick out your favorite this or that. But I didn't know how. My mind didn't categorize that way and I didn't know how to pick anything, so I would just arbitrarily pick things. For example, I knew that my dad liked pineapples and he bought me pineapple lip gloss when we first left. So I said, "OK, pineapple is my favorite scent." Somebody liked the color black in my class, so I said, "Black sounds good. That will be my favorite color."

> *Joseph* (EB): I quickly realized that although I thought I didn't believe any of the Brethren's teachings, I had picked up a lot of unconscious assumptions about the way things are supposed to be from them, and these were being challenged left, right, and center every five minutes. Sometimes the sheer number of new things or weird things felt like sensory overload. It felt like a roller coaster ride: one minute on top of the world, the next in the depths. It was scary not knowing what society expected of me, and every new friend wound up getting the full story from me within about five minutes of meeting because it was easier than pretending I was "normal"! But then I had to learn how to relate "normally" to other people as an adult after I had left the group, which I found very difficult. It seemed contrary to everything I had been led to expect. For example, Brethren always have a circle of social acquaintances, as everyone within the group is expected to socialize with everyone else, and being openly unfriendly to any member would be considered a misdemeanor. Thus, there is little effort required in making or keeping friendships as compared with outside the Brethren, where it seems to me that even having something or a lot in common with someone is not enough to guarantee that they will even like you to start with! And I finally learned that people generally expect privacy, something that I often accidentally violated by asking questions that were considered inappropriate or too inquisitive.

> *Jessica* (FAM): I could eat chips! I could drink beer. It was huge just being able to go to Kmart, to make a phone call, figure out how to do that, you know, figure out how to use a computer. But honestly, at that point, I wasn't looking for any kind of comfort or anything. I hadn't come to terms with what had happened. I didn't talk about it all. I just pretended it never

happened. I just was having a good time doing stuff I always wanted to do, like wear clothes that were in style, not just communal sarongs or somebody's shoes that had been worn by twenty people already. It was just really great being able to not get smacked around for wearing earrings if they weren't the ones we were supposed to be wearing that day. I could do whatever I wanted. It was great. I could listen to music. I always got into so much trouble for listening to music in The Family. I thought that it was fantastic that I could say and do whatever I wanted when I was in my own house and in my own space. You know, the difference between that and basically having a live-in boss who also happens to sleep with you and your mom, is, is huge.

But at that point, I still had absolutely no . . . I was so stupid and naive. I still didn't know about birth control. There were still so many things I just didn't know. I'd never been to a gynecologist. I didn't even know what a gynecologist was, probably. Everything was just like, there's so much to accumulate in just a few years, just basically everything. Just even normal day-to-day things—there's just so much to learn to do. For example, straightening your hair, just simple things. Blow-drying your hair, for Christ's sake. I'd never blow-dried my hair before. I had no idea how to work a blow-dryer! I had to figure that out. It was a really big thing for me to figure out how to work a blow-dryer. I saw it in a movie, didn't know about, went and got it, read the instructions . . . this was like a whole day's worth of discovery. And eating. For example, eating cold cereal. I must have bought every single kind of cold cereal and tried a box of each on all the shelves. I had jam in my fridge—my roommate used to tease me—I had every single jam ever. Because I had never had jam before. At first it was just the stupid things, like little kids' stuff, that we were all discovering. I know all my friends tell me that they were the same way. When we first got out, it was just figuring everything out, the day-to-day stuff. Gosh. None of the girls in The Family were allowed to shave or wax or anything, so you had to figure that out, and everything else practical. And food shopping. You have to go food shopping, right? I didn't know how to food shop.

Matthew (12T): Once I started getting out, I realized I didn't have enough money and I thought I needed to work, but at the same time I wasn't really ready for work. My friend was telling me, "No, you really don't have enough references to try to get a job. You know, working in the commune is different. You're going to have to have a resume, and they're going to do a background check." So there were all these little hoops and I didn't know about any of those and I had to learn about all of this.

Our narrators dealt with many stressors as they learned how to manage in the outside world, yet each of them also had to deal with the effects of having grown up in an environment of prolonged stress and abuse. The pressures of growing up in their groups, and the ways in which cults interfere with normal development, have had long-term effects on each of them.

Emotional and Psychological Aftereffects

While each case of trauma or Post-Traumatic Stress Disorder (PTSD) must be professionally diagnosed, healing professionals agree that "the common denominator of psychological trauma is a feeling of 'intense fear, helplessness, loss of control, and threat of annihilation.'"[4] Typical symptoms include anxiety, sleeplessness, nightmares, anger, floods of feelings or no feelings, a sense of powerlessness, risky behavior, thoughts of suicide, and slipping into dissociative states. Many of these symptoms were shared by our narrators, including thoughts of suicide as well as actual attempts. Among the sixty-five people Janja interviewed, 23 percent (or fifteen individuals) were suicidal at one time or another, either while they were in the cult (six) or after they got out (nine)—for some, it was a chronic problem until they got the help they needed. Of those fifteen, four individuals (or 6 percent of the sixty-five) attempted suicide, and one had a brother in the cult who committed suicide. According to the Centers for Disease Control, the national average for suicidal ideation in the general population is 3.9 percent, while the rate for actual suicide attempts is 0.6 percent.[5] The rate for ideation in the cult survivors we studied was nearly six times higher than the national average, and their rate for suicide attempts was ten times higher. In The Family, for instance, one of Jessica's close friends committed suicide in a very public way.

> *Jessica* (**FAM**): So I decided to do an interview after Ricky died, because he was very near and dear to me, and I didn't feel like his death should be worth nothing.[6] I had so many other friends dying at that point, and I had even been hospitalized because I tried to commit suicide, because everything that I was hiding was just . . . all my emotions had been bottled up for so long, and I just pretended that I hadn't been in a group for so long. I was an absolute wreck, constantly. And it was just getting to be too much. So I decided to go on TV and talk about it. At some point, I just had to deal with it. I had to come out and say, "Yep, these things happened." And they happened to a lot of people. I started talking a while before that. I didn't come out and speak publicly, but I started talking about it a lot. I started therapy, and I started realizing that I was really a mess, and my sister was in therapy, too. She was very depressed; I was very depressed, and it started becoming a real issue for me and for her.
>
> I would have to say that right after I had my daughter is when I started really realizing—and I'm sure a lot of it was postpartum depression—but I started realizing that I was really, really sad all the time. Yeah. I think I

was about twenty years old at the time. I just started realizing that I was sad a lot. And my sister was saying, "You really need to seek some medical help," because at that point she was a sophomore in high school and she was seeing the high school counselor. And he had recommended that she be on anti-depressants. "It's really good. It helps you deal," she was telling me, "You should go see someone." But my ex-husband completely didn't believe in that kind of thing. It was like I was a drama queen. I was really very, very emotional all the time. I had a lot of problems. I was doing really well in school and work, but I was a wreck. Everybody was like, "Oh, you're doing so well," but I knew I was an absolute, absolute wreck. And we were actually having a really bad time in our marriage. I'd just never seen any marriages at all, really. I had no idea how to be married. People were married in The Family, but it wasn't what I would say a marriage is. So really in all honesty, I had no concept about sustaining long-term relationships.

Lily (COL): I started to deal with emotions; I started to get angry. You know, I was dealing with everything since I left the group, you know, living life alone, and you have old habits that you try to get rid of. For example, I discovered that I have spiritual beliefs that aren't true. Why do I think this way? It was *her* belief. It's not really true. But I still think that way sometimes. And I try to get over it. And emotionally, now, I have trust issues. And sometimes I take it to the extreme. I sort of think that everyone is trying to pull the wool over my eyes, because my whole life was a lie with her. It took me some time to realize that I don't trust anybody. It's really hard for me to develop friendships. I have friends, but when I'm making friends and they're like, "Hey let's go out," it's really awkward for me. I don't really know how to keep friends because I think I'm going to end up losing them. You know, I never really experienced close friendships as a child, and I didn't really talk to anyone. I just wanted to get out.

I was really depressed last year. I'm not a suicidal person and I would not hurt myself. But I didn't want to live last year. I would think to myself, why the hell am I not one of those people that just swallows a bottle of pills? I fought with myself: why can't I just do it? But I don't have it in me to do that. I inherently want to live. I'm a person who wants to live. But last year it got to be too much, I couldn't handle any of it. But one thing I did not do was think about going back. Never.

Rachel (12T): Out in the world that was full of evil and killers and sin, the first thing my mom did when we left—and I don't think she did it intentionally; I think she just wasn't thinking—she put me and my sister in these little short shorts. Like spandex short shorts, with these little tiny tank tops that were like belly shirts. And that was the most horrible thing that a little girl could do was wear something like that on top of being out of the Tribes, and so my sister and I just stayed balled up in a corner for days, just sure we were going to die.

I also remember when my dad left the group we had to go back to the cafe to drop off the keys. He was the manager of the cafe and so he had to drop off his keys, and there were some people there. It was at night and they were closing up. The elders heard we were there, and they came and told everybody they weren't allowed to look at us. Everybody had to look away because we were evil and they didn't want us to defile them. That was just like, it was like, yeah, that's it, we're going die. We have been tainted by the world and God has turned his back on us and any minute now the fire bolt of lightning is going to come down (laughs). That feeling stayed with me a long time. Years. I don't know, maybe still today. But the worst of it was the first year. After that, it got gradually better and better.

Joseph (EB): I was not encouraged to make the best of my abilities or interests, and I was prevented from pursuing various types of education, including tertiary education, since this is another thing they do not allow. This has had an impact on me in many ways, including, for example, lower income than I would otherwise have likely had and a loss of self-esteem as a result. I suffered from very low self-esteem generally in the months and years after I left the Brethren, but found some assistance in self-help books. However, I still frequently find it difficult to like or accept myself, and feel somehow that it is unnatural and evil to pursue one's own interests in any way, even when other instincts tell me that I should, for example, in my career.

These aftereffects didn't just affect our narrators' emotional lives; they also affected their sense of who they were, where they belonged, and what they thought and believed. For many cult survivors, identity isn't always stable and reliable; instead, their sense of self may fluctuate, and many struggle with basic issues of self-perception and personal integration.[7]

Who Was I? Who Am I? Who Will I Become?

In a cult, each member's identity is shaped by the group's indoctrination processes, and that collective identity is continually reinforced by the group's systems of control and influence. Leaving a cult, then, can challenge and destabilize a person's beliefs, values, ideas, and basic sense of self. These challenges can be intensified by lingering self-doubt, guilt, shame, and the loss of self-esteem that many people experience when they escape from abusive groups and relationships.

Joseph (EB): I was also told to believe that I was evil—the Brethren believe in the Calvinistic doctrine of original sin and in a literal heaven and hell.

So I experienced, and still sometimes experience, a strong sense of shame even in situations where I now logically know that I have done nothing wrong. I was taught to think of everything in terms of black and white or good and evil, instead of being helped to understand that there are many shades of grey and that individuals have a right to their individual conscience, and to tolerate difference in others. I still feel very uncomfortable with anyone when I know there is a difference of opinion or outlook, and now feel a lot of anxiety about unintentionally offending people with my opinions. In the Brethren, I was told what to believe about everything, important and unimportant, all the time as a child, and I was always taught that what a person believed was of the utmost importance. Thus, at times I find it difficult to express my own opinions or outlook for fear of disapproval. And I still feel considerable anxiety when I am not sure what I believe about any particular issue.

It also took me a long time to learn how to approach belief systems logically, and to be able to feel that "I don't know" is a valid answer to a question about what I think or believe, instead of being swayed by the most aggressive opinion holder or the most eloquent argument. All of this is in spite of me having been a rebellious child who questioned everything I was told.

Rachel (12T): I feel like I am who they made me to be. I don't know if that makes sense, but I felt like whoever I am at the core of me is who I was there. That was really hard for me to deal with because of the way that the world views groups like the Tribes—that they're just really awful. And all the adults in the outside would really make a point to tell me how evil it was. I think that they thought they were helping by telling me that what I had gone through was really horrible, but it had the opposite effect on me. I felt like, well, if everything that I ever knew—the only world I ever knew existed, the only life I've ever known, the only people I've ever known loved me or whom I have ever loved—are evil, then where did that leave me? Or, they said that if the community condemned and shunned me, they couldn't have loved me. So, if everybody I had ever known my whole life didn't love me, then where did that leave me? What kind of person was I? Because that was my world, and if my whole world had been evil, then I must be evil.

So I had a lot of fears about that and a lot of confusion. I felt like I either had to love them or hate them. I either had to think the community was perfect or they were awful. I didn't know how to see them as being both; and the adults in the world seemed to really be telling me, "You can't say there was anything good about them. You cannot." I didn't know how to deal with that and I thought: I know people there loved me. I know I was loved and I know that some people there were really horrible and really sadistic, but I know that not everybody there was.

I always felt this suffering in people there and in a lot of the adults. This was real pain, and pain and suffering are not the same as evil and sadistic. I knew there was a difference; but then at the same time, being raised in the community and being told that adults are always right, adults always know and children are never right—well, I didn't think I could be right. I had this huge doubt in myself, and I thought that if these adults in the outside world are telling me this, then they have to be right. There's no other way. That's just the way the world functions. That's just the way it is.

So I didn't know what to do. I knew I had to become a different person. I had a different name in the community, so when we left, my mom had me go back to my birth name, which is Rachel, and so I just thought of it that way: this is Rachel and she's a new person and I'm just going to create this whole new identity and so that's what I did. I created this whole new identity, this whole new person, and I really separated. I said, "This is who I used to be in the community and now I'm going to pretend to be this other person." And I really saw it as a mask. And I was always into making up stories. So if somebody asked me, "Where did you go to kindergarten?", I had my story all ready: "Oh, you know, we lived in Vermont and I went to kindergarten and I had this friend" or something (laughs). Or I just said I was home-schooled. So I came up with this whole separate person, and people really liked that—and I didn't know what that meant. I didn't know how to merge the two. And when anybody loved me or cared about me, I knew that they didn't, or I thought that they weren't really loving or caring about me because "me" was still the person who was in the community.

Being married has really forced me to try and merge the two finally because now I've reached the point where I'm like . . . for a while I hoped this person over here, this Rachel person, would take over and this other person would disappear, the person from the community would just disappear. But I realized that that person isn't going anywhere, because we are who we are in the first ten years of our lives, and that forms us. And even though maybe I was formed by forces that were fairly negative, I've learned that that doesn't mean I'm a bad person. I realized that this Rachel person whom I created out in the world, she was based on the person in the community. She wasn't just totally a fabricated person. Obviously, I was using parts of myself that were really the good parts of me that had been formed in the community. Learning how to merge those two people meant shedding some of the bad things that I learned in the community and holding onto some of the good things that I learned in the world.

Lily (COL): The first time I got out, it was relief. I was, like, I'm out! And it was like an adventure for me. But life kind of got, you know, I started dating and the guy was a nice, hot guy, and I'm, like, woo-hoo!

I can do anything I want! And then it got hard. You know, I felt so much relief after I left, but I'm still dealing with it. It's twenty years of my life and I'm still dealing with it. And I'm still trying to get over it. Nobody taught me how the dating world works and I learned the hard way, and I've had so many blunders. I just don't know what to expect and what role to play and it's definitely affected me in the dating world. I have a difficult time getting into relationships with men. It's led me to have a bunch of bad relationships because, let's face it, I was neglected. So I choose men who neglect me. I don't mean to, but. . . .

As each of our narrators worked to develop their post-cult selves and their new lives, they found, created, or stumbled upon supportive resources. They didn't find everything they needed, however, and only a few of them found people who understood their unique needs as cult survivors. This lack of understanding, resources, and support slowed their progress, but even so, there were bright spots in their stories.

What Was Helpful?

Our narrators found many things that helped them recover and get their feet on the ground. These included good therapy, developing friendships, going to school, and finding work. Across the board, one of the most helpful things was finding former cult member websites, discussion boards, or blogs, especially if the members were from their own cult.[8] These online groups not only help ex-members share their stories and find validation, many also gather funds and provide resources for escapees, such as housing, clothes, transportation, help applying for services, jobs, schooling, and social and emotional support.

> *Lily* (COL): One day just before I left, I found a former members' website on the Internet. Nothing happened on that website for a good year, and then one day, this girl from one of the COL groups came on and wrote, "This place is a cult and I don't like it anymore and I'm leaving," and we all went crazy and we all joined and wrote about our experiences. And that board has been going strong since. I also talked to a psychiatrist who worked with trauma victims whom I had met through the Graduate School of Psychology. The problem was that I needed an evaluation, and they were all charging me $2,000. This guy did it for $500—a very kind person. He suggested that I get therapy, but I didn't want a strictly professional relationship—I need to know that that person cares about me. Once in a while, he still checks in with me: "How are you doing? Are you doing the steps that I told you to?" It's up to me to do it, but I want a person who cares about me, and the psychiatrist I had before then wasn't caring. And I'm not up for it. I have to spend my money on it, so I want

to make sure that the person cares. And that last one, he really did care and he helped me feel better.

Jessica **(FAM):** My goal was to get an education because for me that was like giving a finger to them, because they absolutely said that education was the Devil. This was like my big revenge—to get an education. It was my goal. I was doing really well at work, and I was doing decently at home, but school was really my focus. I just really, really wanted to get an education. So I went to college and I did really well. And I studied really, really hard because, for me, if I did it any other way, then I was a failure. I had to absolutely do well because they tried to scare me: "You want to leave so bad, but when you leave, you're going to be a crack whore. That's all you're good for." And my response was, "No, I don't think so." So I got involved in a lot of stuff at school. I was made president of the International Students Club because I had been a lot of places, and I worked with all the international students quite a lot. And then I got asked to join Phi Beta Kappa. I became the chapter vice president. My daughter and I would do all the school activities together. I would take her all the time.

Iris **(TM):** I called a counselor who knew about cult stuff. I called her to get into therapy but she was preparing to go away over the holidays. It was December by the time I called her and she asked, "Are you in crisis?" And I said, "Well no. I left the group fifteen years ago and I'm holding down a job. I'm not going to fall apart. I just wanted to talk to someone, to you, when you come back" (laughing). So I went to her for a while. And the next year I deducted $3,000 from my taxes for books I had purchased on Amazon. I really studied cults and mind control and psychology. I was going into real depth to figure it out and really understand why I kept making bad decisions. I wanted to get things right. And it took a long time to get there and a lot of what helped me was reading, yes. Seeing the therapist helped. But the biggest help for me was the fact that I had developed friendships.

I made a real effort to form a friendship community for raising my children with other parents. They became my friends. And when I told them about TM, they were very accepting and made some jokes that were not offensive. They were respectful, warm jokes. And feeling that acceptance removed my own inner stigma from myself. They allowed me to feel that it was safe to start talking—whereas in the cult we learned not to talk and to keep secrets. When you leave, you still can carry that attitude of keeping secrets and being afraid of speaking. But now I found that it was okay to talk. Some people are awkward with it and don't want to be friends, but there were enough people who were totally fine with it, who just said, "You're still a good person. That's okay. You know, we all have skeletons in our closet."

Matthew (12T): There are many, many ex-members of the Tribes—people who have gotten thrown out of the cult and are on the ex-member website. There are many kids as well. We discuss and research for other people, other loved ones, and we share our stories and support each other. There are a lot of great experiences in that group and we discuss different perspectives and different beliefs that we struggle with. It's very, very interesting. I've been involved with that since I left the community eight years ago. It's really helping me.

Joseph (EB): Joining a mainstream church helped. It was a good transition from the fundamentalism and perfectionism of the Brethren. And the online group for ex-Brethren was invaluable.

Rachel (12T): We did have one former cult friend, whom my sister and I stayed very close to. He lived in a city south of us and we would ride the train down on weekends. He had left the group a year before us. We would go down on weekends and just try to catch up on all the movies, all the TV shows we had missed. We would listen to CDs to catch up with music. He really helped us so that we wouldn't be so ostracized at school. And then we would all work on our speech patterns together. For example, "Don't say that word, that's one of *those* words"—so don't say "repent," you know, instead you should say "I'm sorry." In the group it was, "I need to repent." So if we would catch each other, we would say, "No, no, no. You need to say you're sorry." We all really worked with each other and we made sure that we stayed in contact with him.

I think for me, the thing that has been the most helpful was going to college and studying, and being able to look at it in a really logical way, because nobody had ever presented what had happened to me in a logical way. It was always this really emotional thing. So to be able to go to school and study psychology and sociology, especially sociology, and really to be able to . . . you know, these academic authors write about cults and it's just this really matter-of-fact thing. It's not something that is shunned or hidden. It's just something that people are interested in and want to know more about. They don't want to know more about it because they want to make a judgment and say it's good or bad; they are just genuinely interested.

I had some professors who were really amazing. I talked about the community with them and they challenged me to write papers about it and to look at it from a different perspective. For example, what was it like for the adults? I had a psychology instructor who waived all my course work and exams for the semester if I would just write him a paper on the psychological and sociological principles that cause adults to join. And what kind of attributes does a leader have to make him a leader? How does he manipulate people? What does he do to make people stay in these kinds of environments? It was a 22-page paper, and that paper changed my life. Just being able to look at it from the adults' point of view and see it, not from their eyes emotionally, but through their eyes logically. That really, really helped me. The college community really embraced me and said, "What you went through was interesting. This gives you a great perspective on life that other people don't have. You've been given this wonderful tool, an edge." Especially because I'm going into social work, it's really going to give me an ability to empathize that other people don't have: that opportunity to have had those kinds of experiences and that real-life knowledge. So for the first time in my life I feel really accepted—all of me, not just Rachel, but the integrated person.

Our narrators found some very useful resources online and through books, groups, and schooling; however, they still struggled a great deal. As such, they had very good ideas about the resources that they and other cult survivors need to heal, reclaim their lives, and integrate themselves into the outside world.

What *Would Have* Helped?

Toward the end of each interview, Janja asked the narrators what would have helped them. One overwhelming response was to be able to find a therapist or helping professional who had familiarity with or at least some knowledge of the aftermath of life in a cult (we will focus on what helping professionals need to know in Chapter 7).

Joseph (EB): I can think of lots of things that would have been useful: counseling, or mentoring from someone who was skilled and qualified instead of from well-meaning but ignorant friends. That would seem to be the most valuable. I also think that educating the general public about what cults are like and what to expect when they meet a cult survivor would be very valuable. My experience is that most leavers do not think they need help, even when they do, and an educated layperson would be able to help them see where they need help and point them towards qualified people, which would prevent a lot of problems later on.

Rachel (12T): Probably education—really helping people learn the ropes of the world, you know. What do you need? Oh, a GED. And how is society structured? How do people in the world interact with each other? What is that about? And then, I think the most important thing is having support. Knowing that there is someone you can talk to when you're having those moments and you break down and all the pain is just too much. You know, you're thinking about what happened to you or whatever. Having somebody who really understands, not just some therapist who says, "Yeah, yeah, yeah. Now tell me how that makes you feel." You want somebody who really gets it, specifically about controlling groups like that. Exactly what does that mean and how hard it is to break those injunctions—I don't know what other word to use. They really need that place they can go to 24/7 whenever they need it.

Jessica (**FAM**): I guess my biggest suggestion for the kids who are just leaving is a few things. They need a place to go, they need a place to stay, they need help with education, and they need psychological help. I mean, as much as we all tried to deny it, all of us got to a point where we needed psychological help—it was super necessary. That would be my advice to someone. It should be one of the first things you should do is talk to someone. At least someone who can tell you you're not a complete weirdo, even if you completely feel like one (laughs).

Lily (**COL**): We all need to learn to take care of ourselves. All this time I've been struggling to take care of myself. And I mean, people are in their twenties and they're supporting themselves and making good livings—and I'm just renting a room and I need to take care of myself. If there were resources available to me . . . I'm not looking for a free ride. I just can't afford anything right now, you know. I am trying to get myself out of debt and get my life back on track. But I am genuinely interested in somebody that specializes in this. I'm interested in getting objective counseling in how to get over this and open myself up to better relationships with people.

Most of our narrators would have found it easier to get on with life if there were accessible resources to help them with practical matters: how to get a GED (most didn't even know such an option existed), how to find health care, how to write a resume, how to apply to community college or university (and what's the difference between the two?), how to learn computer programs or other skills for finding work, how to file taxes, and so on. The online guide *Starting Out in Mainstream America*[9] by clinical social worker and therapist Livia Bardin was developed to provide such resources. These resources are necessary for people who have lived in a closed and highly controlled group. For instance, one of the young women Janja interviewed spent years of work and borrowed thousands of dollars for a certificate program, only to find out afterward that the institution was not accredited and that the piece of paper she received was worthless. She didn't know how to check on the credibility of a school or program. These are the kinds of experiences we need to help survivors avoid.

Finding Success in the New World

Each of our narrators achieved something wonderful; they all struggled greatly, conquered the seemingly insurmountable, and learned how to build new lives for themselves, and in many cases, for their own children and other cult survivors as well. No one can describe the feeling of being free from cults better than the narrators themselves.

> *Joseph* (**EB**): One of the heartwarming events was that I received secret, independent communications from two or three elderly members of the Brethren indicating obliquely that they secretly agreed with me concerning the leadership and fundamentalism, and expressing their distress at the campaign to denounce me as evil. The existence of even one or two such sympathetic souls was enough to alleviate and dispel a whole mountain of vilification. I also began to relish and enjoy the good things of life that had previously been forbidden, such as literature, poetry, drama, music, and art. I found this sort of cultural enrichment a pure joy. And the friendship of the woman I later married was probably the best experience of all.

> *Matthew* (**12T**): I feel like I left the commune in peace. So I feel much different now, about my struggle, my guilt and everything, everything I held in and suppressed within myself, and the burdens I carried for all those years. A lot of different things that I had suppressed within myself—all the emotion and feelings and just the guilt and everything—I've let it all go. I just let it all go and I feel good about it now. I'm starting to go to school, I'm getting my GED, I'm getting a job and I'm just trying to do whatever I can to get this process going. So that's where I am.

> *Jessica* (**FAM**): Being able to come home and just be able to have down-time—I really, really love that. Just being able to get away and not having somebody on me constantly, watching everything I did, supervising everything. Because they didn't let us be on our own for one minute. I mean, they didn't let us stop quoting or singing or doing or reading, because then we would have time to think, or talk. Just being able to have the time to think, or to be able to say whatever the hell it is I wanted and not get in trouble for "inane babbling," which was talking about anything that was unnecessary. If you said anything at any time, like, "Hey, nice sweater" no, that was inane babbling. You never said anything that wasn't absolutely necessary. And I talk a lot now, but I've got a whole lot of catching up to do!

> *Iris* (**TM**): It's nice now to be out of the closet, really, in terms of just being able to casually say, "Yeah, I was raised in a cult," and kind of roll my eyes. And then people ask me questions. A lot of people find that very unnerving because they want to think that only unintelligent people would be involved in something like that. They don't want to think that it could possibly be them. And so to meet somebody who is functioning relatively normally, not unusual looking, not speaking unusually, someone who's not that off the wall—that's a threat to some people. A lot of mainstream society thinks that they wouldn't fall for Jonestown, they wouldn't fall for Scientology,

or anything along those lines—yet, they're reading Deepak Chopra and Eckhart Tolle and not realizing that it's exactly the same thing. You know, it's threatening. It's awkward for people to be confronted with this reality.

Samantha (**FLDS**): I'm part of the HOPE organization now—I'm the vice president. We're a resource guide for people leaving FLDS towns like Colorado City or Centennial Park. We help with resources. If you need your car registered or if you need a car, we'll try and help you find a car. Depending on what our funds are like, we'll help you with a down payment. We do registration, insurance; and we help with groceries, schooling, and other things for people leaving. We're a resource guide for them: this is what you need, this is where you go. We are the signs.

Lily (**COL**): The best part about leaving is knowing that life can't really get worse. I'm sure drastic things can happen and life could in fact get worse. I could get a disease. But that could happen while I'm in there, too. The best thing is that I have my freedom and I can do whatever I want and I can make the choices I want.

An important response from Janja's interviews with the sixty-five women and men in this study is that no matter how bad things got—and no matter how much they struggled to build new lives for themselves, every person (except one) said they never thought of going back to the cult, even in their darkest moments. For them, even the most painful moments in the outside world were better than life inside their groups.

In our final chapter, we'll explore the resilience that helped all of our narrators escape from their cults and build new lives for themselves. How could professionals or support people have helped them more skillfully? And what advice do our narrators have for people who are thinking about leaving their own abusive groups or relationships?

Notes

1. Colorado City, Arizona, and Hildale, Utah, are neighboring towns that until recently were completely controlled by the FLDS. The twin communities were known as Short Creek. The U.S. Justice Department filed a civil rights lawsuit in 2012, and the breakup of control came after a Phoenix jury found that the two towns "intentionally sabotaged people considered threats and enemies to the imprisoned FLDS prophet Warren Jeffs and his brother and surrogate, Lyle Jeffs. The jury found that the police departments followed, harassed, and intimidated nonbelievers, and that the cities denied services to new residents from outside the faith." www.latimes.com/nation/la-na-ff-polygamy-towns-makeover-20160310-story.html, accessed December 26, 2016.

2. A very helpful online guide developed by Livia Bardin, MSW, a clinical social worker and therapist who specializes in cult-related cases, entitled *Starting Out in Mainstream America* can be found at http://startingout.icsa.name/.

3. See the following for two classic studies on leaving high-control groups: Helen Rose Fuchs Ebaugh, *Becoming an Ex: The Process of Role Exit* (Chicago: University of Chicago Press, 1988); and Janet Liebman Jacobs, *Divine Disenchantment: Deconverting from New Religions* (Bloomington: Indiana University Press, 1989).

4. Judith Lewis Herman, *Trauma and Recovery* (New York: Basic Books, 1992), 33, citing N. C. Andreasen, "Posttraumatic Stress Disorder," in H. I. Kaplan and B. J. Sadock, Eds., *Comprehensive Textbook of Psychiatry*, 4th ed. (Baltimore: Williams & Wilkins, 1985), 918–24.

5. www.cdc.gov/violenceprevention/pdf/suicide-datasheet-a.pdf accessed December 27, 2016.

6. Jessica is referring to Ricky Rodriguez, the son of Family member Karen Zerby, who became the second "wife" of leader, David Berg. Nicknamed "Davidito," Ricky was considered Berg's son and was destined to lead the group to the End-Time. He was also used as the ideal model of adult-child sex education within the group. A book was published and distributed throughout the cult containing countless photographs of his adult nanny having sexual encounters with him throughout his childhood. Ricky left the cult in 2001 at age twenty-six, with much anger and resentment toward his mother, who became leader of the group after Berg's death. In January 2005, while searching for his mother, Ricky stabbed to death a former associate of his mother's and then shot himself in the head. Ricky left behind a video explaining his motives and desire to avenge the many children who were sexually and physically abused in The Family. This event was a major news story for some time, and inspired many children of the cult to speak out publicly for the first time. See www.xfamily.org/index.php/Ricky-Rodriguez and www.xfamily.org/index.php/Story-of-Davidito.

7. Louis Jolyon West and Paul R. Martin, "Pseudo-Identity and the Treatment of Personality Changes in Victims of Captivity and Cults," in *Dissociation: Clinical and Theoretical Perspectives*, Eds., Steven Jay Lynne and Judith W. Rhue (New York: Guilford Press, 1994), 269–88.

8. See Appendix C for a list of some of these websites.

9. This free guide can be downloaded at http://startingout.icsa.name/.

7

SURVIVING AND THRIVING

Trauma, Resilience, and Integration

When you decide to leave, make it definitive. Set up a good plan before you leave, a good game plan. Don't just run away and go out on the street. Set up a good plan; have a good network out there. Find one. If you have one person, find that one person and then make your support group bigger. That ties into making it definitive. Make a strong decision that you're going to get out. Get your mind clear and then stick with it.

Samantha

I can't emphasize enough to just be patient with yourself. It's going to take a long time. But don't be embarrassed!!!! This was done to you. It's nothing to be ashamed of. You might need to learn discretion about sharing of yourself, and discernment, but you don't have anything to be embarrassed about. Whatever was done to you, whatever the spectrum of abuse or manipulation, it was done to you. It was nothing you deserved. You don't have to be embarrassed about anything.

Iris

People should know that when they leave, they're going to struggle. Otherwise, they're going to go back. I would advise people to take it day by day, because that's what it is. Because you're so enthusiastic about trying to get people out that you say, "You should get out. It's great out here. There's freedom!" And what you omit is that it's also really hard. You have nightmares, you doubt your decision, you miss the people you grew up with. And you don't tell people this because you want them to get out. But it is hard. And you're going to deal with a lot of issues. But you have to deal with that, and just take it—take it—it's kind of like bankruptcy, you know. The creditors are calling you, you're drowning, you finally get out of that, and it's great! But then you start your life over and it's hard. You have to revamp your whole way of thinking, which you do when you're out. You have to revamp your whole way of thinking and start over.

Rachel

Don't be ashamed of your past. It is not your fault that you were raised in a group that has different views from the rest of society, and you may well find that the questioning process you go through when thinking about leaving has many benefits for you. In fact, it gives you some advantages over people who have never questioned the culture they were raised in (which includes most of the people you will meet). You are doing a very brave thing in questioning what is right and wrong and how to live your life—be proud of yourself.

Joseph

Trauma and Resilience

Child-development experts know that children require stable, nurturing relationships and supportive environments to grow up healthy, happy, empathic, and resilient. Our narrators grew up with almost none of these things; yet, despite all odds, they survived often-grim childhoods, escaped from bondage, rebuilt their lives, and learned how to thrive. How did our narrators perform these seeming miracles? One answer is resilience.

Resilience is a person's capacity to confront, manage, and heal from stressful and traumatic events. In his hopeful book about human resilience, psychiatrist Robert Jay Lifton introduced the concept of the "protean self," or the evolving self. Lifton writes:

Rather than collapse under these threats and pulls, the self turns out to be surprisingly resilient. It makes use of bits and pieces here and there and somehow keeps going. What may seem to be mere tactical flexibility, or just bungling along, turns out to be much more than that. We find ourselves evolving a self of many possibilities, one that has risks and pitfalls but at the same time holds out considerable promise for the human future.[1]

Our narrators' resilience in the face of their childhood traumas and their post-cult struggles speaks to Lifton's promise. Lifton equates resilience with wisdom, noting that despite childhood trauma, many of us are "able to transmute that trauma into various expressions of insight, compassion, and innovation."[2] We humans appear to have "the capacity to absorb suffering and learn from it,"[3] as evidenced by the recovering and recovered lives of the sixty-five cult survivors Janja interviewed for this book.

Researchers Steven Southwick and Dennis Charney call resilience "complex, multidimensional and dynamic in nature."[4] They studied resilience in relation to PTSD in adults, adolescents, and children. Through in-depth interviews with many highly resilient individuals (former Vietnam prisoners of war, Special Forces instructors, and civilians who endured, and even thrived, after surviving great stress and trauma), Southwick and Charney conclude that "resilience is far more than a simple psychological trait or biological phenomenon."[5] Their book, *Resilience: The Science of Mastering Life's Greatest Challenges*, provides suggestions for becoming stronger and more resilient, and ideas for tackling personal issues with proven coping techniques.

Recent studies have also increased our understanding of resilience, post-traumatic growth, and the positive psychological responses that are surprisingly common among trauma survivors. More than 300 scientific studies have focused on this phenomenon, and this combined research has found that "70 percent of trauma survivors report some positive psychological growth."[6]

The concepts of resilience and post-traumatic growth are important to understand, especially for helping professionals who may encounter cult survivors. Shelly Rosen, a relational psychotherapist who has worked with cult survivors for over thirty years, notes that labeling former cult members as pathological merely increases their guilt, shame, and isolation.[7] This stigma both isolates cult members from the outside world and gives outsiders a very limited and often incorrect view of cult members and cult survivors. Rosen notes that "if trauma from cult involvement is about loss, dissociation, boundary ruptures, and betrayal, then healing impacts growth in connection, integration, self-recovery, self-respect, and trust. Healing is also about learning how to live in a world of ambiguity and multiple relationships, including group involvement. It involves understanding layers of cultural identity and the sense of otherness that comes with a stigmatized experience."[8]

Another factor to consider in regard to cult survivors is that their experience of trauma may be quite extensive, and may lead to PTSD. Risk factors for PTSD include being exposed to sexual assault, interpersonal violence, or physical abuse; witnessing domestic or community violence; being exposed to a traumatic event that elicits extreme fear of injury or death; being victim of neglect by a caregiver; and being exposed to traumatic events that occur repeatedly over time.[9] Additionally, "individuals exposed to multiple traumatic events are also at greater risk for PTSD than those exposed to a single stressor."[10] Rosen also notes that a different form of PTSD called Complex-PTSD (or C-PTSD) may arise after prolonged and repeated trauma. She recommends that therapists with clients who have survived toxic groups or relationships read as much as possible on C-PTSD: "The dilemmas in living for those with C-PTSD can be complicated and painful, and they should be met with informed care."[11]

More research is needed to help us understand why some survivors are resistant to trauma, in that they never develop related mental health problems, while other survivors may develop short-term symptoms but recover naturally.[12] Helping professionals who work with former cult members (especially those who were born and/or raised in a cult) can help by exploring their clients' lives and family issues within the cult, connecting the survivors to social services and educational opportunities, and developing an in-depth knowledge of PTSD, C-PTSD, and effective treatment options. Research data indicates that "the most commonly endorsed interventions [are] cognitive-behavioral therapy, family therapy, and non-directive play therapy."[13] While pharmacologic issues and recommendations are beyond the scope of this book, medication for certain clients, and particularly those with PTSD, should be considered.[14] As our narrator Joseph said, "About eight years after I left the Brethren, I had a major depressive episode. I sought help from my doctor, who prescribed Prozac and referred me for cognitive behavioral therapy, which helped to process a lot of the issues I had."

Cult survivors face many complex issues and hurdles; yet, even without proper support, many find their way to health, integration, and wellness. Of course, this process can be rocky, discouraging, and frustrating—even for individuals whose resilience is high.

Impediments to Healing

Many of our narrators lamented over the fact that it was practically impossible to find a good therapist with knowledge about cults and their aftereffects. Most of the therapists they encountered didn't recognize the symptoms of PTSD or C-PTSD, and therefore couldn't meet their needs. Rachel, for example, shared her dismay and anger at how she was treated in a group therapy setting after she left Twelve Tribes:

> I remember I lived in a homeless shelter for a little while in downtown Los Angeles when I was thirteen, and they would have us all go to group therapy. And in group, everybody else was allowed to talk about what they had gone through, but the therapist in charge told me specifically, "Don't ever tell anybody what you've been through in that group. What you went through was too painful for these people to handle. It's so far out of the norm that they can't handle it. They're trying to cope with whatever pain they have, and you have way too much pain and have gone through much more than they're able to comprehend." So he said, "I just am going to ask you to please keep your mouth shut."
>
> So that's what I would do. I would go to group and I would be quiet and everybody else would talk. That made me really angry and I felt really hurt. I felt like, what is so wrong with me? You know, people were in group talking about how their parents had stabbed them, and this one boy had a scar from the top of his chest all the way down to his belly button where his dad had taken a knife and cut him open. So he had turned around

and killed his father, and he could talk about that! But I couldn't talk about where I came from. I don't know. I just felt like I was this freak of nature, like there was nobody else in the world like me. Like I was this anomaly or something.

Jessica also described some negative experiences; she sought support to explore her painful childhood in The Family, yet she received the opposite of therapeutic help:

No, no, they just pretty much looked at me like I was a bug. It took a really long time to explain and, really, honestly, I saw a couple of counselors and then I stopped because I just felt frustrated. And I thought then that it would be a huge thing to know counselors who know about cults, so we could refer our brothers and sisters who are leaving to them. That would be huge.

Because when I first started seeking counseling, the first few counselors I went to, seriously, I mean, one guy, I thought he was actually a little pervie. He kept wanting to ask me about the sex when I was a little kid. And I was like, "Oh, my God, I don't want to talk about that anymore," you know, but that's all he wanted to talk about. The first thing he said was, "So you mean you had sex when you were a little girl?" And I was like, okay, dude, whatever. I wasn't ready to be cool with that yet. And that's all he wanted to talk about. And the next, a lady, she was like, "Oh my god, I feel so sorry for you," and "You poor thing, you must be so screwed up." And I was like, "Yeah, I am." And so I started drinking a lot, and I experimented with a lot of drugs, you know, just trying them. I wasn't a drug addict or anything, but I did try everything over the next few years, here and there.

Samantha also faced hurdles after she left the FLDS and tried to assimilate into the outside world:

I had to compartmentalize things, all kinds of information. I had to compartmentalize it because it was just so overwhelming. I had so many people around me all of the time. We were really not allowed to cry as children so when I left, I was just emotionally frozen. It was very difficult for me to feel compassion for other people, to relate to their feelings, to relate to them at all, really. But especially to relate to feelings, to think that something I could say would hurt them—and I was so just frozen and had armor on (laughs). When I came out of there, I remember someone said something about my life and gave me just a genuine look of compassion. It was one of my friend's mothers whom I stayed with when I left the community, and it was the most bizarre look. You know, when you see someone give you that look, it just melts you because you know someone really cares and understands. It was the first time I had ever seen a look like that. I don't know . . . I was just frozen when I came out of there.

A young woman who was raised in The Living Word, a fundamentalist group, also mentioned the need for knowledgeable therapists:

I would have loved to have therapists that specialized in cults and a specialist in trauma. Those would have been very helpful, and the whole career issue would have been helpful, but I don't know that I could have dealt with all of it at once. But it seems like it would be good to have that option. There's so much that needs to be rebuilt. It would have been nice to have somebody point out what those things are and how to go about it. It's just so overwhelming to have it all at once.

A woman who was raised in the New Early Christian Church encountered the same difficulties:

Well, if somebody could have identified me as a cult survivor or somebody who had left a cult, or that I fit into a category there, maybe somebody would have known about the typical issues I would have to deal with, like developmental issues. I didn't know the stages of child development, normal child development. When I finally found them out, I looked at them and said, "Well, I haven't done any of these. I haven't even bonded with my parents. The only thing I know is how to do a good job." You know: take a gardening rake and rake up the garden and pick up the pile. I know how to clean the tools; I know how to do a good job, but that's all.

I don't know anything about peer friendships. I don't know anything about how to individuate, bond, and then become a separate person. I didn't know anything about that. Never dated, never made decisions on my own. Now I had to live with the consequences of my own choices. If somebody could notice that about a person who had just entered the world as an adult—well, I don't know what kind of counseling group I would have had to seek in order to find that. There's so much more available now than there was then. Even so, I don't know whether it crosses paths of people who try to make it once they've left their group.

A woman raised in Scientology (whom we refer to later in this chapter as Laura M.) spoke about not being able to recognize or understand the symptoms she had after she escaped:

I think it would have been better if I had had maybe at that particular point some kind of deprogramming. Something to help me understand that what

I was feeling and what I was going through was kind of normal. That was hard. It was hard to understand, or to deal with what I was feeling and these trances and things that I would sort of go into that were completely inappropriate in the middle of school. But I didn't really understand what was happening, and neither did anybody else. And there wasn't any counseling. There wasn't anything at that time. So I think that would have been helpful. But I don't know that the school could have provided that. I would be in class and I'd be listening to the teacher one minute and then I would feel sort of gone and then come back, and I'd realize that I hadn't been hearing what had been happening in the classroom for a while. And those were times when other kids in the classroom noticed, and they would say, like, "Oh, my God, that's the creepy girl, and look what is she doing." Those lasted for a while. I'd say right until I got into high school was the first time I had a counselor, an adult, tell me that I had been in a cult and that I was probably going to need some help to get through some of those things.

A young woman who was raised in the Hare Krishnas shared her ideas about what would have helped her:

What would have helped? Oh, anything (laughs). Oh, God, I wish I would have somehow connected with a guidance counselor, or a counselor at the school, or some teacher because I didn't feel like I really connected with any of my teachers. Somebody who could have been available—a therapist of some sort or parents. They could have been supportive. Even some literature, I think. I know if there was something I could have read, some-thing on ways to help myself, you know, ways to try to reintroduce myself. Written therapy or group therapy, people there who can help support you, who can at least say, "Try this" or "Try that." Even now, if there were some online place where you could go. Or if there are sites like that where you can go and say, "I'm having this problem" or whatnot. Any sort of support in those ways would be great.

A young woman raised in the Church of the Living Word spoke of suffering for more than a decade with intense emotions that were addressed only when she found appropriate therapy:

Frankly, I tend to feel suicidal all the time, where I feel like I'm locked into a situation and then the only option is jumping in front of a train. I have control of it, but that comes up a lot. Suicidal, where I feel locked in: there are no options and I don't know what to do. I get overwhelmed with how damaged I am, in relationships in particular. This is never going to work, I think to myself. I'm thirty-eight. It's never going to work and

I should give up on myself. And I have to cope with that. But I should say that I have been diagnosed with PTSD so I think that also adds to it. I had therapy throughout my fifteen years of being gone and I had lots of depression-focused therapy and grief and all that kind of stuff. But not until this year did I find a PTSD therapist and it changed my life.

Along with an understanding of PTSD and C-PTSD, familiarity with relational trauma can help cult survivors begin to integrate and heal. Leona Furnari, a licensed clinical social worker who has counseled cult survivors for decades, notes that family issues and trauma are linked for many of these survivors.[15]

> Treatment usually focuses on the cult experience first, and then family-of-origin issues, if there are any. In the case of those born or raised in CHDGs [closed high-demand groups] the two are inseparable and must be dealt with simultaneously. Since the trauma is relational and occurs over time, the individual may be dealing with complex PTSD, and professional help may be important for understanding and decreasing the symptoms.
>
> Healing is a process, and adaptation and integration occur over time. It is very important to remember that human beings are resilient. As one begins to experience small successes and builds a foundation of personal strengths and skills, one's sense of safety begins to expand. As one's sense of safety expands, so do self-confidence, autonomy, initiative, and identity, just as in the normal process of healthy childhood development.[16]

This resilience is a shared feature of the people you've met in this book. Though their young lives were painful and traumatizing, and their escapes were often grueling and destabilizing, our narrators found ways to rebuild their lives and reclaim their sense of themselves—even without the support they needed.

Resilience and Integration

Our narrators faced many struggles, issues, roadblocks, and difficulties on their way to healing—yet, heal they did. For instance, Jessica spoke about the discomfort she felt before she left The Family and began her road to recovery:

> I felt like I didn't exist. I felt like nothing I said mattered at all. Like I could be screaming at the top of my lungs about whatever I felt was going wrong, and what was wrong with The Family, and what needed to be changed. And it made absolutely no difference. And, you know, it was wrong. It was just . . . I didn't belong there. And I just didn't fit in with these people. I just couldn't. I just could not ever . . . I just was not happy. It was such a huge thing. I just couldn't. I didn't believe in it anymore, you know. I just didn't. It seemed like lying. All of it. It got so bizarre, and so ridiculous,

and we were so limited in everything we did. And they had no trust. Nobody trusted us with anything because they knew once we started getting out there, we realized it was all foolishness. It was just all made up. And I think that's what was so awesome to realize when I'd left . . . like I'd been so frustrated my whole life, just really frustrated, and I was stuck. And it wasn't right, and it was all ridiculousness that I was trying to fit into this group where they were telling me these things, and I just couldn't deal with it. I mean, I had tried it, and it just didn't work. And when I questioned why it didn't work, they were like "Silence." And that just did not sit well with me. I'm sorry, I'd like to be heard. And like I said, speak out and make a difference, if I can. So . . . here I am.

When our narrators left their groups, they were suddenly faced with many practical issues, certainly; yet they also had to deal with sadness, anxiety, confusion, nightmares, moments of dissociation, and a flurry of emotions. Joseph described his experiences:

I feel a lot of sadness about seven years that were spent in a way that now seems like a waste of very precious time. And I have lost a few friends over it and grown more distant with many others. But I can honestly say that I have never consciously wanted to return to the Brethren. However, the subject has often arisen in dreams. I find myself mysteriously back in the Brethren or living at home again. And in my dream I ask someone or try to remind myself what has happened. And I find the answer that I couldn't survive in the outside world and had to return shortly after leaving. At this point, I am horrified with myself. The dream sometimes ends there, or sometimes I find myself doing ridiculous or horrible things to try to force the Brethren to kick me out (such as beating my mother up), which, of course, it being a dreamworld, they refuse to do, no matter how bad my behavior is. I then wake up with lots of unwelcome emotions.

Fortunately, I have learned to deal with these now, but for many years they would influence the way I felt for the whole of the day. Like ripples on a pond after a stone is thrown in, the effects of my childhood reverberate on through my life. Am I free now of all unconscious influence from the Brethren? I would like to think so, but I feel I can never be certain.

Also, during the first few years after leaving the Brethren there was so much new and exciting that it drew my attention away from what had happened to me. Perhaps that was a good thing, as I don't think I would have been able to endure those emotions if they had erupted at that time. That's not to say that I didn't at times feel awful—I did, and sometimes for quite prolonged periods. But looking back, it feels like the kind of adrenaline reaction you get when you're under threat. I've met a number of other leavers from the group I grew up in and there seems to be a common pattern: they are very bright-eyed and excited in the first few years after leaving, and then they become saddened by the burden of a life alone in an alien culture and the feeling of guilt at leaving their family behind. Most learn to move beyond this to build a new life, fortunately.

Jessica experienced a great deal of turmoil after she left The Family, and she was justifiably skeptical of some of the counselors she met. However, she soon realized how important it was to start talking about her life in the cult:

> They always looked at me like, you poor girl, and that was it. And have some Prozac, and have some Ambien to sleep, and here's some anti-anxiety, and here's some Xanax, and . . . seek counseling, you know (chuckles). And the counselor would just basically let me talk, and then just ask me questions about my life. But I think that it was just learning to talk about it that was my therapy. What I got out of that was just the first time I really talked about it all. And when I started talking about it all, it started getting a little easier. And I started talking about it a little more freely, too. And that really helped.

Being able to talk about life in the cult has been important for many survivors— whether it's with friends, family, coworkers, or even the media. Samantha spoke about being interviewed about the FLDS:

> It's very hard, even after leaving, to speak against it, and it took me a long time. Someone interviewed me in Kalamazoo, Michigan in 1997 or '98, and that article paints Colorado City as this little utopia—only I didn't want to live there. But I couldn't speak against it because I was so afraid that that paper in little Kalamazoo, Michigan would find its way back to Colorado City, and I would be lambasted. I mean, I knew there was nothing they could do to me physically. In fact, I've heard of all the blood atonement,[17] but I have never felt threatened by that. I mean, there was only one time I was afraid of being murdered as a child, and it was the same time as that incident that's written about in *Under the Banner of Heaven*,[18] where that woman and her baby were killed. That was very talked about in Colorado City, and I was terrified. But I was so afraid to speak out about the community because of the way they talk about you when you leave, and especially if you speak out against it. Just in the last ten years, I've gone through incredible growth, an internal growth spurt of being able to see the FLDS more objectively and clearly and talk about it in real terms of what happened and what it's doing to people.

Our narrators also found education to be vital for their healing—whether it occurred on their own, with others, or with a counselor. According to Shelly

Rosen, "Psychoeducation can be the most stabilizing of all interventions."[19] That's why books, articles, and documentaries on toxic groups—and especially former-member websites—are so important. Samantha found this to be true after she left the FLDS:

> I don't know how . . . I was just frozen when I came out of there. Studying, reading. I never went to college, and when people asked me where I went to school, I say Barnes and Noble. I read a lot.

The young woman quoted earlier who grew up in Scientology and left at the age of fourteen describes some of the internal and external turmoil she went through, and the importance of having empathic people around her:

> So I felt kind of like Pippi Longstocking in a way. I felt like I was just on my own and I was going to make it. But I didn't really have any of the social skills to pull it off. And so my first year in public school was really tough. All the other kids knew that I had come from Delphi [a private Scientology school], so there were all kinds of rumors about me. This was the first time where I really felt like, God, I really want to fit in. You know, I really want to belong; it's really important to me. And over time, it got a little easier.
>
> I had a social worker who got me involved with a school counselor who had a group of kids that got together. And I'd say that counselor had a huge impact on me by recognizing that I'd come out of a cult, that I was trying to get over things from that experience, and at the same time, that I was trying to assimilate into a world that I didn't understand. I didn't have any guidance to figure out how to do that.
>
> In the midst of that, I had a father who was sort of nonexistent and a mom who was, um, not so great. So it helped me understand, I think, for the first time, what I had been through and what was going on in my life. Because, I think up until that point it was just about survival. It was just about making it through whatever experience I was getting through. And I didn't really think about how it affected me emotionally. And I didn't really understand why it was so hard for me all the time to make it, to fit in, to get along with other people, to understand what was happening around me. So, yeah, that was kind of a turning point for me.
>
> But when I graduated high school and the older I got, and I looked back on what people really did for me, that was huge, you know. And I'm extremely grateful for the people who took the time to do little things . . . to give me clothes or to give me makeup or just to cut me some slack because they understood that I didn't really know what the heck was going on. And the school counselor at the time knew of my family's situation, which didn't allow me to develop the ability to understand that feelings

are okay. That it's okay to have strong feelings. That it's not going to last forever (laughs), and that it's okay to express them. You know, I struggle with affection in a huge way. It's extremely difficult for me to be affectionate. It's very hard for me to be expressive of how I feel in any sort of consistent way. It's very, very difficult for me to be confrontational, for me to express negative emotions. I have a hard time admitting, you know, that I'm feeling sort of a negative emotion to begin with, and then to outwardly express it. I'm more of a ruminator. That's kind of my way of handling things. So, I think that's a big part of it.

I think the other part of that is something I'm just now beginning to understand, which is the impact it has on me in my hopes for the future in being a parent. I would love to have kids, but I have no idea how I'm going to do that, um, with no memories of my own parents parenting me and no real memories of my childhood. I don't know how I will respond when my kid goes through those kind of, you know, going to school for the first day and kindergarten, just everyday life. I'm petrified that I'm not going to have what it takes to give them what they need, simply because I just don't have it. I haven't experienced it in my own life. School was just something that I did because I had to. I didn't get good grades; I didn't pass a lot of courses. I think I got passed through. I think I got helped along. I think a lot of that is because people knew a little bit about me and I think that they were very empathic towards that. I also think that my counselor was a huge part of that. I'm sure he did as much as he could for me.

The traumas our narrators faced were often overwhelming, and the support they found on the outside was sporadic at best. Even though they all felt painfully lost and lonely, as we noted in Chapter 6, only one of the narrators considered going back to his group. The freedom they experienced after they escaped their toxic utopias was worth the struggle.

Advice from Our Narrators for People Who Want to Break Free

Throughout this book, we've focused on the stories of successful cult escapees. Each of them wanted and needed better support on the outside; nevertheless, even without that support, they persevered and built new lives for themselves. Their hard-won advice is useful for anyone who wants to escape from toxic groups or unhealthy relationships. (*Note:* In this section, we assign pseudonyms to some of the other narrators who share their helpful advice.)

> *Iris* (**TM**): Find whatever it is inside yourself that you're interested in. I don't care what it is, gardening, sewing, astronomy . . . and pursue that, and then

just build from there. Be slow and be patient with yourself. Just really slow. It takes years, but if you find that core part—even when you're raised in a cult, there is some core part that is individual. And that's what's calling you to leave. And if you pursue that, auto racing, I don't care what it is, you will meet other people who have the same interests, and then you can build your life from that.

Lily (COL): Basically, you need to follow your instincts. If your instincts are that this cult is right, stay. You know, because ultimately you need to be happy in life. If you love this place with all your heart and you don't feel any conflict, stay. But if you feel there's any doubt, follow your instincts, because that's what I did. And then just remember it takes time. It's not about getting out and feeling free; it's about getting out and dealing with it, step by step. For me it's been one baby step at a time. It's been really slow.

David G. (FAM): Honestly, my best advice is if you're thinking about it: leave. Do it. You know, there's a reason you've been doubting. There's a reason you've been wondering about these things all these years. There really is; it's not right. Leave. That's my advice.

Mark L. (Scientology): The biggest advice I would give would be not to give up. And not to doubt yourself. But to be careful. Because you're vulnerable and you have to have a little bit of blind hope in that whatever happens, whatever you turn to, however you get out, it's going to be better than where you're coming from. And you have to just believe that, you know. Otherwise it's really hard to get out and stay out. Because it's not easy; it's painful. And it can be lonely and scary. But if you just keep your hope that it's going to get better, and that it's going to definitely be better than where you're leaving from, then you're going to be okay. But definitely, I think it's okay to allow yourself to grieve if you need to grieve. But if you can find someone on the outside whom you feel a connection with, then trust yourself and go for it. And just hang on tight and don't give up.

Jason T. (Tradition, Family, and Property): Don't walk—run! Don't swim—dive! Get away from there as fast as you can. I mean, you're right. If you have the slightest inclination that it's what you think it is—it *is* what you think it is. I think that was a common thread through most of the children raised in groups—we had an uncanny awareness. We knew what it was, a little different from people who went into a cult and sort of got blinded into it. We knew the whole time what it was, but we didn't know how to get out. Most people would go . . . they would leave and go home, but not when your parents put you in something like this. You can't leave and go home because your parents are in it. But by any means possible, get out and find a lifeline because they're out there. There are people who are willing to help. I just hope at some point we'll be able . . . someone will be able to re-form a national organization like the Cult Awareness Network was so that people will have that lifeline. You know, I hate to think that people are finding Scientology as a result of searching for help.[20]

Granted, it's hard. But I would like nothing more than to create a huge . . . sanctuary. I hate using that word because it sounds like a trigger word, but where kids who were raised in cults could go there and just be kids again. Have play rooms, have toys, have big toys, have little toys, teach skills, have computers, have people who can teach them, train them. You know, learn life skills, learn how to balance a checkbook. Get some basic accounting principles. These are all things that can help someone survive in the real world. It's a real adjustment. I mean, my wife sees it. She finally sees it. It's taken years, but she finally sees it. She says, "It's just as if one of us was abducted by an alien spaceship and dropped in their world and now what do you do? I'm in this foreign element. How do I . . . I don't speak the language. I don't understand the customs. I don't recognize the clothes they wear." So that would probably be my biggest dream—to create something like that.

Adriana F. **(New Early Christian Church):** I'd ask, "What does your conscience say?" I left on the basis of my conscience not trusting anything that I saw there. So if a person is thinking about leaving, I think they should probably leave. If they are just thinking about leaving, give it a go. The cult wants you to stay, of course. They'll tell you the outside world is horrible or that some horrible fate will happen to you. But if there's any way to have the courage to just put that thinking on the back burner for a while and do what you think is right, just get out and think about it for a while. Then maybe some more insight will come along.

Laura M. **(Scientology):** I am 100 percent certain that whatever was innate within me to leave at that early of an age [fourteen] has been a huge part of me building character throughout my life. And recognizing that maybe I've got a little bit of a, I don't know, I wouldn't call it rebellion. I think I would just call it this independence that I'm proud of now. That bothered me for a long time, because I felt like it had created all of this damage, but by not giving in—by listening to that little voice inside myself when I was a kid, by not doubting myself even at that young of an age, believing that I was doing what I needed to do has made me in the long run be able to love myself. That's huge.

Because I look back at that now and I go (gasp), "Wow, what a brave kid! I really admire her." And then I go, "Wow, that was me" . . . because it doesn't feel like me. Feels like a really long time ago (laughs), a totally different life. But I realize that is me and I'm still proud of her. And I'm so honored to have that be a part of my life that came out the other side. And when I meet other people who have gone through all different kinds of experiences, I feel lucky that I get that. I get what it is to survive something. I love that I can bond with people about that.

But I know what it is to feel angry. I know what it is to feel sorrow. I know what it is to grieve. You know, I love being part of the human experience. I'm so grateful for that because I know that it could have been so different. I could have been totally and completely kept away from that. And that, to me, would have been the worst.

Joseph **(EB):** Be sure that you can rely on yourself and cope by yourself, at least for short periods of time—others may not understand you, and you will not receive the sort of support you have been used to in the group. Try to be open-minded, even when you are shocked or offended by the behavior of persons who do not share your beliefs or practices. If you realize that you are ignorant about something, ask a friend to explain. Be open about your past with people you meet. They will quickly realize there is something different about you, and you gain nothing by trying to hide these things, as they are part of you.

Seek help when you need it. Particularly, do not be ashamed to get counseling if you feel you are struggling, for getting prompt help may make the problem a lot easier to manage than if you struggle on for years pretending that you are big enough to cope on your own. Try to find your own moral compass rather than relying on what you are told. Be aware that life is like a journey, and you may find that your views change a great deal as you acclimatize to the new society you are in. This is not wrong or unnatural—it's a sign of great maturity to be able to admit you were wrong about something and understand why you used to feel a certain way.

Try to retain some relations with your family in the group if possible. You will miss them, and they will miss you. But don't let them manipulate you, as the group will probably try to make them do. Assert suitable boundaries for yourself in your dealings with them.

Whatever else you do, live your life with zest and make the most of it. Think of the sacrifices you have made to have this life—and make them worthwhile.

With Joseph's help, we end this book on a hopeful note. Cult members and people trapped in abusive groups and relationships can indeed escape and build new lives. They can also offer valuable insights to people who are or have been in toxic groups and relationships. The pain and struggles that our narrators experienced are real—yet, so is resilience. And so is post-traumatic growth, even in a situation where all four aspects of bounded choice are active.

In a small way, you've entered the lives of sixty-seven cult survivors (including Janja and Karla), and their stories have shown you the scope of the problem—yet they've also given you the knowledge that people can and do survive and thrive, even in the midst of toxic groups and abusive relationships. This is a promising sign; yet, as we mentioned in Chapter 1, the cults of our main narrators, Samantha, Iris, Joseph, Jessica, Lily, Matthew, and Rachel, still exist as of 2017. In those cults, and in the others you've read about, and in yet still others in the United States and around the world, there are first-, second-, third-, and fourth-generation members who are trying to escape every day.

We wrote this book not simply to share information about cults and the bounded choice framework and theory, but also to help people on the outside understand the real-life experiences of people on the inside. We want you to understand what cult survivors need: friends and family, skilled social workers and counselors, basic life skills (in many cases) and education, trauma-informed therapy, and empathy. There are resources available for people who want to escape or who need help after they have left their groups. However, these resources can be hard to find, so we've provided resource lists in the appendices.

We also wrote this book to inform helping professionals in any place where cult escapees might land—such as teen centers, churches, college counseling centers, social service agencies, homeless and domestic violence shelters, mental health facilities, and community service organizations. We want these professionals to understand and be able to meet the unique needs of survivors of cultic groups and relationships, especially those who were born or raised in a cult.

We also want survivors of these unhealthy groups and relationships to realize that they're not alone. There are more and more of us getting out every day, and we can help each other rebuild our lives—certainly with tangible support like housing and financial help, but also by simply talking, listening, and sharing our stories.

We thank our narrators for their willingness to share their pain and their triumphs, and we thank you for becoming aware of the serious effects that cultic groups and relationships have on individuals, families, communities, and our world. We end with a helpful reminder about your rights as an individual—and as a member of a group.

Your Personal Bill of Rights

For many individuals in cults or abusive relationships, personal rights do not exist. A key part of their healing comes from learning that they are valuable individuals with unique voices, emotions, ideas, opinions, and rights. Janja created the list below to help escapees from cults and abusive relationships learn about their rights; yet it's important for all of us to be reminded of them from time to time.

If you are not yet familiar with your personal rights, you may want to read this list daily until you are aware of your rights and can assert them. It may also be helpful to post a copy of this list where you can see it regularly.

1. I have a right to ask for what I want.
2. I have a right to say no to requests or demands that I cannot meet.
3. I have a right to express all of my feelings—positive and negative.
4. I have a right to change my mind.
5. I have a right to make mistakes and do not have to be perfect.
6. I have a right to follow my own values and beliefs.
7. I have the right to say "no" to anything if I feel that I am not ready, if it is unsafe, or if it conflicts with my values.
8. I have the right to determine my own priorities.
9. I have the right not to be responsible for the actions, feelings, or behavior of others.
10. I have the right to expect honesty from others.
11. I have the right to be angry at someone I love.
12. I have the right to be myself . . . to be unique.
13. I have the right to express fear.
14. I have the right to say, "I don't know."
15. I have the right not to give excuses or reasons for my behavior.
16. I have the right to make decisions based on my feelings, knowledge, and/or life experiences.
17. I have the right to my own personal space and time.
18. I have the right to be playful.
19. I have the right to be healthy and perhaps even healthier than those around me.
20. I have the right to make friends and be comfortable around people.
21. I have the right to feel safe, and to be in a non-abusive environment.
22. I have the right to change and grow.
23. I have the right to have my wants and needs respected by others.
24. I have the right to be treated with dignity and respect.
25. I have the right to be happy.

Notes

1. Robert Jay Lifton, *The Protean Self: Human Resistance in an Age of Fragmentation* (Chicago: University of Chicago Press, 1993), 1–2.
2. Ibid., 7.
3. Ibid., 217.
4. Steven M. Southwick and Dennis S. Charney, *Resilience: The Science of Mastering Life's Greatest Challenges* (New York: Cambridge University Press, 2015), 7.
5. Ibid., 8–9.
6. Carolyn Gregoire, "The Surprising Benefit of Going Through Hard Times," *The Huffington Post*. January 6, 2016. Accessed January 5, 2017, www.huffingtonpost. com/entry/post-traumatic-growth-creativity_us_568426c0e4b014efe0d9d8e8.
7. Shelly Rosen, "Cults: A Natural Disaster: Looking at Cults Through a Trauma Lens," *International Cultic Studies Journal*, no. 5 (2014): 12–29.
8. Ibid., 17.

9. Daniel W. Smith, Michael R. McCart, and Benjamin E. Saunders, "PTSD in Children and Adolescents: Risk Factors and Treatment Innovations," in *The Psychobiology of Trauma and Resilience Across the Lifespan*, Ed., Douglas L. Delahanty (Lanham, MD: Jason Aronson/Rowman & Littlefield, 2008), 69–72.

10. Ibid., 71.

11. Rosen, "Cults: A Natural Disaster," 20.

12. Smith, McCart, and Saunders, "PTSD in Children and Adolescents," 70.

13. Ibid., 78.

14. See Douglas L. Delahanty and Sarah A. Ostrowski, "Recent Advances in the Pharmacological Treatment/Prevention of PTSD," in Delahanty, Ed., *The Psychobiology of Trauma*, 233–54.

15. Leona Furnari, "Born or Raised in High-Demand Groups: Developmental Considerations," *ICSA e-Newsletter* 4, no. 3 (2005). Accessed January 5, 2017, www.icsahome.com/articles/born-or-raised-funari-en4–4.

16. Ibid.

17. Blood atonement is a form of human sacrifice that early Mormons practiced on people who were considered to have sinned so heinously that the blood of Christ could not heal them. These unforgivable sins included interracial marriage, adultery, murder, theft, and apostasy. The mainstream Mormon church no longer supports blood atonement, but some offshoot Mormon sects do. In those sects, apostasy is still one of the most heinous sins.

18. Jon Krakauer, *Under the Banner of Heaven: A Story of Violent Faith* (New York: Anchor Books, 2004).

19. Rosen, "Cults: A Natural Disaster," 22.

20. The Cult Awareness Network (CAN) was an informational resource for families and former cult members for many years. CAN was founded in 1978, headquartered in Chicago, and CAN affiliates operated in some cities around the country. CAN also organized yearly public conferences. After years of non-stop litigation brought by Scientology and Landmark Education, CAN finally went under in 1996. During bankruptcy proceedings, CAN's assets (including all of its files on cults, which included personal information on many inquirers), its name, and its phone number were auctioned and bought by Scientology and a few other organizations. This was a devastating blow to the public's ability to easily access information on many controversial groups and created a lack of networking opportunities for people who are affected by (or interested in studying) cults.

APPENDIX A

Research Methodology

This book is based on research conducted by coauthor Dr. Janja Lalich, while she was a sociology professor at California State University, Chico. The project was entitled, "On Our Own: How Children of Cults Manage in the 'Outside World,'" and was approved by Chico State's Institutional Review Board. As far as we know, this was the first in-depth research of its kind. The purpose of the study was to explore attitudes, experiences, coping mechanisms, and issues related to societal integration of young people leaving a cultic group and entering mainstream society. A grounded theory approach was used with some document analysis and primarily semi-structured interviews of subjects located through snowball technique.

The subject population was individuals who were born and/or raised in a cult and who left the group on their own—that is, without any inside or outside assistance, an intervention, and so on. These individuals are sometimes referred to as "second-generation" cult members (although some of the participants in this research were third generation) and most don't like that moniker, as they feel they did not choose to be members. They could perhaps be called "adult children of cults," which is the term Dr. Lalich prefers to use.

In most cases, subjects were contacted by e-mail or telephone, and in some cases, in person. Once a subject was identified, he or she was briefly interviewed by telephone to determine whether the requirements of the study were met. During this initial call, an Interviewee Contact Form was filled out that included name, contact information, name of group born or raised in, years in the group, and age when left the group. If the person verbally agreed to the interview, then she or he was sent an Informed Consent Form to sign and send back, as well as a basic demographic questionnaire (age, sex, name of group, years in group, family size, relations with parents and/or siblings, education, how left, marital status, current employment, and so on). Once these documents were returned, an appointment was made for an interview.

Subject interviews were done by telephone or in person. Interviews were semi-structured to allow the person to speak fully. As the researcher, Dr. Lalich used an Interview Guide to ensure covering all desired areas of interest for the research (see Attachment 1). The questions were not necessarily asked or answered in the order they appear in the document. The average length of the interviews was two hours, and all interviews were audio-recorded. Dr. Lalich also took notes during the interviews and immediately afterward. Seven interviews were completed in writing by the subjects who lived abroad and if we were unable to arrange a phone call. Data from these written documents were treated the same as data from the telephone or in-person interviews.

Subjects' confidentiality was preserved in that their identities, as well as other identifying characteristics, were kept in confidence. Subjects were not identified in any report, article, presentation, or publication. Even though several subjects preferred that their real names be used in any publications, subjects' anonymity was preserved through the use of pseudonyms and changing other identifying data, such as nationality, location, and so on. A code key was used to link each interview to the original. During the course of the research, data was kept in a locked file cabinet, and will be destroyed five years after publication of this book.

Sixty-five individuals were interviewed, and they were born and/or raised in thirty-nine different groups that represented a range from Christian fundamentalist to New Age eclectic to political to Eastern meditation to hippie communal. The data from the questionnaires was entered in SPSS by an undergraduate research assistant in the Sociology Department. The interviewees consisted of 50 females, 13 males, 1 transgendered male, and 1 F-T-M transsexual. The number of years spent in the group ranged from 7 to 41 years. Their ages at the time of the interview ranged from 21 to 68.

The audiotapes of the interviews were transcribed by undergraduate research assistants in the Sociology Department, using HyperTranscribe, Express Scribe, and Jodix software. These transcripts were then printed out and hand-coded by Dr. Lalich and a research assistant with a B.A. in Sociology. Two sets of codes were developed for themes that emerged from the interviews. The codes pertained to while the subject was in the cult and after the subject had left the cult. Occasionally new codes were added as the coding progressed.[1]

Once all the interviews were coded, the data were analyzed using Dr. Lalich's bounded-choice theory, as set out in her book, *Bounded Choice: True Believers and Charismatic Cults* (Berkeley: University of California Press, 2004), as well as incorporating theories on attachment, trauma, post-traumatic stress disorder, and resilience.

ATTACHMENT 1

Interview Guide

1. What is the name of the group you were born or raised in? Please describe it for me *briefly*—what type of group, when it was founded, the leader, the size.
2. Did your parents join together or meet in the group?
3. What was your childhood like? If possible, describe this in different age ranges—earliest memories, childhood, middle years, teen years, and so on. Describe where you lived and what your daily life was like. Did you live in the same place with your parents and/or siblings? Did you have friends who were not in the group?
4. Describe how you think the group structure/norms/belief system had an impact on you as a child/adolescent.
5. Were you part of an indoctrination program? Was any part of it especially geared toward children?
6. Tell me as much as you'd like about how you left the group. If that took place over a period of time, please explain.
7. What caused you to leave? How did that come about?
8. What were crucial factors in your decision to leave?
9. Did you leave alone or with others?
10. Where did you go at first? What did it feel like to not be with the group anymore?
11. Whom did you go to for support?
12. What support/aid did you have?
13. What resources were available?
14. What resources would you have liked?
15. Did you, or do you, ever think about going back to the group? What are your thoughts at those times?
16. What, in your opinion, are some positive things about the group experience?
17. Some negatives about the group experience?
18. Describe your relationship with your parents—then and now.
19. Describe your relationship with your siblings or other relatives in the group—then and now.
20. Describe your relationship with the group—then and now.
21. Describe your relationship with the group leader—then and now.
22. There may have been different leaders at different times, or various leaders at different levels who were influential in your life. Please describe that.
23. When you first left the group, did you have contact with other former members?
24. What was new or different about mainstream society from how you grew up? What, if anything, surprised you?

25. On a scale of 1 to 10, how integrated do you feel into regular society? Please explain.
26. What were your best experiences after you left the group?
27. What were you worst experiences?
28. What advice would you give to a young person thinking about leaving a group that he or she was born or raised in?

Note

1. This data were also used in a study for a Master's Degree in Social Science in California State University, Chico, by Susan Latta, who had been raised in a cult. Her thesis, "Adult Children of Cults: The Experiences of Individuals Born and Raised in a Cult as They Transition into Mainstream Society," can be found at http://csuchico-dspace.calstate.edu/bitstream/handle/10211.4/365/Final%20-%20Susan%20Latta. pdf?sequence=1. Dr. Lalich was the Chair of Latta's Thesis Committee.

APPENDIX B

Print and Multi-Media Resources

Useful Books

Bardin, Livia. *Starting Out in Mainstream America*. N.p. N.d. http://startingout.icsa.name/.

Cialdini, Robert B. *Influence: The Psychology of Persuasion*. New York: Harper Business, 2006.

Herman, Judith Lewis. *Trauma and Recovery*. New York: BasicBooks, 1992.

Lalich, Janja, *Bounded Choice: True Believers and Charismatic Cults*. Berkeley: University of California Press, 2004.

Lalich, Janja, Ed. "Women Under the Influence: A Study of Women's Lives in Totalist Groups (Special Issue)." *Cultic Studies Journal* 14, no. 1 (1997).

Lalich, Janja, and Karla McLaren. "Inside and Outcast: Multifaceted Stigma and Redemption in the Lives of Gay and Lesbian Jehovah's Witnesses." *Journal of Homosexuality* 57, no. 10 (2010): 1303–1333.

Lalich, Janja, and Madeleine Tobias. *Take Back Your Life: Recovering from Cults and Abusive Relationships*. Berkeley, CA: Bay Tree, 2006.

McLaren, Karla. *The Language of Emotions*. Boulder, CO: Sounds True, 2010.

McLaren, Karla. *The Art of Empathy: A Complete Guide to Life's Most Essential Skill*. Boulder, CO: Sounds True, 2013.

Shaw, Daniel. *Traumatic Narcissism: Relational Systems of Subjugation*. New York: Routledge, 2014.

Singer, Margaret Thaler, with Janja Lalich. *Cults in Our Midst: The Hidden Menace in Our Everyday Lives*. San Francisco, CA: Jossey-Bass, 1995.

Singer, Margaret Thaler, and Janja Lalich. *"Crazy" Therapies: What Are They? Do They Work?* San Francisco: Jossey-Bass, 1996.

Tavris, Carol and Elliot Aronson. *Mistakes Were Made (but Not by Me): Why We Justify Foolish Beliefs, Bad Decisions, and Hurtful Acts*. New York: Mariner Books, 2015.

Tourish, Dennis. *The Dark Side of Transformational Leadership: A Critical Perspective*. New York: Routledge, 2013.

Workbooks

Allen, Roberta. *The Playful Way to Knowing Yourself: A Creative Workbook to Inspire Self-Discovery*. New York: Houghton Mifflin, 2003.

Kalior, Susan D. *Growing Wings Self-Discovery Workbook*. Tualatin, OR: Blue Wing, 2008.

Marra, Thomas. *Depressed & Anxious: The Dialectical Behavior Therapy Workbook for Overcoming Depression and Anxiety*. Oakland, CA: New Harbinger, 2004.

Rosenbloom, Dena, and Mary Beth Williams. *Life after Trauma: A Workbook for Healing*, 2nd ed. New York: Guilford Press, 2010.

Williams, Mary Beth, and Soili Poijula. *The PTSD Workbook: Simple, Effective Techniques for Overcoming Traumatic Stress Symptoms*. Oakland, CA: New Harbinger, 2002.

Memoirs by Adult Children of Cults

Allred-Solomon, Dorothy. *Daughter of the Saints: Growing Up in Polygamy*. (New York: Norton, 2004.) A memoir of life in a polygamous Mormon fundamentalist cult, and in the family of the leader and naturopathic physician, Rulon C. Allred. The author describes fleeing raids, the assassination of her father by a rival group, and leaving the group over ideological differences.

Arkin, Cassidy Elizabeth. *Little Brown Girl*. (N.p.: Cassidy Elizabeth Productions.) 2015. The author describes her and her mother's experiences reintegrating into mainstream society after living in the Marin County, California, utopian community of Synanon.

Barlow, Kate. *Abode of Love: Growing Up in a Messianic Cult*. (Fredericton, New Brunswick, Canada: Goose Lane Editions, 2006.) Barlow describes her childhood living with her mother, sisters, and twenty women inside the Agapemone, a religious cult led by a man claiming to be the reincarnation of Jesus Christ. Her family is involved in a scandal as her grandfather, the group's founder, takes on "spiritual" brides.

Buhring, Juliana. *This Road I Ride: Sometimes It Takes Losing Everything to Find Yourself*. (New York: Norton, 2016.) A Children of God survivor tells her story of becoming the fastest woman to cycle around the world and reclaiming her life in the process.

Coburn, William. *The Spanking Room*. (Enumclaw, WA: Wine Press, 2008.) An account of the author's abusive childhood in the Jehovah's Witnesses.

Connolly, Ray. *Something Somebody Stole*. (Charleston, SC: CreateSpace Independent Publishing Platform, 2011.) The author's account of his recruitment and twenty-year experience in the Children of God, having parented seventeen children with two women. He discusses notions of self-responsibility, recovery, and the difficulties of leaving the group.

Dugard, Jaycee. *A Stolen Life: A Memoir*. (New York: Simon & Schuster, 2011.) This memoir tells the story of the author's kidnapping in 1991, and her nearly twenty years in captivity as well as her survival and the reclaiming of her life.

Dugard, Jaycee. *Freedom: My Book of Firsts*. (New York: Simon & Schuster, 2016.) The author describes her experience upon gaining her freedom and the many things she did not believe she would do in her life.

Edge, Charlene L. *Undertow: My Escape from the Fundamentalism and Cult Control of The Way International*. (Winter Park, FL: New Wings Press, 2017.) The author describes her teenage recruitment into The Way International, one of the largest cults in the United States, and her seventeen years moving through the ranks of the organization. This memoir highlights the manipulative tactics of the group's leader as well as the author's recognition of the need to escape.

Feldman, Deborah. *Unorthodox: The Scandalous Rejection of My Hasidic Roots.* (New York: Simon & Schuster, 2012.) This is a memoir of the author's youth in and escape from the Satmar sect of Hasidic Judaism, where she found herself in an unhealthy arranged marriage as a teen and forced to live under oppressively strict rules.

Garrett, Ruth Irene. *Crossing Over: One Woman's Escape from Amish Life.* (San Francisco: HarperOne, 2003.) This is a memoir of a member of an Old Order Amish community in Iowa, who recounts the strict traditionalism of the group and her eventual escape from her family and her way of life.

Gingerich, Emma. *Runaway Amish Girl: The Great Escape.* (N.p.: Progressive Rising Press, 2014.) The author's account of her childhood in an Amish community and her eventual escape, which sent her family and friends into turmoil.

Griffin, Misty Elaine. *Tears of the Silenced: A True Crime and an American Tragedy; Severe Child Abuse and Leaving the Amish.* (Charleston, SC: CreateSpace Independent Publishing Platform, 2014.) The author describes her childhood in an abusive Amish sect, the sexual assault that resulted in her escape, and the shock of entering the outside world with minimal education and few resources.

Guest, Tim. *My Life in Orange.* (London: Granta Books, 2004.) An account of the author's experiences growing up in a commune based on the teachings of guru Bhagwan Shree Rajneesh, and the solitude faced as the child of a devoted member of the Sannyasin.

Hoffman, Claire. *Greetings from Utopia Park: Surviving a Transcendent Childhood.* (New York: Harper, 2016.) The author's account of her childhood inside a Transcendental Meditation community in the 1980s and '90s.

Jeffs, Brent W. *Lost Boy.* (New York: Broadway Books, 2009.) The nephew of Warren Jeffs, leader of the Fundamentalist Church of Jesus Christ of the Latter-Day Saints (FLDS), describes his experiences growing up on his uncle's compound and the threatening attitude toward and sexual abuse of young boys in the cult. He describes his choice to leave and the struggle of adjusting to another way of life.

Jessop, Carolyn. *Escape.* (New York: Broadway Books, 2007.) The author describes her life born into the Fundamentalist Church of Jesus Christ of Latter-Day Saints (FLDS), as well as her oppressive polygamous marriage and risky escape with her children.

Jessop, Carolyn, and Laura Palmer. *Triumph: Life After the Cult—A Survivor's Lessons.* (New York: Three Rivers Press, 2011.) An account of Jessop's escape with her children from the FLDS cult, as well as the raid on its Yearning for Zion Ranch, followed by the public trial of leader Warren Jeffs.

Jessop, Flora, and Paul T. Brown. *Church of Lies.* (San Francisco: Jossey-Bass, 2009.) Jessop's account of her childhood of emotional, physical, and sexual abuse inside the polygamous FLDS cult and her attempted escapes. She also discusses her efforts to help other women and children flee similar circumstances.

Jones, Kristina, Celeste Jones, and Juliana Buhring. *Not Without My Sister: The True Story of Three Girls Violated and Betrayed.* (London: Harper Element, 2007.) Three sisters describe their sexually abusive childhoods in the Children of God as well as their three respective escapes and the aftermath of their experiences.

Kelly, Richard E. *Growing Up in Mama's Club.* (N.p.: Richard Kelly, 2008.) The author describes a childhood full of emotional and religious abuse deep inside the Jehovah's Witnesses.

Kelly, Richard E. *The Ghosts from Mama's Club.* (Tucson: Parker Ridge, 2012.) In this sequel to *Growing Up in Mama's Club*, the author tells the story of his escape from the Jehovah's Witnesses.

Kirkby, Mary-Ann. *I Am Hutterite.* (Nashville: Thomas Nelson, 2010.) A look at the life of a Canadian Hutterite family that leaves their colony under dire circumstances, and their struggle to integrate into mainstream society.

Kocsis, Vennie. *Cult Child.* (Tacoma, WA: Angela "Vennie" Kocsis, 2014.) A first-person telling of the author's abusive experience in the fundamentalist cult, Sam Fife's Move of God. The author describes moving around the country with her family, and the leader's violent teachings.

Lee, Brenda. *Out of the Cocoon: A Young Woman's Courageous Flight from the Grip of a Religious Cult.* (Bandon, OR: Robert D. Reed Publishers, 2006.) A memoir and self-help guide based on the author's abusive childhood in the Jehovah's Witnesses, the loss of her family upon leaving, and her personal growth outside of the cult.

Miscavige-Hill, Jenna, and Lisa Pulitzer. *Beyond Belief: My Secret Life Inside Scientology and My Harrowing Escape.* (New York: William Morrow, 2013.) A now-critic of Scientology describes her childhood as the niece of Church of Scientology leader, David Miscavige, her position in the church's highest ministry, and the loss of her family upon leaving.

Musser, Rebecca. *The Witness Wore Red: The 19th Wife Who Brought Polygamous Cult Leaders to Justice.* (New York: Grand Central Publishing, 2014.) The author's account of her upbringing in a polygamous family, her abusive marriage as the nineteenth wife to the FLDS prophet, and her participation in the trial to bring down her former group's leader, Warren Jeffs.

Palmer, Debbie, and Dave Perrin. *Keep Sweet: Children of Polygamy.* (N.p.: Dave's Press, 2004.) Palmer describes her childhood and thirty-three years in the abusive polygamous Mormon fundamentalist community of Bountiful, British Columbia.

Pena, Theresa. *Run.* (Charleston, SC: CreateSpace Independent Publishing Platform, 2013.) A novel based on the true events of a teenage girl's fleeing from a harsh and corrupt drug rehab facility and the aftermath of her escape.

Perks, Micah. *Pagan Time: An American Childhood.* (Washington DC: Counterpoint, 2001.) An account of the author's childhood in a New Age mountain community built by her parents for troubled teens in the 1960s.

Peterson, Grace. *Reaching: A Memoir.* (N.p.: All Things That Matter Press, 2013.) A telling of the author's abusive childhood, followed by a brainwashing relationship with a Luciferian New World Order cult leader and her eventual steps toward recovery.

Powers, Carla. *Matches in the Gas Tank: Trial by Fire in the Armstrong Cult.* (Houston: Bright Sky Press, 2009.) Powers tells the story of her childhood in the Radio Church of God, which included harsh restrictions, arranged marriages, and deprivation. She flees the group and finds great success on the outside.

Prophet, Erin. *Prophet's Daughter: My Life with Elizabeth Clare Prophet Inside the Church Universal and Triumphant.* (Guilford, CT: Lyons Press, 2008.) The author describes growing up in her mother's End-Times cult, and having to reassess her life, her beliefs, and her relationship with her mother as her mother's prophesies repeatedly fail.

Richmond, Ivan. *Silence and Noise: Growing Up Zen in America.* (New York: Atria Books, 2003.) The author describes his childhood living in silence in a Zen Buddhist monastery with his family in Northern California, followed by his family's leaving in the early 1980s and his acclimation to mainstream society.

Rugullies, Christine. *Caryatid: Memoir of Life in a Religious Cult.* (Brooklyn: Long Dash, 2008.) A memoir of the author's thirty-three years in a Christian cult in mid-century America, written over the course of twenty-five years.

Sand, Marlowe. *Paradise and Promises*. (N.p.: O-Books, 2015.) The author's recollection of her recruitment and fifteen years of experience as a student of guru Andrew Cohen, a self-professed radical Buddha.

Sayrafiezadeh, Saïd. *When Skateboards Will Be Free*. (New York: Dial Press, 2010.) Growing up in the Socialist Workers Party, the author's memoir discusses negotiating his Iranian-Jewish heritage as well as the instability of childhood in the midst of the cult's preparations for the revolution that never was to come.

Schmidt, Susan. *Favorite Wife: Escape from Polygamy*. (New York: Lyons Press, 2009.) The author tells the story of her upbringing in a polygamous Mormon cult (in which nearly two dozen people are killed), and her eventual escape.

Spencer, Irene. *Shattered Dreams: My Life as a Polygamist's Wife*. (N.p.: Central Street, 2007.) The author describes her experience in a polygamous marriage and the fundamentalist Mormon village of Short Creek, Arizona. The village is raided, and she and her family flee to the Mexican desert.

Spencer, Irene. *Cult Insanity: A Memoir of Polygamy, Prophets, and Blood Atonement*. (N.p.: Central Street, 2009.) The author's experience being raised in polygamy is described in this account of her life of abuse and a polygamous marriage in a cult in which her brother-in-law proclaimed himself to be a prophet and murdered any who questioned his authority.

Tamm, Jayanti. *Cartwheels in a Sari: A Memoir of Growing Up in a Cult*. (New York: Harmony Books, 2009.) The author describes her childhood as the "Chosen One" in the widely popular cult of guru Sri Chinmoy. She discusses her relationship with the guru, her appointed path to enlightenment, and her decision to leave.

Tate, Sonsyrea. *Little X: Growing Up in the Nation of Islam*. (San Francisco: HarperSan Francisco, 1997.) The author shares her experiences as a girl growing up in this radical and mysterious group, shedding light on the contradictions of life in the group, and bringing new insights to its controversial leaders.

Taylor, Kim. *Daughters of Zion: A Family's Conversion to Polygamy*. (Grants Pass, OR: Rogue Hill, 2008.) Taylor tells the story of her childhood as she is uprooted from Utah to live in a Mormon polygamous colony in Mexico. She describes her experiences being courted for plural marriage and the violence that ensued in her colony.

Wagler, Ira. *Growing Up Amish: A Memoir*. (Carol Stream, IL: Tyndale House, 2011.) Wagler describes his childhood in an Amish settlement in Iowa and his decision to leave upon entering adulthood.

Walker, Jerald. *The World in Flames: A Black Boyhood in a White Supremacist Doomsday Cult*. (Boston: Beacon Press, 2016.) Walker describes his childhood in the 1970s with two blind parents and six siblings in Herbert W. Armstrong's Worldwide Church of God. He details the group's strict rules regarding medicine and the belief in members being the chosen people as well as the group's failed apocalyptic prophecy of the Great Tribulation.

Wall, Elissa, and Lisa Pulitzer. *Stolen Innocence: My Story of Growing Up in a Polygamous Sect, Becoming a Teenage Bride, and Breaking Free of Warren Jeffs*. (New York: Harper, 2009.) A memoir by a young woman born into the Fundamentalist Church of the Latter-Day Saints (FLDS) and her experience providing testimony to aid in the conviction of cult leader, Warren Jeffs.

Walsh, Mikey. *Gypsy Boy: My Life in the Secret World of the Romany Gypsies*. (New York: Thomas Dunne, 2009.) A memoir of a young boy's unconventional childhood and upbringing in a Romany Gypsy community. As he grows up, he must decide whether to stay in the secretive group or escape.

Wariner, Ruth. *The Sound of Gravel: A Memoir.* (London: Flatiron, 2016.) Wariner describes her childhood as one of forty-two children growing up in rural Mexico in a polygamous family. Upon the death of her father, she and her siblings live in poverty between Mexico and the United States.

Wilson, Barbara. *Blue Windows: A Christian Science Childhood.* (New York: Picador, 1997.) The author's account of life in a Christian Science family, in which she watches her mother fatally refuse treatment for breast cancer as a result of religious doctrine.

Documentaries, Films, and Television Series

Aaron Bacon. Directed by Nick Gaglia. New York, NY: Justice Films, 2010.

Children of God: Lost and Found. Directed by Noah Thomson. New York, NY: HBO Films, 2007.

Cult Witness. Directed by Samuel Stefan and Nick Oakley. Gwatt, Switzerland: Arthio Productions, 2010.

Dangerous Persuasions. "Revolution Isn't a Tea Party." Season 2, Episode 6. Directed by Peter Norry. Discovery Channel, May 20 2015. Available on YouTube.

God Willing. Directed by Evangeline Griego. Los Angeles, CA: About Time Productions, 2010.

Going Clear: Scientology, Hollywood, and the Prison of Belief. Directed by Alex Gibney. New York, NY: HBO Films, 2015.

Holy Hell. Directed by Will Allen. New York, NY: FilmRise, 2016.

I Escaped a Cult. Directed by Sally Howell. Washington, DC: National Geographic Society, 2012.

Inside a Cult. Directed by Ben Anthony. Washington, DC: National Geographic Society, 2008.

Jesus Camp. Directed by Rachel Grady and Heidi E. Ewing. Los Angeles, CA: Magnolia Home Entertainment, 2006.

Scientology: The Aftermath. Directed by Erin Gamble, Rachelle Mendez, and Eli Holzman. New York, NY: A & E Television Networks, 2016 and 2017.

The Devil's Playground. Directed by Lucy Walker. New York, NY: HBO Films, 2002.

The Devil's Trap. Directed by Mitchell Stafiej. Montreal, Canada: Parabola Films, 2016.

APPENDIX C

Cult Information and Resource Websites

Specific Cultic Groups and Churches

International Churches of Christ/International Christian Church/Sold Out Discipling Movement

Reveal.org—Nonprofit organization of former members of the International Churches of Christ (ICoC), the International Christian Church (ICC)/Sold Out Discipling Movement/Boston Church of Christ/"Boston Movement," and Crossroads Church of Christ/"Crossroads Movement." www.reveal.org

Jehovah's Witnesses/Watchtower Society

AAWA.co—Advocates for Awareness of Watchtower Abuses offers support for people who have been negatively affected by involvement with Watchtower teachings and practices. http://aawa.co/

FreeMinds.org—A nonprofit organization keeping a critical eye on the Watchtower/Jehovah's Witnesses. Includes information on recruiting techniques used by other groups. Includes current news, ways to avoid recruitment by cults, an online store to purchase its materials, plus information on legal issues, women's issues, and more. Information available in several languages. www.freeminds.org

Gayxjw.org—An organization that offers a worldwide support network for gay, lesbian, bisexual, and transgender individuals who were, or still are, associated with Jehovah's Witnesses. http://gayxjw.org

YourTakeOnSpirituality.com—Collective of sites providing support for former members of Jehovah's Witnesses (and those questioning their beliefs), monitoring activity within the Watchtower Society, and endeavoring to provide information to the general public about this religious denomination. http://hub.yourtakeonspirituality.com/hub/jehovex

Mormon Church/Latter-Day Saints

ExMormon.org—For those who are questioning their faith in the Mormon Church, and for those who need support as they transition out. Not affiliated with any religion and does not advocate any religion. http://www.exmor mon.org/

QuitMormon.com—Offers free legal representation to streamline resignation from The Church of Jesus Christ of Latter-Day Saints. https://quitmormon. com/

Scientology

ExScientologyKids.com—This site is designed, owned, and operated by three young women who grew up in Scientology, and later left the Church. www.exscientologykids.com

Xenu.net—Anonymous site protesting Scientology and its alleged crimes against members and ex-members. http://www.xenu.net/

Seventh-Day Adventist Church

ExAdventist.com—A ministry of former Adventists for those seeking biblical answers on Adventism. www.exadventist.com

LeavingSDA.com—Online guide and resource center for leaving the Seventh-Day Adventist Church. http://leavingsda.com/

The Family International/Children of God (COG)

ExFamily.org—Source information about The Family/COG and resource for former members. www.exfamily.org/index.htm

MovingOn.org—Created by and for young adults with parents who joined The Family/COG and who were born and/or raised in the group. www. movingon.org

See also: Archives of the original MovingOn.org website at http://archive. movingon.org

XFamily.org—Collaboratively edited encyclopedia about The Family International/COG. http://xFamily.org

The Gentle Wind Project

WindofChanges.org—Hosted by former members of the Gentle Wind Project. www.windofchanges.org

The Way International

GreaseSpotCafe.com—Forum for those who have been affected by The Way International. www.greasespotcafe.com/ipb/

The Worldwide Church of God

HWAmstrong.com—Collection of facts, opinions, and comments from survivors of The Worldwide Church of God and its Daughters. http://hwarm strong.com/index.htm

Twelve Tribes

TwelveTribesEx.org—A website to help parents and other affected by the Twelve Tribes, initiated by a former member of the group. www.twelve tribes-ex.org

Ultra-Orthodox & Hasidic Judaism

FootStepsOrg.org—Provides educational, vocational, and social support to those seeking to enter or explore the world beyond the insular ultra-religious communities in which they were raised. www.footstepsorg.org

Word of Faith Fellowship

ReligiousCultsInfo.com—Hosted by an ex-member of the Word of Faith Fellowship. http://religiouscultsinfo.com/

Cult Information and Recovery Websites

Cult Research & Information

ApologeticsIndex.org—The Apologetics Index provides 47,863+ pages of research resources on religious cults, sects, new religious movements, and alternative religions. www.apologeticsindex.org

ApologeticsSearch.com—Information on religious cults, churches, movements, preachers, or doctrines from a mainstream Christian theological perspective. http://apologeticssearch.com

Caic.org—Informational site of the Cult Awareness and Information Center, based in Australia. www.caic.org.au

Cifs.org—Cult Information and Family Support, Inc., Australian support and information network, originally started by parents and family members of those affected by cults. www.cifs.org.au

CounterCultSearch.com—This search engine returns results primarily from websites and blogs that address cults from a sociological perspective. http://countercultsearch.com

CultInformation.org—Cult Information Center (CIC) is a charity providing advice and information for victims of cults, their families and friends, researchers, and the media. http://cultinformation.org.uk/

Ex-Cult.org—General information regarding cults, plus links to articles, books, and resources for people seeking more information. www.ex-cult.org

FactNet.org—Provides information about cults, covers many expert organizations and individuals, and includes posts on articles pertaining to cults, recovery, and specific accounts by former cult members. http://factnet.org/

FamiliesAgainstCultTeachings.org—Education and awareness, victim support, and cultic group investigation. www.familiesagainstcultteachings.org

Hjalpkallan.se—Help source and support network in Sweden for people exiting cults, funded through the Swedish National Board of Health and Welfare and the Swedish Agency for Youth and Civil Society. http://hjalpkallan.se/

ICSAHome.com—International Cultic Studies Association (ICSA)—Network of people concerned about psychological manipulation and abuse in cultic or high-demand groups, alternative movements, and other environments. Provides an extensive listing of cult-related information, articles, books, hard to find documents, listings of experts, and other valuable resources and information. www.icsahome.com

InfoSect.Freeshell.org—Based in Montreal (Quebec, Canada), offers help and information about cults, new religious movements, and related groups and subjects. http://infosect.freeshell.org/infocult/ic-home.html

JourneyFree.org—Dedicated to helping people transition out of harmful religions, recover from trauma, and rebuild their lives. http://journeyfree.org

OutofTheSnare.co.uk—Out of the Snare tells the story of a journey out of an abusive church, plus information on the signs of spiritual abuse and resources for anyone with questions about abuse in a church setting. www.outofthesnare.co.uk/home

PerryBulwer.com—Blog by a former member of a fundamentalist Protestant cult, with an archive of news articles about child abuse in a religious context. http://perry-bulwer.blogspot.com

SpiritualAbuseResources.com—Spiritual Abuse Resources provides information and assistance to victims of spiritual abuse, clergy and other religious professionals, mental health professionals, families, and anyone concerned about spiritual abuse. www.spiritualabuseresources.com

Watchman.org—Watchman Fellowship is an independent Christian research and apologetics ministry focusing on new religious movements, cults, the occult, and the New Age. Serves the Christian and secular community as a resource for education, counseling, and non-coercive intervention and evangelism training. www.watchman.org

Recovery Resources

EnCourageCultSuvivors.org—EnCourage offers support to those who have left a cult, abusive group, one-on-one cult or have been spiritually abused, including first-generation (joined or recruited) and second-/third-generation (born and or raised). www.encourage-cult-survivors.org

Ex-CultSupport—A mailing list for anyone who has been in a cultic, high-demand, or spiritually abusive group. https://groups.yahoo.com/neo/groups/ex-cult-support/info

Refocus.org—Recovering Former Cultists' Support Network provides a network of referral and support for former members of closed, high-demand groups, relationships, or cults. Supports the creation and exchange of related information that educates, encourages, or informs, such as books, articles, journals, newsletters, video and audio materials, surveys and research data, etc. www.refocus.org

SafePassageFoundation.org—Safe Passage Foundation (EIN: 30–0188676)—Nonprofit 501(c)3 tax-exempt organization providing resources, support, and advocacy for youth raised in restrictive, isolated, or high-demand communities. SPF was cofounded by the late Julia McNeil and has dedicated its scholarships to her memory. http://safepassagefoundation.org/

SpiritualAbuse.com—Spiritual Abuse Recovery Resources is a conservative Christian site primarily concerned with Bible-based groups. www.spiritual abuse.com

Treatment Centers

MeadowHaven.org—The New England Institute for Religious Research hosts a transitional home for people leaving high-control and communal cults. www.meadowhaven.org

WellspringRetreat.org—Treatment center for those who have been abused in relationships, cults, situations of trauma, and by destructive therapeutic alliances resulting in emotional betrayal and/or physical harm. Offers hope and help through a program of counseling and education. http://wellspring retreat.org/

APPENDIX D

Influence Methods that Support a Behavioral-Control System

This list can help you identify toxic influence in groups or relationships. Note that not all groups or individuals use all of the influence methods listed here. For example, some groups may be quite efficient using a select few, coupled with the charm and manipulations of a powerful leader. Other groups may have no need for isolation, inadequate diet, or fatigue to exert considerable control over members; however, most authoritarian leaders utilize an assortment of influence techniques as needed to control their followers. Some of these are as follows:

- Isolation of the person and manipulation of his or her environment
- Control of information going in and out of the group environment
- Separation and/or alienation from family and friends
- Induced dissociation and other altered states by putting the person in mild form of trance—through speaking in tongues, chanting, repeating affirmations, extended periods of meditation or prayer, lengthy denunciation sessions, long hours of lectures or study, public trials or group humiliation, "hot seat" criticisms focusing on one individual, sexual abuse, torture, etc.
- Control of the person's financial resources
- Debilitation through inadequate diet, fatigue, and sleep deprivation
- Degradation of the person's sense of self in individual or group sessions—through confession, self-reporting, rebuking, criticism and self-criticism, humiliation, and so on, in individual or group sessions
- Peer and leadership pressure, especially using powerful guilt mechanisms
- Induced anxiety, fear, and confusion, with joy and certainty being offered only through surrender to the group
- Instilling the belief that the person's survival (physical, emotional, and spiritual) depends on remaining with the group

- Induced crises that force the person to perform symbolic (or real) acts of submission to the group via betrayal and renunciation of self, family, and previously held values
- Control of personal life, and in many cases, sexual life
- Extensive indoctrination sessions—through Bible lessons, political training, recruitment training, self-awareness lessons, criticism sessions, group rituals, lectures by leaders, etc.
- Assignment of monotonous tasks or repetitive activities, such as chanting or meditating, cleaning, copying written materials, rote administrative work, etc.
- Rigid security regulations and daily rules
- Alternation of harshness and leniency in a context of compulsory discipline

REFERENCES

Allen, Ashley. "Impact on Children of Being Born into/Raised in a Cultic Group." *ICSA Today* 7, no. 1 (2016): 17–21.

Arendt, Hannah. *Totalitariansism.* New York: Harcourt Brace, 1951.

Aronson, Elliot. *The Social Animal.* New York: Worth, 2011.

Aronson, Elliot, Timothy D. Wilson, and Samuel R. Sommers. *Social Psychology.* Upper Saddle River, NJ: Pearson, 2015.

Ayella, Marybeth. "'They Must Be Crazy': Some of the Difficulties in Researching 'Cults.'" *American Behavioral Scientist* 33, no. 5 (1990): 562–77.

Balch, Rob. "How the Problem of Malfeasance Gets Overlooked in Studies of New Religions: An Examination of the AWARE Study of the Church Universal and Triumphant." In *Wolves within the Fold: Religious Leadership and Abuses of Power*, edited by A. Shupe, 191–211. New Brunswick, NJ: Rutgers University Press, 1998.

Bardin, Livia. *Starting Out in Mainstream America.* N.p. N.d. http://startingout.icsa.name/

Bowlby, John. *Attachment and Loss, Vol. I: Attachment*, 2nd ed. New York: Basic Books, 1969/1982.

Cialdini, Robert B. *Influence: How and Why People Agree to Things.* New York: Quill, 1984.

Delahanty, Douglas L, and Sarah A. Ostrowski. "Recent Advances in the Pharmacological Treatment/Prevention of PTSD." In *The Psychobiology of Trauma and Resilience Across the Lifespan*, edited by D.L. Delanty, 233–54. Lanham, MD: Jason Aronson/Rowman & Littlefield, 2008.

DeLamater, John D, and Daniel J. Myers. *Social Psychology*, 7th ed. Belmont, CA: Wadsworth, 2011.

De Waal, Frans. *The Age of Empathy: Nature's Lessons for a Kinder Society.* New York: Harmony Books, 2009.

Durkheim, Emile. *The Elementary Forms of the Religious Life.* New York: The Free Press, 1915.

Ebaugh, Helen Rose Fuchs. *Becoming an Ex: The Process of Role Exit.* Chicago: University of Chicago Press, 1988.

Edge, Charlene L. "Why I Had to Escape a Fundamentalist Cult." *ICSA Today* 7, no. 2 (2016): 15–17.

Festinger, Leon, Henry W. Riecken, and Stanley Schachter. *When Prophecy Fails: A Social and Psychological Study of a Modern Group that Predicted the Destruction of the World*. New York: Harper Torchbook, 1964.

Fromm, Erich. *Escape from Freedom*. New York: Avon Books, 1941.

Funari, Leona. "Born or Raised in High-Demand Groups: Developmental Considerations." *ICSA e-Newsletter* 4, no. 3 (2005). http://icsahome.com/articles/born-or-raised-funari-en4-4.

Goffman, Erving. *Asylums*. Garden City, NY: Anchors Books, 1961.

Gregoire, Carolyn. "The Surprising Benefit of Going Through Hard Times." *The Huffington Post* (January 6, 2016). http://huffingtonpost.com/entry/post-traumatic-growth-creativity_us_568426c0e4b014efe0d9d8e8.

Hall, John R. *Gone from the Promised Land: Jonestown in American Cultural History*. New Brunswick, NJ: Transaction, 1987.

Hamilton, Marci A. *God vs. The Gavel: Religion and the Rule of Law*. New York: Cambridge University Press, 2005.

Heimlich, Janet. *Breaking Their Will: Shedding Light on Religious Child Maltreatment*. New York: Prometheus Books, 2011.

Herman, Judith Lewis. *Trauma and Recovery*. New York: Basic Books, 1992.

Jacobs, Janet Liebman. *Divine Disenchantment: Deconverting from New Religions*. Bloomington: Indiana University Press, 1989.

Keillor, Garrison. *Lake Wobegon Days*. New York: Penguin Books, 1985.

Kelman, Herbert C, and V. Lee Hamilton. *Crimes of Obedience: Toward a Social Psychology of Authority and Responsibility*. New Haven, CT: Yale University Press, 1989.

Kent, Stephen A. "Generational Revolt by the Adult Children of First-Generation Members of the Children of God/The Family." *Cultic Studies Journal* 3, no. 1 (2004): 56–72.

Kent, Stephen A, and Deanna Hall. "Brainwashing and Re-Indoctrination Programs in the Children of God/The Family." *Cultic Studies Journal* 17 (2000): 56–78.

Krakauer, Jon. *Under the Banner of Heaven: A Story of Violent Faith*. New York: Anchor Books, 2004.

Kristina, Celeste and Juliana. *Not Without My Sister*. London: Harper Element, 2007.

Kutz, Paddy. "What Are the Effects of Child Abuse on the Brain?" (n.d.). http://newark advocate.com/fdcp/?unique=1334335352843.

Lalich, Janja. "The Cadre Ideal: Origins and Development of a Political Cult." *Cultic Studies Journal* 9, no. 1 (1992): 1–77.

Lalich, Janja. "Pitfalls in the Sociological Study of Cults." In *Misunderstanding Cults: Searching for Objectivity in a Controversial Field*, edited by B. Zablocki and T. Robbins, 123–55. Toronto: University of Toronto Press, 2001.

Lalich, Janja. *Bounded Choice: True Believers and Charismatic Cults*. Berkeley: University of California Press, 2004.

Lalich, Janja, and Madeleine Tobias. *Take Back Your Life: Recovering from Cults and Abusive Relationships*. Berkeley, CA: Bay Tree, 2006.

Latta, Susan. "Adult Children of Cults: The Experiences of Individuals Born and Raised in a Cult as They Transition into Mainstream Society." Master's thesis, California State University, Chico, 2011. http://csuchico-dspace.calstate.edu/bitstream/handle/10211.4/365/Final%20-%20Susan%20Latta.pdf?sequence=1

Layton, Deborah. *Seductive Poison: A Jonestown Survivor's Story of Life and Death in the Peoples Temple*. New York: Anchor Books, 1998.

Lifton, Robert Jay. *Thought Reform and the Psychology of Totalism: A Study of "Brainwashing" in China*. New York, Norton, 1961.

Lifton, Robert Jay. *The Protean Self: Human Resilience in an Age of Fragmentation*. Chicago: University of Chicago Press, 1993.

Lifton, Robert Jay. *Destroying the World to Save It: Aum Shinrikyo, Apocalyptic Violence, and the New Global Terrorism*. New York: Metropolitan Books, 1999.

McCants, William. *The ISIS Apocalypse: The History, Strategy, and Doomsday Vision of the Islamic State*. New York: St. Martin's Press, 2015.

McWilliams, Nancy. *Psychoanalytic Diagnosis: Understanding Personality Structure in the Clinical Process*. New York: Guilford, 2011.

Milgram, Stanley. *Obedience to Authority: An Experimental View*. New York: Harper & Row, 1974.

Narisetti, Innaiah. *Forced into Faith: How Religion Abuses Children's Rights*. New York: Prometheus Books, 2009.

Oakes, Len. *Prophetic Charisma: The Psychology of Revolutionary Religious Personalities*. Syracuse, NY: Syracuse University Press, 1997.

Oswaks, M. "Tiny Tombstones: Inside the FLDS Graveyard for Babies Born from Incest." *Broadly*, March 9, 2006. https://broadly.vice.com/en_us/article/tiny-tombstones-inside-the-flds-graveyard-for-babies-born-from-incest.

Perez-De-Albeniz, Alberto, and Jeremy Holmes. "Meditation: Concepts, Effects and Uses in Therapy." *International Journal of Psychotherapy* 5, no. 1 (2000): 49–58.

Perry, Bruce Duncan, and Maia Szalavitz. *The Boy Who Was Raised as a Dog and Other Stories from a Child Psychiatrist's Notebook*. New York: Basic Books, 2006.

Pfeffer, Jeffrey, and Robert B. Cialdini. "Illusions of Influence." In *Power and Influence in Organizations*, edited by R.M. Kramer and M.A. Neale, 1–20. Thousand Oaks, CA: Sage, 1998.

Rosen, Shelly. "Cults: A Natural Disaster—Looking at Cult Involvement Through a Trauma Lens." *International Cultic Studies Journal* 5 (2014): 12–29.

Shaw, Daniel. *Traumatic Narcissism: Relational Systems of Subjugation*. New York: Routledge, 2014.

Shaw, Daniel. "The Insanity of Narcissism." *The Huffington Post*, August 15, 2016. http://huffingtonpost.com/entry/the-insanity-of-narcissism_us_57b25a19e4b0567d4f12b90b.

Smith, Daniel W, Michael R. McCart, and Benjamin E. Saunders. "PTSD in Children and Adolescents: Risk Factors and Treatment Innovations." In *The Psychobiology of Trauma and Resilience Across the Lifespan*, edited by Douglas L. Delahanty, 69–88. Lanham, MD: Jason Aronson/Rowman & Littlefield, 2008.

Southwick, Steven M, and Dennis S. Charney. *Resilience: The Science of Mastering Life's Greatest Challenges*. New York: Cambridge University Press, 2015.

Stein, Alexandra. "Mothers in Cults: The Influence of Cults on the Relationship of Mothers to Their Children." *Cultic Studies Journal* 14, no. 1 (1997): 40–57.

Stein, Alexandra. *Terror, Love and Brainwashing: Attachment in Cults and Totalitarian Systems*. East Sussex, UK: Routledge, 2016.

Stein, Alexandra, and Mary Russell. "Attachment Theory and Post-Cult Recovery." *Therapy Today*, September (2016): 18–21.

Stern, Jessica. *Terror in the Name of God: Why Religious Militants Kill*. New York: HarperCollins, 2003.

Tavris, Carol, and Elliot Aronson. *Mistakes Were Made (but Not by Me): Why We Justify Foolish Beliefs, Bad Decisions, and Hurtful Acts*. New York: Mariner Books, 2015.

Tourish, Dennis. *The Dark Side of Transformational Leadership: A Critical Perspective*. East Sussex, UK: Routledge, 2013.

Tourish, Dennis, and Naheed Vatcha. "Charismatic Leadership and Corporate Cultism at Enron: The Elimination of Dissent, The Promotion of Conformity and Organizational Collapse." *Leadership* 1, no. 4 (2005): 455–80.

Tourish, Dennis, and Tim Wohlforth. *On the Edge: Political Cults Right and Left*. New York: Sharpe, 2000.

Weber, Max. "The Sociology of Charismatic Authority." In *From Max Weber: Essays in Sociology*, edited by H. H. Gerth and C. Wright Mills, 196–252. New York: Oxford University Press, 1946.

Weber, Max. *The Sociology of Religion*. Translated by Ephraim Fischoff. Boston: Beacon Press, 1947/1968.

Weber, Max. "The Nature of Charismatic Authority and Its Routinization." In *Max Weber: On Charisma and Institution Building*, edited by S. N. Eisenstadt, 48–65. Chicago: University of Chicago Press, 1968.

West, Louis J, and Margaret T. Singer. "Cults, Quacks, and Nonprofessional Therapies." In *Comprehensive Textbook of Psychiatry/III*, edited by Harold I. Kaplan, Alfred M. Freedman, and Benjamin J. Sadock, 3245–57. Baltimore: Williams & Wilkins, 1980.

West, Louis J, and Paul R. Martin. "Pseudo-Identity and the Treatment of Personality Changes in Victims of Captivity and Cults." In *Dissociation: Clinical and Theoretical Perspectives*, edited by S.J. Lynne and J.W. Rhue, 269–88. New York: Guilford Press, 1994.

Williams, Miriam. *Heaven's Harlots: My Fifteen Years in a Sex Cult*. New York: Morrow, 1998.

Zablocki, Benjamin. "Hyper-Compliance in Charismatic Groups." In *Mind, Brain and Society: Toward a Neurosociology of Emotion*, edited by D.D. Franks and T.S. Smith, 287–310. Stamford, CT: JAI Press, 1999.

Zablocki, Benjamin, and Thomas Robbins, eds. *Misunderstanding Cults: Searching for Objectivity in a Controversial Field*. Toronto: University of Toronto Press, 2001.

Zimbardo, Philip G, and Michael R. Leippe. *The Psychology of Attitude Change and Social Influence*. New York: McGraw Hill, 1991.

INDEX

abandonment issues 49
abuse see child abuse; child labor; sexual abuse
acceptance 118, 119–120
accessible resources 121
addiction 7, 9n10
Aesthetic Realism 35–36, 54–55
aftereffects 112–114
alienation and loss, sense of 107–109
all-encompassing belief systems 32
all-exclusive belief systems 32
all-or-nothing belief systems 93
alternative social structures 37–38
American Buddhist Movement 4
anger 24, 59–60n1, 66, 124n6
anxiety 15, 16, 89, 97, 115, 158
apocalyptic groups 93, 103n7 *see also* end-times predictions
Arizona, Fundamentalist Mormons in 12
Arquette, Alexis 1, 9n1
Arquette, David 1, 9n1
Arquette, Patricia 1, 9n1
Arquette, Richmond 1, 9n1
Arquette, Rosanna 1, 9n1
Assemblies of God 90–91
Asylums (Goffman) 63
atheist cults 4
attachment behavior system 47
attachment theory 46–47
Aum Shinrikyo 103n7
authoritarianism 51
authority 6, 87 *see also* charismatic authority

bankruptcy metaphor 125–126
Bardin, Livia 121
Beatles 14
behavioral modification processes 93
belief issues, post-cult 114–115
believe in yourself 137
Berg, David "Moses" 20, 21, 35–36, 45–46, 54, 124n6
bonding: healthy 7, 46–47; with parents, not permitted 10, 19, 21, 25, 34–35, 34–35n10, 46, 55–56, 68
boundaries, loss of 94
boundary violations 52
bounded choice 3, 8, 9n4, 58; four dimensions 5–6, 11, 24, 31–33, 39–40; *see* charismatic authority; systems of control; systems of influence; transcendent belief system
Bounded Choice: True Believers and Charismatic Cults (Lalich) 9n4, 40n6, 59n13, 59n14, 60n24, 103n4, 144
bounded reality 7, 45
Bowlby, John 46
brainwashing 88
Branch Davidians 68
Braxton, Toni 1, 9n1
Brotherhood of the Spirit/Renaissance Community 45, 53
Buddhism 4

Camping, Harold 2, 9n2
capturing and retaining followers 33–37
career issues 120–121

caregiving system 47
Celestial Kingdom 12
Celestial Marriage (plural marriage) 12
Centennial Park (FLDS) 104, 123
changing the world 3
charisma, concept of 42–44
charisma by proxy 6, 54–55
charismatic authority 5, 6–7, 31, 41–60;
    coping mechanisms for surviving
    55–56; defined 42; dynamics 52–53;
    egotism of leader 43–44, 51–54;
    evaluating in your own life 56–58;
    followers required 43; healthy 58; how
    charism becomes toxic 44–48;
    narcissism in 51–54; toxic narcissism of
    cultic groups 54–55; Weber on 42–44
Charney, Dennis 127
checks and balances, lack of 44, 57, 58,
    80, 90
child abuse 68, 75
childcare duties 10, 15
child labor 16, 75, 76–77
child protection agencies 26
children of cults 1; caretaking roles
    assumed by 34, 37; children of cult
    leaders 48–50; not there by choice 10
    see also sexual abuse of children
The Children of God (The Family)
    20–22, 30, 35, 56
ChildTrauma Academy (Houston) 68
China 103n7
Chinese Communist schools 93
Chopra, Deepak 123
Christian groups 2, 9n2 see also Children
    of God; Church of the Living Word;
    Fundamentalist Mormons
    (Fundamentalist Church of Jesus Christ
    of Latter-Day Saints, FLDS); New
    Early Christian Church; Worldwide
    Church of God
Church of Jesus Christ of Latter-Day
    Saints (LDS) 12
Church of the Living Word 36–37, 90,
    131–132
Cialdini, Robert 86–87, 97
Close, Glenn 1, 9n1
closed high-demand groups (CHDGs) 132
codes, secret 37, 38
cognitive dissonance 97
collective homes 10
College of Learning (Jung SuWon martial
    arts) 25–27, 34, 44, 45, 46, 55–56, 74;
    escape from 108, 116–117, 121;

families separated 69–71; system of
    control 79
Colorado City (FLDS) 104, 123, 134
commitment 97, 101; testimony of 32
communal intimacy 88
communication, control of 63, 93, 100,
    101
compartmentalization 129
Complex-PTSD (C-PTSD) 127–128, 132
compliance 91; hyper-compliance 96–97
confession, public 89, 94, 100
conscience 138
consistency 87, 97
control 38 see also systems of control
coping mechanisms for survival:
    charismatic authority 55–56; systems of
    control 78–79; systems of influence
    98–99; transcendent belief system
    37–38
core self 95
corporal punishment 19, 20, 21, 26, 35;
    touted as benefit 36–37
corporate cults 5, 31, 63
countries, as cults 52
critical judgment 96–97
critical-thinking capacities 94
criticism 30, 38, 52, 84, 88–89, 92; self-
    criticism 40n6, 88, 89
Cult Awareness Network (CAN) 138,
    142n20
cult behavior, as human behavior 1, 8
cults: defined 5–8; as term 3–4; what cults
    are not 4–5
Cultural Revolution 103n7

daily rules 64, 73–78
Deadheads 17, 88
"death-to-outsiders" feature 6, 9n9
dedication/devotion 14, 31, 93–94, 101
defense mechanisms 95
defiance 56
"Deliverance Ministry" 74–75
Delphi (Scientology school) 88–89, 135
Democratic Worker's Party 81n3, 103n4
denial 33
deprogramming 130–131
deviance, inner 52
dialectic of freedom and necessity 92
disability 19–20, 21, 65–66
discipline 19, 20, 33, 57; corporal
    punishment 19, 20, 21, 26, 69–70, 74;
    systems of control 69
discretion 125

disfellowshipping 78
dispensing of existence 96
dissociation 37, 60n30, 112, 131
doctrine over person 94
double and triple standards 51
Durkheim, Emile 40nn2, 4, 5
duty and obedience 43–44, 64; systems of influence 91

education/schools: after escape 118, 119–120; College of Learning 27; Exclusive Brethren 23–24; for healing 134–135; public, Fundamentalist Mormon 15; re-indoctrination of public school students 66; Transcendental Meditation 15–16
The Elementary Forms of the Religious Life (Durkheim) 40nn2, 4, 5
end-times predictions 2, 9n3; Children of God 20, 35; The Family 36; Twelve Tribes 18
Enron 5, 31, 63
entrapment 38, 40, 42, 45, 56, 64, 73
escape from cults 16, 19, 104–124; acceptance 118, 119–120; alienation and loss 107–109; helpful resources 117–120; identity and self-esteem 114–117; plan for leaving 125; reading supportive literature 118; roller-coaster of world outside 109–112; second- and third-generation cult members 106–107; stigma about cults 106, 107, 108, 109; what would have helped 120–121; work experience 111, 114 *see also* surviving and thriving
evaluation: charismatic authority 56–58; systems of control 79; systems of influence 99–101; transcendent belief systems 38–39
exceptionalism 32
exclusion 39; disfellowshipping 78
Exclusive Brethren 22–24, 28n12, 29, 32, 41, 46, 56, 61–62, 66; escape from 104–105, 107, 110, 114–115, 119, 120, 122, 133, 139; social restrictions 72
excommunication 22, 24, 41; after escape from group 105, 107
"exorcism" 74–75, 95
expulsion, threats of 15, 16, 53, 57, 77–78
extremism 93, 96

Fairfield, Iowa 15
false sense of freedom 7

The Family International, The Family, Children of God 20–22, 30, 35, 46, 56, 61; child labor 75; education 65; escape from 104, 109–113, 121, 122, 132–133, 134, 137; "Flirty Fishing" 20; Law of Love 20, 21, 75; murder/suicide 112, 124n6; rebellion 79; social restrictions 72; system of influence 85, 95; teen training camps 67; Turkish compound 69–70
family life: control of 64; restrictions on 68–71 *see also* parents
Family Radio station 9n2
family units, as cults 5
fatigue, debilitation through 63
"favorites" not allowed 76, 110
fear, state of 73, 91–92
Fellowship Tabernacle 66
first-, second-, third-, and fourth-generation members 140
First Amendment rights 4
"Flirty Fishing" 20
food stamps 12, 27n3
foster families 104
four dimensions of bounded choice 5–6, 11, 24, 31–33, 39–40
freedoms, restriction of 66–67
free will 96
friends 16, 18; contact not allowed or difficult 25, 26, 36, 71–72, 83–84; loss of through excommunication 83; as recruits 86
friendship communities for child raising 118
Fromm, Erich 52, 60n27
fundamental attribution error 59n7
Fundamentalist Mormons (Fundamentalist Church of Jesus Christ of Latter-Day Saints, FLDS) 11–14, 27n3, 30, 34, 56, 61; escape from 104, 109, 123, 129–130; increase in groups 13–14; systems of influence 89–90
Furnari, Leona 132

Gabriel of Sedona 45
Gallaudet University for the Deaf 20
GED (General Educational Development) 120, 121
"gentile world" 30
Germany, Nazi 52
Goffman, Erving 63
goodness, cult's definition of 47

Grandmaster Kim (Tae Yun Kim) 25, 41, 44, 45, 55–56, 65, 74, 108
Grateful Dead 17, 88
Greater Bethel Temple 51, 53–54
grieving 137, 139
group, needs of 7, 43–45, 54, 84
group therapy 128–129

Haas, Anne 54
Hare Krishnas 70–71, 131
healing process 127, 132–134
healthcare *see* medical issues; mental health
healthy groups 6, 31; charismatic authority 56, 58; family bonding 7, 46–47; signs of 39–40; systems of control 62, 81
healthy relationships 42
heart rates 68
Heaven's Gate 9n4, 51, 52
helping professionals 1, 106, 127–128; group therapy 128–129
hero worship 6, 7, 42
hierarchy 6, 39, 62
higher power 6
hippies 20
Holiness Movement 91
homelessness 3, 22, 105, 140
home-schooling 18, 65
hope 43, 137
HOPE Organization 13, 123
Hubbard, L. Ron 47–48
human nature 2, 8
humiliation 38, 57, 69, 74, 76, 93, 100, 158
hyper-compliance 7, 9n10, 96
hyper-credulity 96
hyper-responsibility 37

identity, after escaping cult 114–117
ideological totalism 93
imaginary history 45
imagination/daydreams 37, 78
immediate environment, manipulation of 63
inadequacy, feeling of 33
inbreeding 13
individuality suppressed 31, 53, 56, 95
individuation 50, 85–86, 137, 138
indoctrination: mind-numbing effects of 64–68; negative 62; sessions 11, 33–35, 38, 47–48
infant and child mortality rate 13
influence *see* systems of influence

Influence: How and Why People Agree to Things (Cialdini) 86–87
inner circle 6, 15, 25–26, 39, 56; charisma by proxy 54–55; different rules for 80, 100; in healthy groups 101
Inside Edition 26
instincts, trusting 137, 138
intense focus 3, 5, 6
interests, cultivating 136–137
internal conflict 97
internalization 64, 100
internal life 37
International Churches of Christ 89
interrogation 63, 73
Iowa, TM community 15
Ireland, Exclusive Brethren 22–24
isolation 32, 63, 105; by helping professionals 127; systems of control and 7

jargon 94, 100, 119
jealousy 49
Jeffs, Lyle 27n3, 123n1
Jeffs, Warren 27n3, 123n1
Jehovah's Witnesses 72–73
"Jesus babies" 20
Jesus Movement 17, 20
job skills/life skills 16, 111, 114
Jones, Jim 51, 52
Jonestown 51, 52
Jung SuWon martial arts *see* College of Learning (Jung SuWon)

Keillor, Garrison 1, 28n12
ki, chi (life energy) 25
Kutz, Paddy 68

Lake Wobegon Days (Keillor) 28n12
language, loading 94, 100, 119
Law of Love (The Family) 20, 21, 75
leaders/leadership teams 6, 31, 39
Lifton, Robert Jay 93, 126
liking 87
The Living Word 67, 73
loading the language 94, 100, 119
London, Exclusive Brethren 23
love relationships 6–7, 45
loyalty to leader 51, 100; defense of leader 52; families defer to 68

madly-in-love feelings 6
Maharishi Mahesh Yogi (Mahesh Prasad Varma) 14, 15, 48, 54

Maharishi School of the Age of Enlightenment (Transcendental Meditation) 15–16
"malignant narcissists" 52
Manson Family 52
Mao Zedong 93, 103n7
marriage 56; after escape from cult 113, 116; arranged, for young girls 13, 21–22; divorce 69; Fundamentalist Mormons 11–12
martial arts cults 4, 25–27, 65 see also College of Learning (Jung SuWon martial arts)
Marxist political cult 3, 4
McGowan, Rose 1, 9n1, 28n10
media approaches 2, 3
medical issues 16, 17, 46, 128; corporal punishment for 19, 21, 33, 35; disability 19–20; heart rates 68; prayer- or meditation-based healthcare 18, 29, 35; as satanic 21, 33, 35, 38, 79
meditation 14–15, 27–28n7 see also Transcendental Meditation (TM)
mental health 13, 19; dissociation 37; Fundamentalist Mormons 13, 89–90; Transcendental Meditation 15, 105
Mental Health America 68
Mexico, Mormons in 27n2
middle management 54
milieu control 93
"Mo Letters" (Berg) 65
moral imperative 40n6
Mormons see Church of Jesus Christ of Latter-Day Saints (LDS); Fundamentalist Mormons (Fundamentalist Church of Jesus Christ of Latter-Day Saints, FLDS)
Morningland 48–49
mother-child bond 47
multinational groups: Children of God 20–22; Exclusive Brethren 22–24
murder 51
mystical manipulation 93

names/nicknames 100, 116
narcissism 51–54
Narcissistic Personality Disorder (NPD) 52
Nazi Germany 52
neglect 10, 47; children of cult leaders 48–50
never-ending cycle 40

New Age cults 3, 27, 54, 105; Brotherhood of the Spirit/Renaissance Community 45, 53
New Early Christian Church 130, 138
new religious movement (NRM) 4, 24
New York, Twelve Tribes see Twelve Tribes
North Korea 52
nutrition, inadequate 27n3, 63, 77; eating disorders as result of 96

obligation, sense of 32
"Open Heart Reports" (OHR) 95
open-mindedness 139
outsiders 6, 9n9; as corrective 90–91; within cult 38; escapees as 114; kindness of 109–110; restrictions on social life with 71–73, 100; as worldly evil influences 23, 24, 26, 32, 39, 72, 114, 138
outside world see escape from cults

pain, emotional 68
parents 59–60n21; bonding not permitted with 10, 19, 21, 25, 34–35, 34–35n10, 46, 55–56, 68; children of cult leaders 48–50; devotion to cult rather than children 32, 68; former cult members as 136; healthy 104–105; idolization of as requirement 50; neglect by 26, 95–96, 108 see also family life
past lives, belief in 45
patience with self 125, 136–137
peer involvement not allowed 77
peer pressure 7–8, 84, 88–89, 91
Pentecostal churches 36
perfection 16, 38, 52; corporal punishment and 19; expected of children 29–30, 35
Perry, Bruce 68
personal bill of rights 140–141
personal closure 93
philosophically-based cults 4, 54–55; Aesthetic Realism 35–36
Phoenix, River 1, 9n1, 28n10
plural marriage (Celestial Marriage) 12
police departments, cult 123
political cults 3, 4, 44, 92; leaving 105
polygamist families 11–13, 30
post-traumatic growth 127
Post-Traumatic Stress Disorder (PTSD) 112, 127–128, 132

pregnancies 13
Presley, Lisa Marie 1, 9n1
prisoners of war, American 93
privacy, learning about after escape 110
protean self 126
protection, need for 46–47
psychoeducation 134–135
psychological development 37, 50, 68, 71, 72, 126
public self-reporting rituals 89
purity, demand for 93–94 *see also* dedication/devotion
purpose, higher 6, 38

raids on cults 68, 75
"Rank & Yank" performance review 63
rapture 9n2
Raven/Taylor/Hales group (Exclusive Brethren) 23
rebellion 78–80, 138–139
rebuke 51, 88, 89
reciprocity 87
reincarnation 14, 15
relational psychotherapy 127
religions 4–5
Remini, Leah 1, 9n1
repetitive activities 63
reporting of self and others 80, 88, 89, 93–94, 100
resilience 8, 37, 55, 123; emotions 129–130, 135–136; integration and 132–136; stages of healing 132–134; trauma and 126–128
Resilience: The Science of Mastering Life's Greatest Challenges (Southwick and Charney) 127
resistance 19, 55; literature and art 90; turned against people 78
resocialization 64, 96
resources: print and multi-media 147–152; recovery 157; treatment center 157; websites and online resources 153–156
return to cults 18, 19, 22
"right" ideas, approaches, and people 6, 30–31, 38, 47
Rodriguez, Ricky 112, 124n6
Romney, Gaskell 27n2
Romney, George 27n2
Romney, Miles Park 27n2
Romney, Mitt 27n2
Rosen, Shelley 60n30, 78, 127, 134–135
Russia, Stalinist 52
Ryder, Winona 1, 9n1

sacred science 94
Safe Passages 22
Sanctified Brethren 28n12
scarcity 87
schisms in cults 23
school counselors 131, 135–136
Scientology 47–48, 64, 130–131, 142n20; escape from 137, 138; systems of influence 88–89
secrecy 71, 118, 122
self: core self 95; protean 126; as socially constructed 85
self- and other-policing 7–8
self-communication 93
self-condemning behaviors 33
self-criticism 40n6, 88, 89
self-deception 96–97
self-denial 43, 84, 92
self-esteem 114
self-exposure 94
"Separation from Evil" 23
Seventh Day Adventists 86
sexual abuse of children 53; Children of God 20, 21, 22, 46, 124n6; Fundamentalist Mormons 13
shame about past 106, 114–115, 125, 126
shaming 70, 80, 114–115
Shaw, Daniel 52
Short Creek 123n1
Siegel, Eli 54
silence restriction 67, 75–76
"Silence Restriction" signs 67
Singer, Margaret 63
Smart, Elizabeth 13–14
Smith, Joseph 12, 43
social and cultural life, control of 63
social proof 87
social-psychological influence techniques 93–95
Southeast Asia, Children of God 20–22
Southern Baptist churches 92
Southwick, Steven 127
"spiritual but not religious" cults 4
Starting Out in Mainstream America (Bardin) 121
Stein, Alexandra 46–47
stigma about cults 106, 107, 108, 109, 115–116; damaging to former members 127
stress response 78
suicide, mass 9n4, 15, 51
suicide attempts/suicides 19, 21–22, 105, 131; after escape 105, 112–113

support needs 1–2, 105
support organizations 106; HOPE
    Organization 13; online groups 27,
    117, 119; Safe Passages 22
surveillance 100, 101, 122; reporting of
    others 80, 88, 89
surviving and thriving 125–42; advice
    from narrators 125; helping
    professionals and 127–128;
    impediments to healing 128–132;
    personal bill of rights 140–141;
    resilience and integration 132–136 *see
    also* coping mechanisms for survival;
    escape from cults
systems of control 5, 7, 23, 31, 43,
    61–82; avoidance of scrutiny 2;
    coping mechanisms for surviving
    78–79; daily rules 73–78; defined
    62–63; escape from cult and 106;
    evaluating in your own life 79; family-
    damaging 70–71; family life, restrictions
    on 68–71; four areas 63–64; healthy 80;
    indoctrination, mind-numbing 64–68;
    influence methods that support
    behavioral control system 158–59;
    social life, restrictions on 71–73;
    Transcendental Meditation 15; unique
    features 63–78; women's reproduction
    10–11
systems of influence 5, 7–8, 31, 63,
    83–103; bounded choice 84–85;
    coping mechanisms for surviving
    98–99; criticism, perfectionism, and
    constant monitoring 88–92; defined
    84–85; entrapment by 93–96;
    evaluating in your own life 99–101;
    healthy 86–87, 99, 101–103; how
    followers learn to entrap themselves
    96–97; influence tactics 87; social-
    psychological influence techniques
    93–95; unique features 85–88

Taylor, Jim 41
terrorist groups 9n9
therapy 139; group 128–129; helping
    professionals 127–128
threats 34; of expulsion 15, 16, 53, 57,
    77–78, 80
Tolle, Eckhart 123
"total institutions" 63
Tradition, Family, and Property 138
Transcendental Meditation (TM) 4,
    14–16, 29, 32, 41, 46, 48, 56; escape

from 122–123; escape from group 105,
    107; social restrictions 72, 77–78
transcendent belief system 5, 6, 29–40, 45,
    94; capturing and retaining followers
    33–37; coping mechanisms for survival
    37–38; defined 30–31; evaluating in
    your own life 38–39; healthy 39–40;
    internalization of 33; narcissism and 52;
    perfection required 30, 32; systems of
    influence and 100; unique features
    31–33
trauma 68; resilience and 126–128
trauma psychologists 117–118
"traumatizing narcissists" 52, 53
trust 113
Truth 32
Turkey, Family compound 69–70
Turner, Bishop Nelson 51, 53–54
Twelve Tribes 16–20, 29–30, 35, 42, 46,
    56, 65–66, 128; child labor 76;
    corporal punishment 74; escape from
    106, 108, 110, 111, 113, 115–116, 119,
    120–121, 122; families, limits on
    68–69; social restrictions 71–72;
    support networks 119; system of
    influence 88

Under the Banner of Heaven (Krakauer)
    134
unhealthy relationships 6–7, 45, 79–80
urgency, sense of 52
us-versus-them polarization 6
Utah 12
utopias 3, 8, 42, 136

Vermont, martial arts cult 25
Vietnam War 17

Weber, Max 42–44
welfare 12, 27n3
West, Louis 63
wisdom 126
women: in Exclusive Brethren 23; mental
    health 13
women's reproduction 10–11, 11–12, 23,
    76
Woodstock Festival 17, 88
Word of Life Fellowship 44, 74–75
working conditions 80
Worldwide Church of God 78, 91–92

Zablocki, Benjamin 96–97
Zerby, Karen 124n6